ALSO BY BEN RAINES

Saving America's Amazon:
The Threat to Our Nation's
Most Biodiverse River System

Simon & Schuster
1230 Avenue of the Americas
New York, NY 10020

First Simon & Schuster hardcover edition January 2022

SIMON & SCHUSTER and colophon are registered
trademarks of Simon & Schuster, Inc.

For information about special discounts for bulk purchases,
please contact Simon & Schuster Special Sales
at 1-866-506-1949 or business@simonandschuster.com.

The Simon & Schuster Speakers Bureau can bring authors to your live event.
For more information or to book an event, contact the Simon & Schuster Speakers
Bureau at 1-866-248-3049 or visit our website at www.simonspeakers.com.

Interior design by Ruth Lee-Mui

Manufactured in the United States of America

1   3   5   7   9   10   8   6   4   2

Library of Congress Cataloging-in-Publication Data

Names: Raines, Ben, author.
Title: The last slave ship : the true story of how Clotilda was found,
her descendants, and an extraordinary reckoning / Ben Raines.
Description: First Simon & Schuster hardcover edition. | New York : Simon
& Schuster, 2022. | Includes bibliographical references and index.
Summary: "The incredible true story of the last ship to carry enslaved people
to America, the remarkable town its survivors founded after emancipation,
and the complicated legacy their descendants carry with them to this day-by
the journalist who discovered the ship's remains"— Provided by publisher.
Identifiers: LCCN 2021042307 | ISBN 9781982136048
(hardcover) | ISBN 9781982136161 (ebook)
Subjects: LCSH: Clotilda (Ship) | Slavery—Alabama—Mobile—History—
19th century. | Slave trade—Alabama—Mobile—History—19th century. |
West Africans—Alabama—History—19th century. | | African Americans—
Alabama—Mobile—History. | Africatown (Ala.)—History.
Classification: LCC E445.A3 R35 2022 | DDC 306.36/20976122—dc23
LC record available at https://lccn.loc.gov/2021042307

ISBN 978-1-9821-3604-8
ISBN 978-1-9821-3616-1 (ebook)

THE LAST SLAVE SHIP

The True Story of How Clotilda
Was Found, Her Descendants, and
an Extraordinary Reckoning

BEN RAINES

SIMON & SCHUSTER

New York   London   Toronto   Sydney   New Delhi

For the millions whose lives were stolen,
and whose stories will never be known.

Contents

Introduction

A secret beneath the murky waters of an Alabama swamp has been revealed. One hundred and sixty years after she was burned and sunk to hide evidence of a ghastly crime, the wreck of the *Clotilda*—the last ship to bring enslaved Africans to America— was finally discovered. The ship has haunted those associated with her final voyage for generations. This is the story of that ship, the people shaped by her complex legacy, and the healing that began on both sides of the Atlantic when her wooden carcass finally came to the surface.

Joycelyn Davis's ancestors were among those chained in the *Clotilda*'s hold on July 9, 1860, smuggled into America under the cover of night by a man named Timothy Meaher, who'd made a bet on the eve of the Civil War that he could import a load of enslaved people from Africa despite a federal law outlawing the international slave trade. After successfully returning to Alabama from Ouidah, one of Africa's most notorious slave ports, in modern-day Benin, with 110 captives, Meaher and his confederates immediately tried to destroy the *Clotilda* to escape prosecution. Though the fire failed to fully consume the ship before it sank, their efforts were enough to hide it from view and allow them to escape punishment. Joycelyn already knew the story of the *Clotilda* when she encountered it as a nine-year-old in her textbook in fourth grade. The tale had been passed down through her family for generations. Seeing a picture of Cudjo Lewis in her schoolbook, her reaction was fear— fear that her classmates would figure out "that I was related to those Africans." Even in the 1990s, being related to the Africans who founded Africatown, her hometown, was cause for derision from some in the community. Since the earliest days after the *Clotilda* Africans arrived, they were mocked by American-born Black people for their accents, facial scarifications, tattoos, and other "savage" traditions. That ostracism was still prominent toward descendants of the *Clotilda* passengers through the 1950s and '60s within the Africatown community, when, in the words of one resident, "anything African was painted as bad, you didn't want to be associated with Africa." Joycelyn felt keenly that way in the 1990s. She continued trying to hide her family legacy through high school. The shame she felt came to a head in history class in her junior year when her teacher, Ms. Crocker, told the class that her ancestors were from France and asked if anyone knew where their family came from. Joycelyn started to raise her hand.

"But I did not do it. I was ready to tell . . . then I thought about my friends, and that's crazy, but I didn't say anything. I knew people knew. I mean, my great-grandmother lived over here in the Quarters and we went to her house every week," Joycelyn remembered. "This is a small town. People knew, 'OK, they came from those Africans.' I wasn't teased or anything. My family wasn't ashamed. It was really just me. I don't know why

I was ashamed. The story I guess. You know, there was a dispute between tribes in Africa. Then there was a bet here in Alabama. So you were sold by your own. Then there are these guys making a bet that they can come over and get you. Why would you tell anybody that? Why would you tell anybody? As you become older and wiser, you learn more. But growing up, I didn't have that."

While some hid from their history, others, like Darron Patterson, the president of the *Clotilda* Descendants Association, had it hidden from them. Patterson was unaware that he was a direct descendant of the Africans until he was sixty because his mother, ashamed of her connection to the former slaves, lied to him about it until the day she died. After she passed away, Darron finally learned of his birthright through a chance encounter on the street with two of his mother's old friends. He was stunned to discover that his great-grandmother and his great-aunt—a prominent figure in his life—had been born to the *Clotilda* slaves.

"My momma would say, 'I'm not an African.' So we didn't know. We knew people who lived around us were related to the Africans, but my mother always insisted we weren't. . . . She didn't want us to think about slavery and where we came from. She was ashamed to a degree about how we got here," Patterson said. "The crazy thing is her aunt, Eva Allen, who I knew all my life, was actually one of the last children born to one of the slaves. . . . Aunt Eva lived until 1992 and would always say we were related to the Africans. But my mother just always said, 'Don't believe anything she says. She's crazy. She's not African and neither are you.'"

To the nation at large, the story of the arrival of the last enslaved Africans on the *Clotilda* was little more than a historical footnote. Around Mobile, Alabama, where many of the *Clotilda's* passengers ended up living after emancipation, the story had, conveniently for some, come to be treated as myth. Without the shipwreck, people said there was no proof the story was true. That remained the case until April 9, 2018, when, after an extensive search, I dove underwater in scuba gear and came up holding the first piece of *Clotilda* to see the light of day in 160 years. It took a team of archaeologists a year to confirm my find.

"You don't know what this means. They've been calling us liars for years," said Lorna Woods, Joycelyn Davis's aunt, after the ship was found. "Back in the day, they just thought we was talking nonsense. They didn't want to hear about that old stuff."

Woods said it has been a struggle to get people to cherish their *Clotilda* ancestors and recognize Africatown's story. She has spent decades trying to assemble as much of her family's history as she could, gathering city records and any documents she could find, backing up the family lore shared by her grandmother, whose parents arrived on the *Clotilda*.

"People I met, they didn't have a story like ours. They didn't know anything about where they'd come from or when their people arrived here. . . . I got it from my grandmomma, Eugenia Bond. She lived right next to the church and tried to make sure we learned this history. She would talk it all the time, and she'd say, 'Don't y'all ever forget this history.'"

For decades, Mrs. Woods has visited schools with a homemade fold-out display covered in yellowed newspaper clippings and black-and-white photos of her ancestors that have been saved as family keepsakes. "My grandmother and my mother, they were proud we came from the Africans, but most people tried to hide it. We've lost so much of the history because people were ashamed to be called African. The people in Mobile started saying none of it was true. But now, with the ship, they can't do that anymore. We've been telling the truth all along."

Out of twenty thousand ships used in the global slave trade, just thirteen have been found, and the *Clotilda* is the only ship ever found that brought enslaved people to America. Remarkably, descendants of those smuggled aboard the ship still live in Africatown, a community founded after the Civil War by the *Clotilda* survivors, on land they bought from the plantation owners who had enslaved them. The original name was African Town, because the thirty-plus founders, who had only been in America for five years at the war's end, ruled it according to the laws and customs of their African homeland. By the early 1900s, Africatown was the fourth largest community in the nation governed by African-Americans, attracting the attention of Booker T. Washington, Zora Neale Hurston, and others. By the 1950s, there were movie theaters, grocery stores, barbershops, restaurants, and twelve thousand residents.

Today, Africatown is on the brink of disappearing. All the businesses and most of the people are gone. Fewer than two thousand people live in the old neighborhoods. The Meahers, the same family that removed the *Clotilda*'s passengers from Africa, have in effect continued to oppress their descendents into the twentieth century. Deciding to get out of the house rental business after nearly a century as one of Africatown's most prominent landlords, the Meaher family suddenly bulldozed hundreds of rental properties they had built, destroying much of Africatown's housing stock, rendering entire city blocks into vacant lots. They leased or sold their old plantation land surrounding the community for paper mills and other heavy industry, leaving residents saddled with high rates of cancers associated with environmental pollution. Even today, the Meaher Family Land Trust Group seeks to rezone property it owns in Africatown to bring more industry into the community.

The heroes of this story are the enslaved Africans who survived slaughter and bondage to build the first autonomous African-American community in America, beginning days after the end of slavery. The *Clotilda* Africans were likely the first Black people to demand reparations from their former enslavers, doing so just weeks after gaining their freedom. Their legacy is carried forward in the modern age by men and women on both sides of the Atlantic, in America and in Benin, who remain determined to unearth this suppressed history for the sake of mending a wound almost too deep to heal. The discovery of the ship animates and propels their longtime efforts. With it, the town's history has been made real and can no longer be ignored.

We owe a tremendous debt to four women, without whom I could not have found the ship. These women are responsible for preserving the story of the *Clotilda* and, more importantly, the stories of this last group of Africans brought to the United States in bondage. The books written by each of the women, published over the course of one hundred years, together document the forces that led to the creation of Africatown, Alabama, the only community in the nation started by people who were born in Africa. Because of these women, we have some of the only firsthand accounts of an African slaving raid as experienced by the victims. We have a half dozen voices describing the horrors of the Middle Passage, the forced voyage of enslaved Africans to the New World. We know how desperately the *Clotilda* captives longed for home and family left behind. What's more, we know more about the fate of the 110 souls imprisoned on board *Clotilda* than is known about any of the millions of other people who were enslaved in the Americas. We know exactly what part of Africa they came from, who captured and sold them, who bought them, exactly when they arrived in America, and what happened to them once they were here. The record of their experience illuminates and informs the lost histories of millions of African-American families who know only that their forebears were also stolen and shipped across the ocean.

Emma Langdon Roche, born in Mobile in 1878, published *Historical Sketches of the South* in 1914. It is the first and most important history, written while eight of the *Clotilda* survivors were still alive. Roche was the daughter of a Mobile, Alabama, funeral director and Confederate Civil War hero. She first came to know the story through one of the *Clotilda* Africans who worked for her father as a gravedigger for many years. Fascinated, she made herself a regular visitor to African Town, sketching and photographing the *Clotilda* survivors. She conducted numerous interviews with the Africans, and knew several personally over the course of decades. She expertly recorded intimate details of their capture, their longing for home, and their new lives in America, fifty-four years after they arrived.

Zora Neale Hurston, an Alabama native, came to Mobile from her home in Harlem in 1927 and 1928 to interview Cudjo Lewis, the last survivor from Africatown's original settlers. He was eighty-six when they met. She knew of Cudjo through Roche's book and spent several months in Alabama interviewing him in the one-room cabin he'd built after emancipation and lived in until he died seventy years later. *Barracoon*, her masterful account of his life, which she finished in 1931, languished in the archives of Howard University until it was finally published in 2018. "All these words from the seller," she writes in the opening. "Not one word from the sold." With Roche's book as her guide, Hurston becomes Cudjo's conduit to "get in a word for the sold," producing one of the most definitive accounts in the historical record of a slave raid, life in a barracoon (an African prison where captives were held until they were sold), the ocean crossing, and life during and after enslavement.

Dr. Natalie Robertson, author of *The Slave Ship Clotilda and the Making of Africatown, USA*, began work on her PhD dissertation in Africatown in 1992, when the *Clotilda* story was nothing but a historical footnote, completely unknown to the world at large. She captured the last interviews with the generation of people who grew up knowing personally the men, women, and children who arrived on *Clotilda*, and provided an invaluable record for future historians.

Finally, there is historian Dr. Sylviane Diouf, who published *Dreams of Africa in Alabama* in 2007 to national acclaim, sparking widespread interest in the *Clotilda* story. More importantly, using clues from the Africans' names, religious ceremonies, and the words they spoke in their native tongues, Diouf figured out where many of the *Clotilda* captives were born, what tribes they belonged to, and the languages they spoke. It was through her work that the descendants living in Africatown and around the United States learned definitively where their forebears were from, down to the level of individual towns. To Ms. Diouf I am most indebted. Her work informed my search for the ship, and she was generous with her time and scholarship as I hunted for it.

But even with their inspired work, these women did not have the power to liberate the descendants of the *Clotilda* saga from its corrupting history. When the ship was discovered, some Africatown residents still buried the truth of a past they were ashamed of. The people of Benin still buried the truth of their nation's complicity in centuries' worth of crimes they were ashamed of. And the white descendants of the enslavers still buried their connection to a legacy they were ashamed of. What this story shows is that the past corrupts souls through the centuries, and that physical evidence is sometimes the only way that the past cannot be ignored. *Clotilda* was a ghost that haunted three communities—the descendants of those transported into slavery in her hold, the descendants of their fellow Africans who sold them, and the descendants of their American enslavers—and the only way that ghost could begin to be expelled was for the ship to be revealed.

Chapter 1

THE BET

There are multiple historical accounts that describe the moment the saga of the *Clotilda* was set in motion. None of the accounts agree on all the details, and only two of them rely on actual interviews with Timothy Meaher, the Alabama steamboat captain at the center of the entire affair. The most accepted version of the story suggests Meaher and some of the passengers on his steamboat were discussing the future of slavery in April of 1859 against the backdrop of a nation edging toward war.

Meaher routinely dined with the passengers on board his ships, and after the evening meal would often sit in the richly furnished main salon or out on the upper deck for lively talk and cigars. On this night, Meaher was captaining the *Roger B. Taney*, the latest addition to his fleet of steamboats. It was a side-wheeler—configured with a paddle wheel on each side of the vessel, rather than one large one in the stern—so as to be more maneuverable in Alabama's fast and twisting rivers. An advertisement of the day described the boat as having "elegant and spacious staterooms and large, well-ventilated cabins." Meaher had named the steamer in honor of Roger Taney, then chief justice of the U.S. Supreme Court. Justice Taney wrote the majority opinion in the Dred Scott decision of 1857, which denied citizenship to Black people, regardless of whether they were enslaved or free.

At the time, Meaher and his brothers collectively owned dozens of people purchased at the slave markets in Mobile. In some measure, the story of the *Clotilda* begins and ends in Mobile, where the ship was built, where the culprits behind the crime lived and worked, and where the Africans imprisoned aboard her toiled for their captors and settled once they were free.

Today, Mobile is a Gulf Coast seaport whose diminutive skyline sports just a handful of buildings more than fifteen stories tall. It is an old city, one of the oldest in the nation, founded in 1702 as the capital of French Louisiana. Mobile was home to the first Catholic diocese in America, and also to the first Mardi Gras celebrations. Most of the real estate downtown, and all of the several miles of waterfront except for a small public park, is taken up by the port, which business in Mobile revolves around, as it has since the heyday of King Cotton, when the city was rivaled only by New Orleans for prominence and wealth along the Gulf Coast.

If you live in Mobile today, the words written by visiting British journalist Hiram Fuller a decade before the Civil War are well known: "The people live in cotton houses and ride in cotton carriages. They buy cotton, sell cotton, think cotton, eat cotton, drink cotton, and dream cotton. They marry cotton wives, and unto them are born cotton children. In enumerating the charms of a fair widow, they begin by saying she makes so many bales of cotton. It is the great staple—the sum and substance of Alabama. It has made Mobile, and all its citizens." He wrote those words in 1858, two years before the *Clotilda* voyage, a year before Timothy Meaher made his bet. At the time, Alabama grew more cotton than any other state. The entire voyage of the *Clotilda*, which cost more than $1 million in today's dollars, was financed with wealth Meaher earned moving cotton downriver from the plantations to Mobile's cotton wharves, and from the cotton grown on his own plantation. In his 1892 obituary in the *Mobile Daily Register*, Meaher is credited with having transported 1,700,000 bales of cotton, a staggering amount weighing 850 million pounds. Meaher's three oldest descendants, his great-grandsons Joseph, Augustine, and Robert, who together inherited Timothy's cotton wealth, were considered Mobile's largest and wealthiest landowners until a family spat a few years ago caused them to divide their holdings.

Cotton money is still everywhere in Mobile. The city's science museum, art museum, libraries, symphony, ballet, and other cultural resources all benefit from donations given by families made wealthy during the cotton era. Alabama remains one of the largest cotton producers in the nation. Wrangler even sells a line of premium blue jeans with an outline of the state of Alabama on the buttons and a promise that the pants are made of nothing but cotton grown in the state. Head out of Mobile in any direction in the summertime and you'll pass cotton fields, hundreds of thousands of acres of deep green leaves punctuated by millions of snow-white puffs.

During the fateful run of the *Roger B. Taney* from Mobile to Montgomery, one of the group—which included a New Yorker, a Southern plantation owner, and a pharmaceutical manufacturer from the East Coast, among others—suggested that slavery was unsustainable due to the ever-increasing price of enslaved people in the South. Prices at the slave markets had indeed increased rapidly across the South in the fifty years since Congress made it illegal to import new slaves from Africa. Known as the Act Prohibiting the Importation of Slaves, the law was signed in 1807 by slave-owning president Thomas Jefferson. It did not affect the domestic slave trade or the right to own people in the United States, but made the importation of Africans a capital offense. The origin of the law dates to the Constitutional Convention of 1787, and the debate there over whether to abolish slavery outright. In a nod toward the states where slavery was prominent, the framers included Article 1, Section 9—which made it expressely illegal to outlaw slavery for at least twenty years, or until the year 1808. Seen in this historical context, the act, which went into effect on January 1, 1808, was a first step toward ending slavery, beginning at the very start of the first year abolition was legally allowed under the Constitution. While the law did not end slavery within the United States, it ultimately made it so expensive to purchase another human that it began to destabilize the Southern economy. In the account relayed by Meaher's son, one of the Northern passengers described the institution of slavery as "doomed," because public opinion in the North and in England and Europe was solidifying against the practice. The discussion moved on to the lengths the government had gone toward curtailing the illegal trade, including U.S. Navy boats patrolling the slave coast of Africa and the jumping-off points for slave traders in the Caribbean. The New York passenger suggested that anyone caught trying to enslave people should be killed, as called for in federal law.

"Hanging the worst of them will scare the rest off," the New Yorker said.

"Nonsense! They'll hang nobody," Meaher countered, boasting that he would "import a cargo in less than two years, and no one be hanged for it." The captain then proposed a bet.

"A thousand dollars that inside two years I myself can bring a shipful of niggers right into Mobile Bay under the officers' noses." The officers Meaher referenced would have been U.S. Army officers manning the twin forts located on barrier islands on each side of the mouth of Mobile Bay. For Meaher, the $1,000 bet was inconsequential, even though it would amount to about $30,000 today. He made the bet because he wanted to thumb his nose at the federal government in the most visible way possible, following a path of resistance to federal authority then being charted by several men Meaher admired.

By 1859, there were loud rumblings in the press and Congress that the ban on the international slave trade was putting the South at a growing competitive disadvantage. American-grown cotton had supplanted Indian-grown in European markets and most countries of the world, including England, where as much as 80 percent of the cotton was imported from the American South. The American raw material was better and made for stronger fabric. It was also considerably cheaper than Indian cotton. But the cotton coming out of the South was cheaper thanks solely to the labor of enslaved people. Cotton picked with this "free" labor was the base of the entire Southern economy, and the rising prices in the slave markets threatened to limit production. You can see the growth in cotton farming in this era in the annual value of exports leaving Mobile, which climbed from an average of $9 million per year in the 1840s to $38 million by 1860. That's equivalent to $1.1 billion in today's dollars, just from the port of Mobile. As more and more land in the South was stolen from native tribes and put under cultivation, more and more people were needed to plant, pick, and process the cotton. But thanks to the international trade ban, there was now a finite supply.

After the African trade was ended, the legal slave trade simply shifted to the Northeast. Instead of importing new captives from the Côte d'Ivoire, Angola, and Dahomey, the people for sale at the markets in Alabama and Mississippi were coming from the most northern of the slave states—Maryland, Delaware, Virginia, and the Carolinas. By the 1850s, prices were twice as expensive in Mobile as they were in Virginia. A November 1859 article in the *Mobile Daily Register* reports that "prime" males, which means aged eighteen to thirty-three, cost between $1,400 and $1,800 each at auction. That's the equivalent of more than $50,000 in today's dollars. To the plantation set, the vast price discrepancy between the North and the premium prices paid in the South was nothing so much as a way for Yankees to siphon money from the South, almost like a tariff Southerners were forced to pay. So many plantation owners, the Meahers among them, bought slaves from points north.

The illegal trade in humans, which Meaher sought to participate in, began as soon as the 1808 law was on the books. Even American hero Jim Bowie participated in illegal slaving, in an ongoing scam with the pirate Jean Lafitte, who specialized in sneaking captives into America through the Louisiana marshes.

At the time, slavery's proponents argued that the law was a slavery ban in name only, partially an attempt to keep in step with the British, who'd passed a similar law, the Abolition of the Slave Trade Act, in 1807. Like the American law, England's put a stop to its participation in the international slave trade but did not outlaw slavery in England or her colonies. That didn't happen for another twenty-six years, until 1833, when Parliament formally ended slavery in the British Empire, freeing about eight hundred thousand people, mostly working on sugar plantations in the Caribbean. It is worth noting that the English accomplished this without a war, though British sugar plantation owners argued to keep the practice. Parliament created a compensation fund, offering the modern equivalent of about $14,000 per enslaved person. The amount spent to appease the enslavers added up to 40 percent of the national budget that year, and was equal to about 16 billion pounds (approximately $22 billion) today. But compared to the cost of the U.S. Civil War in lives and treasure, $22 billion sounds like a bargain.

With the abolition of slavery in the entire British Empire, the largest navy in the world turned its full attention to interrupting the slave trade globally. Prince Albert, newly married to Queen Victoria, made his first public remarks in 1840 as president of the Society for the Extinction of the Slave Trade and for the Civilization of Africa, condemning the "atrocious traffic in human beings" as "repugnant to the spirit of Christianity," and a stain upon the nations engaged in slavery. A treaty signed in 1842 meant that the United States and Britain established a twin naval presence along the West African coast to catch slavers. In the ensuing years, the anti-slaving squadrons captured dozens of American-flagged vessels caught with loads of captives. By the

1850s, the illegal trade had become much more hazardous, and most captives coming out of Africa were sent to Brazil.

Together, the resulting high prices at the slave markets and the increased risks of illegal slaving manifested in a growing movement in the South to reopen the African slave trade, even as the nations of Europe were abolishing slavery altogether. In South Carolina, the state studied the issue through a grand jury proceeding in 1854. "We present, as our unanimous opinion, that the Federal law abolishing the African Slave Trade is a public grievance. We hold this trade has been and would be, if re-established, a blessing to the American people, and a benefit to the African himself. We would show further that this trade is consistent with the true policy of the south; that slavery itself is authorized and sanctioned by Holy Writ, and experience has taught us that, by introducing African Slavery into the United States, the African has been elevated from a condition of absolute barbarism, to one of comparative civilization; from a condition of heathen darkness, to one of Christian light. . . . We hold that slavery is forbidden by no principle of policy or religion, except that which springs from the frenzied imagination of fanatic philanthropy, which arrogantly assumes to be purer and holier 'than what is written.'"

To Meaher and his fellow plantation owners, reopening the African slave trade was seen as the only salvation for the collapsing Southern economy. In 1857, Robert Bunch, the British consul in South Carolina, was alarmed enough by popular sentiment that he sent a missive to his handlers back in England with the headline "Increase in the value of Negroes: scarcity of Labor in the Cotton Fields: probable result." He noted that cotton production had increased 3,000 percent in the fifty years since importation of Africans was banned, while the enslaved population required to pick the ever-growing yield had barely increased at all. Bunch speculated that war was on the horizon between North and South, threatening shipments of the Southern cotton that accounted for 80 percent of English imports. Bunch suggested the Crown should begin thinking about growing the white gold in Africa with paid labor, instead of relying on the American crop.

The price difference between North and South and the frustration with the import ban begin to get at the rationale for the *Clotilda* bet, but don't fully explain it. Meaher was already wealthy. Fabulously so, even by the standards of the day. He and his brothers owned many enslaved people, and his position as the most prominent riverboat captain working the Alabama and Tombigbee Rivers during the heyday of the cotton economy had made him one of the richest men in Mobile, itself one of the wealthiest cities in the antebellum South. Why risk it all to bring in a load of slaves? Especially when the legal penalty was death.

In the end, there were two well-publicized events that served to radicalize Timothy Meaher—the failure of the *Susan*, and the success of the *Wanderer*.

The *Susan* was a fast schooner built in the Meaher shipyard, and she and Timothy Meaher played a role in a failed effort to turn Central America into a haven for slavery. At the center of the strange escapade of the *Susan* is a most unusual character in U.S. history, William Walker, a doctor, lawyer, journalist, and filibuster. In this original context, filibuster refers to a person seeking to cause a revolution in a foreign country, not the act of talking for twenty-four hours in the well of the U.S. Senate to defeat legislation. Walker's road to attacking other countries was an odd one. He was apparently something of a genius, graduating from college at the age of fourteen, then studying medicine in Pennsylvania, Scotland, and Germany. He practiced medicine for a few years, but decided then to go to law school. He similarly worked as a lawyer for a time, but then bought a newspaper in New Orleans and became enamored with journalism, ultimately moving to California as part of that career. It was there that Walker was shot twice in a duel by a law clerk upset by a critical article.

Having been born in the slave state of Tennessee in 1824, Walker then hit on the idea of invading Mexico and taking control of the portion closest to California, which he would name the Republic of Sonora. He imagined it would ultimately be admitted to the Union as a slave state. This was essentially what had happened in Texas, when American settlers revolted and created the Republic of Texas. But this time, Mexican authorities had other ideas and chased Walker out of the country. Still, the attempt won Walker many admirers, including forces within the government of Nicaragua. When a civil war broke out there, one side invited Walker to intervene on its behalf, which he did with a group of Americans who sailed from San Francisco. Walker famously conquered Nicaragua with a band of soldiers from Southern states, including Alabama. Just thirty-one years old, he ruled the nation for more than a year during 1855 and 1856, and was recognized as the president of Nicaragua by U.S. president James Buchanan before being overthrown by the Costa Rican Army.

After losing power, Walker, then going by "General Walker," though he was never in the U.S. military, washed up in Mobile in 1858, where he began loudly recruiting money and men for another invasion. Among those contributing to the expedition were both Timothy Meaher and a Captain William Foster, who hailed from Nova Scotia and would soon gain infamy for his role as the captain of the *Clotilda* voyage. Foster and Meaher owned stakes in the *Susan*, which had been given to Walker to carry the filibuster force to Nicaragua. It was Meaher's first act of open rebellion. Others would follow.

Neither Meaher nor Foster signed on to take part in Walker's pending attempt to invade Nicaragua again, but both, like many wealthy Southerners, supported his plan. Walker's stated goal was to establish slavery in Central American countries, hopefully bolstering the case to reopen the African slave trade in America. At this juncture, President Buchanan turned on Walker and put the full power of the federal government against the "leaders of former illegal expeditions who had expressed their intention of open hostilities against Nicaragua," and ordered the military and port officials to be "active, vigilant, and faithful in suppressing these illegal enterprises." Knowing Walker was assembling men and money for his planned attack on Nicaragua, Buchanan went further, forbidding any ships to leave from Mobile or New Orleans headed to Central America without express permission from federal officials in Washington, D.C. The people controlling cotton money in the South believed Buchanan's order was an attempt to weaken the South financially. Roche writes that this was "received with indignation throughout the whole of the lower South." In Mobile, the pending voyage of the *Susan* drew widespread popular support, including of a financial nature.

The departure of the *Susan* from the port of Mobile was anything but secret. The *McClelland*, a federal revenue cutter gunboat, was waiting for the ship to set sail, and captured the

Susan and the *Walker*'s crew of 240 men almost immediately as the wind died just after the *Susan* set sail in Mobile Bay, leaving the ship dead in the water just a few miles south of the downtown port. The gunboat forced the *Susan* to drop anchor near Dog River, one of the coastal rivers that flows into the bay. A standoff ensued, with the federal soldiers demanding that the heavily armed crew of the *Susan* surrender and return to port. The would-be invading army on board refused, and prepared to fight any attempt by the federal forces to board their ship. The standoff continued into the night. Hours later, a heavy fog settled over the bay, obscuring the anchored *Susan* from view of the federal gunboat. Under cover of the fog, Walker and the crew quietly weighed anchor and sailed down the bay, escaping into the Gulf of Mexico and headed for Nicaragua.

The whole affair fizzled before it began, after Walker and crew wrecked the *Susan* on a coral reef off Honduras, destroying the ship. The British Navy rescued the soldiers and returned the erstwhile general and his men to Mobile. Walker would attempt to take over a Central American nation one more time a year later, this time landing in Honduras in another borrowed ship. He was not well received. The government executed Walker by firing squad in Honduras at age thirty-six. Still, his example lit a fire in Timothy Meaher to do something, to be a man of action, to take matters into his own hands. We can see Meaher's embrace of Walker and the dream of creating a Central American slave state in the gift of the *Susan*, which would have been worth nearly $1 million in today's currency. Soon, like Walker, Meaher would be putting his own life on the line to further the cause of slavery.

The other galvanizing force that pushed Meaher toward

illegal slaving was the exploits of a wealthy Georgian named Charles Augustus Lafayette Lamar, who bought the *Wanderer*, a luxury yacht, in New York and outfitted her for slaving. Around the time Meaher made his bet, Lamar was being lionized as a hero in newspapers across the nation as tales of the Africans he smuggled into the country spread.

Relying on family money to make his start, Lamar was involved in horse racing, gold mining, road building, and the shipping of cotton. However, it appears he was not particularly good at any of those endeavors, and was repeatedly bailed out of financial disasters by his father, Gazaway. A family history going back three hundred years contains a small mention of Charles, describing him as "a dangerous man, and with all his apparent recklessness and lawlessness, a cautious man, too." Perhaps not too cautious, as he was known to often resort to violence. While serving as an alderman on the Savannah City Council in 1853, he was arrested for "disorderly conduct and fighting in the streets." In 1858, he shot out a friend's eye while attempting to defend his uncle in a fight. Ultimately, he was the last person killed in the Civil War, in a small battle fought in Columbus, Georgia, seven days after the surrender at Appomattox.

In the years before the war, Lamar championed the reopening of the Atlantic slave trade. Like Meaher, his first act of rebellion was to invest money in a filibustering attempt, this one to take over Cuba in 1857, again with the dream of turning it into a slave state.

As for the dangers involved with slaving, namely prosecution, Lamar was as dismissive of the federal government as Meaher was when he made his bet. "The collector of the port is a Lone Star man, and can be sent away for a few days," Lamar wrote, suggesting he could arrange for the man in charge of the port of Savannah to look the other way when one of his slave ships arrived or departed. He also believed his local political connections would protect him. "The Judge [Circuit Court, U.S.] will not trouble himself, nor do anything more than his duty requires of him. I have no fear myself of the consequences of an infringement of the neutrality laws. [President] Pierce and his whole Cabinet, were they here, could not convict me or my friends. That is the advantage of a small place. A man of influence can do as he pleases," Lamar wrote.

Interestingly, the *Wanderer* was outfitted as a slaver on Long Island, which involved building huge cisterns to hold fifteen thousand gallons of water and structures to accommodate the slaves during the Middle Passage. *Lalor's Cyclopaedia* from 1881 quotes a *New York Evening Post* article stating that eighty-five ships were modified for slaving in New York during an eighteen-month period in 1859 and 1860. And numerous accounts place a handful of corrupt New York port officials as being actively involved in looking the other way when it came to the slave ships leaving for Africa from the port. Those ships would most likely have deposited their illicit cargo in Cuba or Brazil, where Americans ran a brisk business trafficking slaves to the places where importation was still legal. But those ships also still sometimes went to the South. The historic record is rife with proof that slaves continued to pour into the country from Africa, with some estimates suggesting as many as ten thousand a year. The federal census from 1870 lists close to two thousand people born in Africa among the country's population of freed people, a number that is certain to be a vast understatement of the true total.

In November of 1858, Meaher, like people all across the

country, read media accounts reporting that the *Wanderer* was newly arrived back in Georgia with 471 enslaved Africans on board. Robert Bunch, the British consul, described the reaction in South Carolina to the news as a "general feeling of delight," in "the outwitting of the United States' authorities, and in the second, at the success of this importation of fresh laborers into the Southern country."

According to Lamar's letters, his prisoners were landed on Jekyll Island off the Georgia coast. They were then moved upriver via smaller boats, or overland to buyers in Alabama, Mississippi, and Louisiana. The Africans attracted attention everywhere they went. "The correspondent of the New York Times writes from Montgomery, Alabama, that some forty of the slaves introduced into Georgia by the Wanderer, had arrived in that place from Macon, and would be sent down that river to the plantations to which they are destined. We take it for granted that they will be arrested by officers of the federal government."

The slaves were not arrested, but Lamar and a number of his minions were. As the news spread of the *Wanderer*'s arrival, the very port collector whom Lamar had bragged about having in his pocket sent word to the district attorney for the Georgia District that he suspected Lamar and the ship of slaving. The *Wanderer* was seized. A hearing was held in admiralty court to decide ownership of the vessel. The hearing was presided over by Lamar's father-in-law, Judge John Nicoll, who ruled that the ship had been used for slaving and should be auctioned off. That his own father-in-law ruled against Lamar is telling. It could not be reassuring for a parent in the South to know that his daughter's spouse was flamboyantly breaking a federal law that carried the death penalty.

In the end, Lamar was the only person convicted of anything during the six trials related to the *Wanderer* and its illicit cargo. But Lamar wasn't convicted of slaving. Instead, he was sentenced to thirty days of home confinement because he broke one of his coconspirators out of jail during his trial so the man could come to a party Lamar was putting on in a nearby hotel. When lawmen turned up to return the escapee to jail, they were turned away by Lamar and other partygoers armed with pistols. The next morning, the prisoner turned himself in and the trial continued. During the trial, Lamar challenged one of the witnesses, a commodore in the U.S. Navy, to a duel over his testimony. Both men missed their shots and the trial continued. The only penalty Lamar or anyone else suffered for participating in the *Wanderer* episode was thirty days of house arrest and a fine of $250.

A *New York Times* story about the final outcome of the trials in May of 1860 bore the headline "The Savannah Slave Case. Lamar and His Associates Go Unpunished."

By then, Timothy Meaher, like people all around the country, had been fascinated by the well-publicized story for more than a year and a half, since word of the arrival of the Africans first hit newspapers in November of 1858. The story remained a hot conversation topic in salons from New York to Alabama, and it was well known that Lamar had challenged the editors of both the *New York Times* and the *New York Tribune* to duels in protest of their coverage. His involvement in slaving had made him a swashbuckling figure in the public's mind, bravely poking the federal government and Yankee elites in Washington in the eye.

The city of Mobile was ripe ground for such sentiments, with a long-standing antipathy toward federal rule tied to unpopular laws such as the "Tariff of Abominations," and several others, which protected goods manufactured in the North from foreign competition at the expense of the export economies of the Southern states. Timothy Meaher had been shaped by the political climate of Mobile from an early age.

He and his brother James, also a prominent figure in the *Clotilda* saga, moved to Mobile in 1835, when Timothy was twenty-three, and James twenty-five. When they arrived, Alabama was known as a place where a man could start with nothing and become rich, much like the early settlers in the original colonies had built fortunes in the new world that transformed them and their descendants into aristocrats instead of laborers. This possibility is precisely what attracted the Meahers, whose father was an Irish immigrant stonemason back in Maine. The Meaher boys sought work as deckhands on river steamboats upon their arrival in Mobile. They encountered a radically different world than the home they'd abandoned in Maine. First, Maine was never a slave state. It was considered a free state from the moment it entered the Union in 1820. Federal census records recorded fourteen hundred Blacks in Maine in 1840, five years after the Meahers migrated south. Alabama, by contrast, was home to hundreds of thousands of enslaved African-Americans, representing nearly half of the state's population. Mobile had several active slave markets located in the center of town, though by the time of the Meahers' arrival they were used only for the trade of enslaved people already living in the United States, not new imports from Africa.

As cotton boomed, so did Mobile, exploding from a city of fifteen hundred souls in 1820 to more than thirty thousand by 1860, making it Alabama's largest city, by far. The state's next largest city, the capital city Montgomery, had a mere eighty-eight hundred people in 1860. In the antebellum South, only the cities of Charleston and New Orleans had larger populations than Mobile. And nationwide, only New York and New Orleans topped Mobile in terms of exports. As the Meaher brothers' fortunes quickly improved in the booming port city, several of their siblings and spouses moved to Mobile. For four of them, the move proved fatal as they succumbed to yellow fever during the repetitive outbreaks that plagued the city throughout the 1800s.

A picture of Timothy Meaher from around the time of his arrival shows a young man with a round face and high forehead. He sports large mutton chops, a wide and squat nose, and chin-length hair swept mostly to one side of his head. The *Mobile Daily Register* routinely documented the arrival of ships bearing immigrants like the Meahers. One, the cargo ship *Eliza Morrison*, captained by a John McCullock and carrying seventy-nine Irish immigrants, was representative of these vessels arriving nearly every day loaded with poor, mostly uneducated and unskilled people hoping for a better life in Alabama. The *Eliza Morrison* carried farmers, laborers, children, and women, including one Jane Stain listed in the ship logs as a "spinster" though she was but fifteen years old. At the time, a third of Mobile's population had been born in another country or another state. Imagine then the scene along Mobile's wharves, with the chatter of immigrants coming in various languages, the calls of oystermen hawking their catch, the hiss of steam boilers firing up amid the clanking of anchor chains and the constant screeching of seagulls. Old photographs of the port area show the masts of dozens of ships tied up alongside the miles of docks. Enormous cotton warehouses butt right up to the water, surrounded by the various businesses vital to the shipping industry.

Visitors to the city remarked on its lovely architecture, a mix of Greek Revival for large public buildings, such as churches and schools, with Italianate homes and villas of the wealthy lining broad, tree-shaded avenues. William Howard Russell, a correspondent for the *Times* of London, visited Mobile—"the most foreign-looking city I have yet seen in the States"—in 1861, arriving aboard a steamboat captained by Timothy Meaher. He describes a carriage ride through town: "I sallied forth, and had a drive on a shell road by the head of the bay, where there were pretty villarettes in charming groves of magnolia, orange trees and lime-oaks. Wide streets of similar houses spring out to meet the country through sandy roads; some worthy of Streatham or Belham [tony neighborhoods in London], and all surrounded in such vegetation as Kew might envy."

Russell's journalistic eye captured the nightlife of Mobile as well. "After dinner we walked through the city, which abounds in oyster saloons, drinking houses, lager-bier and wine shops, and gambling and dancing places. The market was well worthy of a visit—something like St. John's at Liverpool on a Saturday night, crowded with negroes, mulattoes, quadroons, and mestizos of all sorts, Spanish, Italian, and French, speaking their own tongues, or a quaint lingua franca, and dressed in very striking and pretty costumes."

A copy of the *Mobile Mercantile Advertiser*, one of the city's earliest forms of news and advertising, from November 1835, paints a vivid picture of Mobile in the year the Meaher brothers arrived. I found this particular copy hanging on the wall of my friend Erk Ashbee's office in Mobile. He found it in a stack of old newspapers in a Mobile garage.

The city it depicts was a place of wealth, industry, and

culture. There are ads for violin and waltzing lessons, sealskin boots, velvet vests, and places for sailors to meet women. Waterfront hotels welcomed "bachelors," promising that "Oysters and other refreshments will be served up in any variety of style that may be desired," and "an assortment of the very best of liquors will be found. . . . For the accommodation of gentlemen disposed to amuse themselves." One of the more prominent ads in these pages is for the night's entertainment offered at a local theater. There, a Mr. Barton—also star of the show—promises first a popular tragedy, known as *Virginus*, which debuted in New York City in 1820, and after that a pair of songs, including a "comic song" titled "Puff! Puff! Puff!" The night's entertainment finished up with a farce called *Day After the Wedding*, which debuted in London's Covent Garden in 1808. A total of seven theaters offered programs at the time in Mobile, a testament to the size and spending power of the city's most elegant society set. Internationally famed Irish actor Tyrone Power, great-grandfather of the 1940s-era American movie star of the same name, even trod the boards in old Mobile.

On an afternoon in the city, one could acquire Moroccan raisins, Spanish saddles, Havana "seegars," handmade men's "dancing pumps," and champagne from France. Many of the ads in the paper are designed to cater to the thousands of sailors who passed through the city each year aboard schooners, barks, steamships, and riverboats. For instance, St. John, Price, and Co., a downtown haberdashery, "have received per ship Lorena and other recent arrivals, a handsome assortment of Fashionable Seasonal Clothing direct from our Manufactury in New York." The haul includes goat hair coats, boiled camel hair coats, "fancy colored pants," collars, suspenders, gloves, and, specifically for the sailor, "black lion skin great coats, pea coats, monkey coats . . . ," and many more. It is unclear if the black lion skin coat was actually made of lion pelts, but the monkey coat was definitely not made of monkey fur. Instead, the term is a reference to the short, nipped waist jackets worn by sailors before the Civil War.

Perhaps the oddest advertisement is for a dentist who will pull your rotten teeth and install a full set of "Teri Metalic Incorruptible Teeth," which, I imagine, were metal dentures. "Having passed through the ordeal of fire in making them, they do not absorb the saliva so as to become offensive either to the taste or smell: no particle of food can adhere to them, so the breath remains sweet. These Incorruptible Teeth retain color, solidity, durability, polish, strength, and beauty not surpassed by any." Another Dauphin Street dentist offers a carrot to lure customers: "Operations performed at the residence of the patient without extra charge."

The world of luxury available to Mobilians from the constant arrival of ships is a testament to the amount of money flowing through the city, with merchants bragging of the dresses in the latest styles from New York and the European capitals, rendered in velvet, cashmere, and handmade lace. And then there are the ads for runaway slaves.

The slave markets were also downtown, three according to advertisements in a copy of the *Railroad Time Table and Guide* published in 1863. (The city of Mobile today recognizes only one slave market site downtown.) One of the advertisements is for a "Negro Mart," where slaves were sold on commission.

It seems certain that Meaher, who by the end of his life ranked among the five or six wealthiest men in Mobile, would have interacted with Dr. Josiah Clark Nott, a Paris-trained physician who arrived in Mobile in 1833, two years before Meaher. Nott founded Alabama's first medical school in Mobile, and was one of the first scientists to suspect that insects, namely mosquitoes, were responsible for transmitting yellow fever, which ultimately killed four of Nott's children in one week. During the three decades the two men spent climbing to the top of Mobile society, Nott rose to prominence as one of the nation's leading architects of racist thought. In 1854, he was celebrated as the coauthor of a now notorious text, *Introduction to the Types of Mankind.* The book was a best seller, going to twelve printings. It is described by Dr. Scott Trafton, a George Mason University professor, as "one of the most racist texts ever written, a classic of American racism as much as American science, and is today considered the highwater mark of American scientific racism."

Nott enslaved nine people at his home and promoted the idea that blacks and whites were different species, which "differ as much as the swan from the goose, the horse and the ass." He preached a sort of pseudoscientific racism, relying on biological markers such as cranial measurements and facial features to create a hierarchy of races, with whites, naturally, at the top. He gave lectures in Mobile with titles such as "The Natural History of the Caucasian and Negro Races," and was a celebrated member of the city's society. Writing a bizarre quasi-medical analysis conducted for the life insurance industry, regarding the benefits of insuring the people one enslaved to protect your investment in case they died, Nott explained his worldview succinctly: "The negro achieves his greatest perfection, physical and moral, and also greatest longevity, in a state of slavery."

That attitude, that being enslaved was a gift to Africans, was common in the Mobile that Nott and Meaher inhabited. Such was the spirit of the place and its people as Timothy Meaher rose from his beginning as a deckhand to become a first mate on several boats, then captain of his own steamboat in 1846, eleven years after his arrival in Alabama. Along the way, he also bought timberland and then built a sawmill on a parcel he purchased between Three Mile Creek and Chickasabogue, a bayou just north of downtown Mobile. The mill was soon doing a robust business sawing Alabama pine and oak into planks and shipping them around the Gulf Coast and to foreign ports. With the additional income generated by the sawmill and his plantations, Meaher and his surviving brothers, James and Burns, opened a shipyard adjacent to the mill. The Meahers quickly increased their holdings, constructing a total of eight river steamboats, "all built at Mobile, owned and commanded by myself," according to Meaher.

By the 1850s, the Meaher brothers enslaved more than five dozen people, who worked the fields on their plantations, harvested timber from their forests, worked in their homes, ran the sawmill, and labored on the steamboat fleet they commanded. By the year 1858, twenty-three years after they arrived in Mobile, the Meahers were indisputably wealthy and fully invested in the Southern slave culture. The family's allegiance was as plain as the name they put on the latest steamboat built in the Meaher shipyard, the *Southern Republic*. This blatant endorsement for the creation of an autonomous slave nation offers proof of the total conversion of Timothy Meaher—from native-born son of the free state of Maine to wealthy Alabama plantation owner engaged in saber-rattling against Yankee abolitionists.

Given the timing of Meaher's bet aboard the *Roger B. Taney* in 1859, it is almost certain that the tale of the *Wanderer* then unfolding in the press was at the center of the conversation on the deck of the steamboat. When Meaher retorted, "No one will be hanged," to the New Yorker, he was defending Charles Lamar and his conspirators. When he made his bet, he was casting his lot with Lamar and Walker, as men of principled action. All Meaher needed to accomplish his goal was a ship capable of sailing to Africa.

Chapter 2

THE VOYAGE OF THE *CLOTILDA*

*E*ven as he made his blustering bet, Timothy Meaher had a ship and a captain in mind for the voyage to Africa: the *Clotilda*, owned by his neighbor and sometimes business partner William Foster. The ship had already proven an exceptionally fast and yar vessel, and seemed purpose-made for the sort of quiet and discreet slaving trip Meaher envisioned. Many of the historical accounts claim Meaher built the *Clotilda* specifically for the slaving run to Africa. This is not true. Foster built the ship in 1855, five years before the trip to Dahomey. The historical record is confused on the question of whether Meaher bought the *Clotilda* from Foster for the voyage or simply chartered the ship and the captain's services. In a newspaper interview thirty years after the trip, Meaher said that he bought the *Clotilda* from Foster for $35,000, then hired him as captain. This would have been enough to purchase a sailing ship like the

Clotilda. However, a survey of the records in the City of Mobile archives shows no formal change in ownership, nor do the insurance papers filed for the voyage. And one of Meaher's surviving descendants told me that according to family lore, Timothy never owned the *Clotilda*. But, with $35,000 from Meaher in his pocket, and the promise of ten of the captives on his successful return to Mobile, Foster stood to make more than $1 million in profit in today's currency for making the run, enabling him to buy his way into Mobile aristocracy.

We know the precise dimensions of the *Clotilda* thanks to the rapid growth of federal bureaucracy in the 1800s, including a law passed by Congress entitled "An Act concerning the registering of Ships or Vessels." We know exactly when *Clotilda* was built, what types of wood were used, the style of rigging, and precisely how much she could carry. Gross tonnage, after all, was used to calculate taxes related to shipping. The federal license lists Foster as owner and builder of *Clotilda*, but another man as captain. We also have detailed records of the cargoes she carried in her first five years on the high seas. Schooners like *Clotilda* were the 18-wheelers of their day, designed to move commodities such as rum, lumber, rice, and turpentine in and out of the shallow ports ringing the Gulf, from Mexico and Central America to the Caribbean and the United States. Foster's carefully detailed ship logs show that he put the ship to work right away. The first voyage left for Havana loaded with 75,000 feet of Alabama yellow pine lumber, 62 barrels of beef tallow, and 24 casks of turpentine. On another trip, her hold was jammed with 38 tons of sugar, 80 baskets of oranges, 100 bunches of bananas, 26 bunches of plantains, and baskets of yams and various plants.

But *Clotilda* was also unique. There were only eight schooners ever built for Gulf Coast service that were similar. In essence, she was built for speed. Her hull was even coated in an expensive shield of copper plating, which served to make her faster by reducing drag from the caulked seams joining every plank on the hull, and by eliminating the growth of barnacles and algae while she sat in port. Foster was a master shipwright, coming from a long line of shipwrights in Nova Scotia, where he learned the trade growing up. He was thirty-seven and in full command of his craft when he built *Clotilda* in 1855. Upon her launching, the *Mobile Daily Advertiser* described the schooner-style vessel as "light and commodious. . . . Her model is of that graceful turn which confers assurance that she will prove a fast sailer." This and the fact that she could sail in less than four feet of water were perfect for her home waters around the Gulf Coast, where the bays and inlets are notoriously shallow. The *Clotilda* even had a retractable centerboard, which would give the vessel more stability when deployed in the open sea, but could be pulled up into the hold near shore to avoid grounding. This is not the typical design for ships making regular runs across the big waters and rolling waves of the open Atlantic Ocean. Likewise, *Clotilda* would certainly not have been the vessel of choice for running a transatlantic slaving operation.

At eighty-six feet, she was small, a two-masted coastal schooner with a shallow hold belowdecks.

This meant she would be able to carry relatively few prisoners, but it also meant the ship was less likely to attract the attention of the authorities, who had become much more involved in interrupting the slave trade of late. But the British and American fleets were hunting big game, as most slave ships carried at least five hundred captives, and often more than a thousand. The anti-slaving squadrons would be more likely to ignore the sighting of a small schooner like *Clotilda* on the horizon, guessing it would be full of corn or oranges instead of enslaved Africans. Meaher knew it would be difficult to shoehorn even a hundred captives in its hold, along with the water and food required to survive the journey. The *Wanderer*, by contrast, had a longer and much deeper hull. It arrived with 371 people aboard, and was reported to have left Africa carrying another hundred who died en route and were pitched into the sea. Many of the vessels hauling prisoners to Cuba and Brazil carried between one and two thousand people per trip.

Foster, like Meaher, was a transplant from the far North, in his case Nova Scotia. The men both lived on Three Mile Creek, where each operated a shipyard, and where Foster built the *Clotilda*. The two had been partners in several business endeavors, and Meaher regarded Foster as a man who could be trusted. Their shared convictions regarding enslavement were well known. Just a few years before, each had contributed his share in the ship the *Susan* to Walker's Nicaraguan folly. Foster's resources were meager enough that he lived in a rooming house. He owned no land or people, and so that became part of the lure Meaher used to enlist the younger captain in his scheme—ten of the captives, worth close to half a million dollars in today's currency, paid to Foster on delivery of a boatload of Africans. While the value of that payment might seem excessive for sailing a boat across the ocean and back, the trip was hazardous in the extreme, and would turn Foster into a literal pirate and expose him to the death penalty if caught. There could be no mistake by early 1860, when the *Clotilda* was being provisioned for the voyage, that news of the *Wanderer* and the rumored arrival of other ships carrying Africans had increased the likelihood of getting caught. No one had yet been hanged, even when the perpetrators had been apprehended on board ships full of prisoners. (In fact, no one had ever been hanged for illegal slaving under the 1807 act, though every president since Thomas Jefferson— a list that includes founding fathers James Madison, James Monroe, John Quincy Adams, Andrew Jackson, and seven other presidents—had pardoned convicted slavers.) Despite that, it must have weighed on Foster that he was about to risk his freedom to become a pirate sailing through a gauntlet of ships whose sole mission was to capture people like him.

By the 1850s, the thirty-six ships that Britain had assigned to its West African Squadron had captured sixteen hundred slave ships and freed 150,000 Africans en route to the United States, Brazil, and other nations where slavery was still legal. The success of the British fleet—particularly the constant capture of American-flagged vessels, most of which sailed to Africa from New York—finally embarrassed the United States into standing up a fairly robust fleet of eight steam-powered ships to interdict slavers. Foster certainly would have seen the news that the U.S. fleet had been augmented again after the adventures of the *Wanderer*. Likewise, he would have known that in May of 1860, just as he was outfitting the *Clotilda* for its slaving run, U.S. revenue cutters around Key West intercepted three ships headed to port with 1,432 enslaved Africans on board.

The U.S. consul in Puerto Rico, Charles De Ronceray, laid out the continuing attraction of slave trading by Americans succinctly in a message to his superiors in Washington, stating, "The trade cannot be checked while such great percentages are made in the business. The outlay of $35,000 often brings $500,000." He reported that the price for an adult male in the slave markets of Ouidah, in modern-day Benin, was $34 in 1860. That same captive would bring more than $1,500 in Mobile. "No wonder Boston, New York, and Philadelphia have so much interest in the business," De Ronceray concluded.

To finance the venture, Meaher enlisted his brothers and a few close friends who owned plantations along the river north of Mobile. Each was guaranteed a share of the human cargo as reward, with any leftover captives to be sold once the ship returned. Foster set to work in the shipyard, altering *Clotilda*'s rigging so she could fly more canvas and catch more wind. Taller masts were installed, with longer spars and booms, allowing the use of larger sails. The work was designed to make an already fast ship even faster in the hopes of outrunning both the steam-powered vessels of the slaving squadrons, and the gossip mill of antebellum Mobile, where word of the mission was bound to leak out and spread. Even before the ship sailed, news of Mea-her's bet had made the rounds. Using the sleek, copper-hulled *Clotilda* flying a conspicuous amount of extra sail was a good strategy, so long as the wind kept blowing. Foster kept a detailed log of his preparations for the ship, of the voyage itself, and of his experience in Dahomey purchasing captives. Thanks to that, we know precisely what he loaded on board before departure for a round trip expected to take at least four months, if every-thing went according to plan.

The ship's hold was crowded with 25 casks of rice, 30 bar-rels of salted beef, 40 barrels of salted pork, 3 barrels of sugar, 25 barrels of flour, 4 barrels of bread, 4 barrels of molasses, 125 casks of water, and 80 casks of cheap rum for trading with the slave dealers. Foster also lists 25 boxes of dry goods and sundries, which included presents for bribing port officials along the way. Meaher gave him $9,000 in gold (worth more than $250,000 today) to be used to purchase 125 Africans.

Foster searched the port for sailors from out of town when he hired "nine men for the mast" to do the hard work of sailing the ship. It took a lot of hands to hoist the heavy canvas sails, anchor, centerboard, etc., on a nineteenth-century sailing ship, and the men Foster selected were "scoundrels of no certain nativity anywhere, no common interest save love of adventure, drink, and rascality in general." In other words, he chose a bunch of itinerant sailors for his crew, men he thought would be hardened enough to become slavers without complaint. He added first and second mates to round out the crew, but told no one on board that they were about to become pirates on an illegal slaving run.

We have two primary sources for information about the *Clotilda*'s voyage. The first was written by Captain Foster himself thirty years after the fact. I suspect he wrote it in an attempt to garner some of the publicity surrounding the voyage, which for decades had all gone to the voluble Meaher. Captain Tim gave frequent interviews to newspapers and magazines in the years after the war, and when he died he was celebrated in a *New York Times* obituary as the last person to bring enslaved Africans into the country. The obit made no mention of Foster, even though he was still alive. This must have galled Foster a bit, as Meaher had stayed safely behind in Mobile while he risked his neck sailing to Africa. Foster's account is twelve pages long, handwritten in a tight and precise cursive script. The old fountain pen ink has faded to a washed out gray, as if it had been written in watercolors. The other primary account comes in Emma Langdon Roche's book. Roche interviewed Foster's widow about details of the trip, adding color to her husband's fascinating but brief memoir.

Just before midnight, March 3, 1860, Foster kissed his wife goodbye and made the short walk from the boardinghouse where they lived (after several years, the captain had married the daughter of the boardinghouse's proprietor) to the wharf at the shipyard on Chickasabogue Creek. A heavy bag slung over his shoulder hid twenty-seven pounds of gold, currency of the realm in slave transactions. Foster stashed the gold behind a bulkhead in his cabin and waited for the crew. The eleven hired sailors clambered aboard, still in the dark about the purpose of their trip, blind even to the telltale evidence of a slaving mission down below in the hold. That was by design. In order to fool both the crew and the slave squadron patrols who might board the boat en route to Africa, trusted workers from Meaher's shipyard had been employed to hide the huge amount of water and meat on board beneath stacks of lumber. Piles of pine boards were also stacked on deck, camouflaging the vessel as an ordinary schooner delivering lumber to the Caribbean. Once the ship arrived on the slave coast, the lumber would be used to refashion the area belowdecks into a prison for its human cargo.

Steering by the light of a waxing half moon hanging in the sky, the *Clotilda* loosed her moorings and slipped into the river current. Timothy Meaher waved from the dock. It was to be the last he'd see of the ship for five months. The destination was the infamous slave-trading nation of Dahomey. The king there had only recently abandoned an 1852 treaty with the British, renouncing the profitable trade in human beings that had made Dahomey rich and notorious. King Ghezo's return to the business of selling members of neighboring tribes captured in turf wars was international news. Meaher and Foster read about it in the *Mobile Daily Register* in November of 1858. "From the west coast of Africa we have advice dated September 21st. The quarreling of the tribes on Sierra Leone River rendered the aspect of things very unsatisfactory. The King of Dahomey was driving a brisk trade in slaves at from fifty to sixty dollars apiece at Whydah. Immense numbers of negroes were collected along the coast for export." Shortly after the article appeared, King Ghezo died, and was replaced by his son, King Glele, who was responsible for the capture and sale of the *Clotilda* captives.

Foster carried papers clearing the ship for a run to St. Thomas to deliver lumber. He had other false papers at the ready as well. Three and a half days after crossing the bar at the mouth of Mobile Bay, the *Clotilda* made it to Cuba, 614 miles away. During the crossing, Foster steered by compass heading, checking the ship's position at night using a sextant and the stars. But the *Clotilda* was never where she was supposed to be according to the course plotted on his chart. The ship drifted steadily off course all through the day, though the compass heading appeared true. This was concerning, because being "a little off course" on the open ocean can result in missing your destination by hundreds of miles. Lying in his bed, it suddenly hit him. It was the gold. Twenty-seven pounds is a lot of gold, certainly enough to affect the magnetic field around it. The bulkhead he'd stashed the gold behind was in his cabin, directly beneath the helm of the ship. He moved the treasure and the compass swung back to the true course.

But that mattered little, for by the next day, as the *Clotilda* rode the Gulf Stream current north toward Bermuda, a fierce storm blew up, knocking the ship far off course. Foster's journal notes a "sprung main boom and other damages," meaning the ship was seriously crippled until repairs could be effected. With the main boom detached from the mast, it would be impossible to use the ship's largest sails until the boom was fixed. Stopping to repair it just four days into the journey, while passing through the heavily patrolled Florida Straits, was necessary, and nerve-racking. The British routinely captured slave ships along this corridor. Luckily, Foster was a master shipwright, and had the know-how to fix the boom while at sea, rather than having to venture into a port, where they would be sure to attract unwanted attention. But the troubles only increased as *Clotilda* passed south of Bermuda and "encountered a heavy gale of wind lasting nine days with great damage to vessel." A giant wave crashed over the ship and swept all of the lumber that had been stacked on the deck as camouflage overboard, along with all but two of the small rowboats used to get to shore in ports without deepwater docking facilities. As the lumber washed across the ship's decks, it tore off half the steering wheel and split the rudder head—the point where the rudder attached to the ship—into three pieces.

Foster knew he was going to have to put into a port for proper repairs. Fixing the enormous, heavy rudder while at sea was simply impossible, and the bulk of the journey—another four months of sailing—lay ahead. It would be impossible to cross the Atlantic so crippled. Sailing for Porto Playa, in the Dutch West Indies, to perform the repairs, the damaged *Clotilda* suddenly found itself pursued by a man-of-war Foster identified as a ship from the Portuguese anti-slaving squadron. The large, heavy gunboat gave chase from 8 a.m. to 6 p.m. as thunderstorms crashed overhead. Undamaged, the *Clotilda* would have easily outrun the ship, but crippled as she was, she had barely escaped when darkness fell. In his journal, Foster calls it "the most exciting race I ever saw." Early morning a few days later, still making for Porto Playa, "we sighted a Portuguese Man of War running for us. We changed course to get away from her not wishing to be boarded so early in the voyage as he would follow us for capture. . . . Now having arrived at Porto Playa Cape D.V. came the trouble to save the vessel. My crew refused duty and I thought my voyage broken up."

This was the first of several mutinies during the slaving run. It occurred on April 14, just a few weeks into the four-month trip. The crew, alerted by Foster's refusal to surrender to two heavily armed gunboats, had figured out the true nature of their trip. They were pirates, albeit unwitting, aboard a slaving ship sailing through heavily patrolled waters. The crew threatened to turn Foster in to the port authorities. "However, I made a bargain with my crew to double their wages from first agreement in Mobile and they went to work cheerfully to repair the vessel," Foster wrote in his journal. When Foster's widow was interviewed by Roche nearly forty years after the trip, she said the captain had a favorite saying, "Promises were like piecrust—made to be broken." While the crew worked on the ship, he went ashore to get the clearances needed for permission to sail to Africa, using the fake papers Meaher had obtained through bribing port officials back in Mobile.

Foster wrote that the American consul approved his travel documents, despite the official guessing that the *Clotilda* was actually sailing for Africa on an illegal slave run, rather than delivering lumber. Of course the captain had greased the bureaucratic skids upon arrival in Porto Playa, presenting generous gifts to both Portuguese officials and the consul, who agreed to look the other way for a fellow American off to enslave Africans. Among the twenty-five boxes of sundries listed in the shipping manifest were various jewels and items of ladies' clothing, such as shawls, that Foster had brought specifically for the wives of the government officials he met during the voyage. This sort of bribery was common in the far-flung colonial ports dotting the islands of the Caribbean, and gold was often part of the equation. The American consul of Puerto Rico acknowledged as much in a report to Congress in 1860, writing, "the business is winked at by all officials, and nearly all the governors of districts make large fortunes by the bonus given to them for permits to land cargoes of Africans."

The bribed consular official authorized the African leg of Foster's journey. The *Clotilda* now had official papers that said she was sailing to Luando (sometimes spelled "Loando" in old texts), on the west coast of Africa for a load of red palm oil. The fake destination was actually far south of Dahomey, providing cover for the voyage unless they were caught with a cargo of captives on board. Additional fake papers were set for another stop. But before the last part of the voyage could even begin, another trip-threatening disaster struck the newly repaired *Clotilda* as she headed out of port. In his journal, Foster blames his unfamiliarity with the local currents and channels for what transpired. Somehow, heading out the channel for open water, the *Clotilda* slammed into an anchored man-of-war gunship that was part of the anti-slaving squadron. The accident did heavy damage to the warship, ripping the boom and mainsail from the mast, leaving the military vessel dead in the water and unable to pursue the

Clotilda. It appears this was simply a case of bad seamanship on Foster's part. According to the shipping manifests, he had never captained the *Clotilda* prior to the Africa run. Instead, he hired other captains to make all his runs. It is possible that both the crippling damages from the storms and the hit-and-run on the man-of-war were simply the result of Foster being out of practice as a captain.

"I thought she would intercept us with shots but did not," Foster wrote, describing his getaway after accidentally ramming the warship. This appears to have been the last noteworthy moment of what had so far been a most unlucky start to the voyage. Things improved from that point on. "Blowing a fine breeze at the time we were soon out of reach of guns, had fine breeze off coast of Cape Palmas; Arrived at Whyda May15th and anchored 1 1/2 miles from the shore at 4 p.m."

It had taken seventy-three days to reach Africa, including a week in Port Playa for the repairs. Ouidah, then as now, had no natural port. In Foster's time, the only way to make it ashore was to paddle through a fearsome line of breakers in a small boat. The two rowboats that remained on the *Clotilda* after the Bermuda storm swept everything else off the decks were much too small for such seas. But even as the *Clotilda* dropped anchor just beyond the crashing surf, more than a mile offshore, a stirring could be seen on the beach and Africans were soon making their way to the ship. The Dahomeans were far too savvy and eager for trade to let a potential customer linger for long, especially with the anti-slavery patrol lurking.

"The sea rolling at a fearful height at the time we could not land in our boats," Foster recorded in his journal. "But the natives had boats 60 feet long manned by 20 natives," long enough to stretch from the crest of one wave to the crest of the next, without tumbling into the trough between the waves and capsizing. In short order, a group of five representing the king and his slave traders climbed rope ladders up onto the deck. Negotiations commenced and it was agreed Foster would have to come ashore to conclude the transaction.

Preliminary negotiations complete, Captain Foster and the band of slave traders boarded one of the enormous landing craft that had come to greet the ship, a canoe nearly as long as the *Clotilda* itself. Foster writes that it "darted through waves like fish," apparently quite literally. According to the account relayed by his wife, Foster was warned to plug his nose each time the craft cut through a breaker, suggesting the waves washed right over the passengers on board.

Beyond the dangers posed by the heavy seas, it must have been an uneasy feeling for the captain to board the native craft, leaving behind his ship at anchor in the open sea, easily visible from a great distance off. First, Foster had to worry his crew would mutiny again and simply decide to pull anchor and sail away as soon as he was onshore. It would be a simple enough thing to claim something foul happened to him in the custody of the traders. Then there was the very real possibility that one of the thirty-six British ships patrolling the slave coast might happen upon *Clotilda*. If the crew ran an American flag up the mast, the British would not board thanks to a treaty between the two countries (a fact that largely enabled American vessels to trade slaves in Brazil and the Caribbean almost unimpeded for decades after Jefferson made it a crime). But if she were discovered anchored at one of the world's most notorious slave ports, Her Majesty's navy would probably refuse to leave *Clo-*

tilda's side until she weighed anchor for the journey home. It would be impossible to load a cargo of slaves right under the guns of the warship, treaty or not. The final concern would be an old-fashioned double cross, where the slave traders obtained his twenty-seven pounds of gold, and then betrayed Foster to either British or American interests.

Foster made it ashore safely, but many were not so lucky. There are numerous records of boats full of captives being ferried from shore to a slave ship in chains and drowning when the surf boats overturned. Likewise, there are records of slave traders drowning in the same fashion as they tried to make it ashore. The dangerous coastline at Ouidah was well known by the 1600s, when one slave trader described it as worse "than at any other part of that surf-beaten coast, and from April to July, the sea became so violent that any attempt to land was at the imminent risk of life."

The beach at Ouidah is several hundred yards wide, the broad expanse of sand giving way directly to coconut palms and jungle growing from rusty red clay. Coming up from the water, the soaking wet Foster was matched with an English-speaking interpreter, who congratulated him on making it ashore. The infamous barracoons of Dahomey beckoned, crowded with thousands of captives. All that remained was for Foster to trade his gold for as many wretched souls as it would bring.

Chapter 3

THE KING OF
THE AMAZONS

*B*y the time of the *Clotilda*'s voyage, the Kingdom of Dahomey was well known as one of the most violent and ruthless societies in human history. The kingdom was built on war, and was always at war. Attacking neighboring nations was an annual and predictable event. The primary purpose was to collect people from neighboring kingdoms and villages to sell into slavery. The sale of these prisoners, numbering in the tens of thousands each year, kept the kingdom's coffers full and was the central pillar of the Dahomean economy. Historians estimate the Kingdom of Dahomey may have been responsible for capturing and deporting about 30 percent of all the Africans sold into bondage worldwide between 1600 and the 1880s.

The seemingly unstoppable supply of slaves coming out of Ouidah for the preceding centuries did not escape the notice of the British when they decided to stamp out slavery. The Brits, who had been longtime customers of the Dahomeans, came to regard shutting down the Dahomean operation as a keystone to ending slavery on a global scale. To that end, British naval officer Commander Frederick Forbes made two missions to Dahomey to negotiate with the king in 1849 and 1850. The British tried to convince the Dahomeans to give up slave trading and refocus their economy on harvesting and selling palm oil. Clearly, Forbes did not succeed in his mission of transforming Dahomey into a peaceful society. But his accounts of the style of dress, forms of currency in use (primarily heaps of shells), and social customs are among the most informative and reliable we have when it comes to painting a portrait of daily life around the time of the *Clotilda*'s arrival.

Forbes published a book about his time there, which was excerpted widely around the world in newspapers and periodicals and would fuel many of the racial stereotypes of Africans— particularly as bloodthirsty heathens—popularized in the next one hundred years. But as a piece of journalism, Forbes's book does an impressive job documenting the world of Dahomey as it was. His account paints a picture of a regime that is at once built on politeness and respect for authority and position, and on cruelty.

The British considered the Dahomeans the preeminent military power in West Africa, and the wealth generated by two centuries of slaving meant the Dahomeans were well supplied with guns from Europe. Forbes estimated that the Dahomean Army marched with a force about fifty thousand strong, roughly one-fourth of the nation's population. The large army would have been necessary both to subjugate thousands of prisoners, but also to manage and feed them on the march back to Dahomey from the conquered lands. The most surprising feature of the Dahomean Army was an elite shock troop unit composed of five thousand female warriors. "The Amazons spoken of in these journals are not deprived, like the ancient female warriors, of their left breast, but are perfect women. . . . All dress alike, diet alike, and male and female emulate each other: what the males do, the Amazons will endeavor to surpass," Forbes wrote, describing this most unusual combat force. Historians in Benin—modern-day Dahomey—say the female force arose after the death of a Dahomean king who had a twin sister. The sister chose to keep her brother's death secret and assume power in his place. To keep her ruse hidden, she surrounded herself with an all-female army so none would know her secret. The female warriors proved so loyal and fierce in battle that subsequent kings kept the force intact.

A lithograph based on a drawing of King Ghezo made by Forbes gives us a window into Dahomean dress and royal customs. It shows a rakish monarch, wearing a plumed hat as ostentatious as anything you would encounter in the salons of Europe or America at the time. The wide hat sports concentric rings of red and yellow bands, several enormous and colorful feathers, and a rim of gold tassels hanging from the brim. The king has a trim, pencil-thin mustache, and large hooped earrings in each ear. A blue tunic, perhaps silk, carries a decidedly European-looking print. In his right hand, just below a prominent gold bracelet, he holds a vicious-looking hatchet. Behind him, a female attendant, undoubtedly one of the "Amazon" warriors who always guarded the king, holds a large red umbrella over Ghezo's head. The rim of the umbrella, like the king's hat, features an elaborate trim of golden tassels. The warrior's breasts are covered, as the

Amazons dressed in the same uniform as the male soldiers, but she has much plumper lips than the king, and they are noticeably red. Given what we know of the Amazons, this application of lipstick was probably the product of the lithographer's imagination.

From historical accounts, including those provided by the *Clotilda* captives, we know the Dahomeans often relied on traitorous members of a competing tribe to ensure a successful attack. Even without the help of traitors, the size of Dahomey's army alone was enough to ensure victory over almost any enemy. "On every side, conquest has increased its territories, as each successive annual slave-hunt has annexed some one or other of the neighboring states, which [Dahomey] depopulated in its merciless progress." The depopulation Forbes mentions refers to the Dahomean practice of killing everyone in a village deemed either too young or too old to serve as a slave. This meant they left behind a swath of destroyed ghost towns in the wake of every slaving run, which were easier to control than if any survivors had remained alive. For the millions of Africans subjugated by Dahomey's warriors during a 250-year reign of violence, there were only two outcomes: death or enslavement, for Dahomey left none behind in conquered lands.

There are few parallels in history for a nation whose government and economy were totally predicated on the capture and sale of people in neighboring lands. Perhaps even fewer parallels exist for the ritualistic slaughter of captives that was integral to annual festivals and celebrations tied to the native religion in Dahomey. Forbes wrote that more than two hundred captives were sacrificed in honor of the deceased father of King Ghezo during a celebration in 1848, some beheaded, some killed slowly with many cuts. The festivals sometimes lasted a month and kept "the nation in a fever of excitement, dancing, singing, haranguing, firing and cutting off heads." The kingdom was the birthplace of Vodun, the parent religion of the forms of Voodoo exported to Brazil, the Caribbean, and the American South through the global trade in humans. Vodun is still one of the dominant religions in Benin today, with a national celebration every January that attracts adherents from across the globe. Its chief religious figure globally, His Majesty Dada Daagbo Hounon Houna II, King of Seas and Oceans, still resides in a palace in Ouidah. Sacrifice and offerings to the souls of departed ancestors remain a central tenet of the religion. Today, chickens, goats, and other animals are sacrificed, and then eaten.

Captain Foster, sopping wet from the shore landing, was carried into Ouidah in a canopied hammock borne by three men. The city was home to one of the king's palaces and five or six barracoons—huge prisons built by the colonial slaving powers, including France, Portugal, and Britain. The sprawling slave prisons and the royal compound were situated a few miles inland so as to be out of the reach of the cannons of the slave squadron ships. The entourage that greeted Foster would have been wearing the latest in Dahomean working-class fashions, which included "a small cloth round the loins, and a large country or foreign cloth, or silk thrown over the left shoulder, leaving the right arm and breast bare, and reaching to the ancles," according to Frederick Forbes. "The women wear a cloth reaching to the knee, fastened under their breasts and leaving them exposed."

Foster described his accommodations in the "Merchant's Exchange" as splendid. His journals offer a few cursory tidbits about the sights that greeted him as he wandered around the city, waiting for his meeting with a prince. Others who visited around the same time described an active merchant market, run largely by women. There were numerous restaurants catering to the working class, and a "gin palace; the material, bottles and decanters of Brazilian rum and cheap French liqueurs, with glasses of all sizes—stands on white cloths, and business seems brisk."

In terms of the natural world, the city was close to the equator and tropical in nature, with the temperature seldom dropping below seventy degrees, or rising above ninety. Coconut palms and papayas were among the most common trees. As early as the 1600s, a visitor described Dahomey as "exceedingly fertile, and so populous that the villages in many places were contiguous. The huts were made of bamboo with round thatched roofs, and enclosed fencing, while magnificent tropical trees planted with design enhanced the beauty of the prospect."

Among the sites Foster visited was the Temple of Pythons, which still stands today and is one of the central sites of Benin's Vodun religion, which reveres snakes. Foster ventured into the temple's walled courtyard, where he found devotees with snakes "wound around their necks and waists" and the limbs of the trees crawling with constrictors. Leaving the temple, Foster reports in his journal that he was summoned to the palace to see "the ebony Prince, a man of 250 pounds," who was King Glele's nephew.

We have an account of King Glele's bearing from Brit Richard Burton, who encountered the king in 1864. He describes Glele as "in the full vigor of life, from forty to forty-five, before the days of increasing belly and decreasing leg. He looks like a king of negro men, without tenderness of heart or weakness of head. . . . His person is athletic, upwards of six feet high, lithe, agile, thin flanked and broad shouldered, with muscular limbs, well turned wrists and ankles, but a distinctly cucumber shaped shin." As to his clothing, "the body cloth was fine white stuff, with narrow edging for watered green silk, and as it sat loose around the middle, decorum was consulted by drawers of purple flowered silk hardly reaching to mid-thigh . . . altogether, the dress, though simple, was effective, and it admirably set off the manly and stalwart form."

Other visitors remarked on the devotion shown to King Glele. "If perspiration appears upon the royal brow, it is instantly removed with the softest cloth by the gentlest hands; if the royal dress be disarranged, it is at once adjusted; if the royal lips moved, a plated spittoon, which . . . was gold, held by one of the wives, is moved within convenient distance; if the king sneezes, all present touch the ground with their foreheads; if he drinks, every lip utters an exclamation of blessing. This intense personal veneration reminded me of the accounts of Mohammed the apostle."

When William Makepeace Thackeray, author of *Vanity Fair*, the cutting satire of English aristocracy, was made editor of a new publication, the *Cornhill Magazine*, in 1860, he immediately published journal accounts from a slave trader who had frequented the Dahomean king's palace 170 years before. The accounts would have aligned with popular sentiment in Britain at the time, and served to reveal the barbarity of the slave trade. Titled "A Slave Dealer of 1690," the accounts of a trader named Bosman provide an unusual window into a kingdom that by several accounts appeared to have changed little over two hundred years. The king's word was absolute; even his most outrageous orders carried out without question. But in all the accounts, one thing is clear: Dahomey's business throughout its history was capturing neighboring tribes and selling them into slavery. Bosman describes the Dahomeans he conducted his business with "as being, without exception, civil and obliging to white men, in which they had an excellent example set them by their king. Their bearing, too, towards each other was marked with courtesy, distinctions of rank being observed, and the inferior showing respect to the superior." Bosman also reports that unlike at some ports, where a trader might be able to pick up just three or four slaves in a week by the 1700s, a trader visiting Ouidah could expect to "soon procure a couple of thousand, and fill four ships."

Foster arrived in May, just after the conclusion of a large slave hunt, and found himself something of a captive to Prince Akode, Glele's nephew, and his court. The young prince dragged negotiations over the slaves out for more than a week, surprising Foster, who had expected to conclude the deal in short order and be on his way. "After detaining me eight days, I thought him purposing my capture," Foster worried. Finally, Akode agreed to entertain Foster's request, in front of fifty courtiers who fell to their knees when the prince entered. "We then partook of social drink, and then I told him my business, that I had nine thousand dollars in gold and merchandise and wanted to buy a cargo of negroes for which I agreed to pay one hundred dollars per head for one hundred and twenty five."

At this point, the king flattered Foster for "his superior wisdom and exalted taste," and invited him to choose a member of the royal court as a personal slave. Foster chose a man known as Gumpa, a ranking member of the court who was a citizen of Dahomey, possibly related to the king, but most certainly not an imprisoned victim of a slave raid waiting to be sold. He spoke

Fon, the language of Dahomey, and was a high-ranking official in court. This man, known later as African Peter, was the first of the *Clotilda* captives selected by Foster. Decades later, as a freed slave living in Africatown on the edge of Mobile, Gumpa would explain the course of his life this way: "My people sold me and your people bought me."

Finally, eight days after dropping anchor on the coast, Foster was escorted to the barracoons to select his cargo.

Chapter 4

CAPTURED

As the Americans were sailing across the Atlantic, the main actors in the *Clotilda* saga were being ripped from their homes and dragged onto the stage. We know this from one of the most vivid and wrenching first-person accounts of a slaving raid in the historical record. It comes from Cudjo Lewis, a victim of the Kingdom of Dahomey, one of the most brutal slaving regimes in world history. When his story begins, he is a nineteen-year-old Yoruban villager living an idyllic life in a land of plenty. Per custom, he had several small, bent lines cut into his cheeks in childhood to identify his tribe. In addition, six of his teeth, three on top and three on bottom, were purposefully chipped in such a way that it made a hollow oval on one side of his smile when his teeth were clenched together. His mother, he says, named him Kossula. Cudjo is the name he adopted during slavery.

When Cudjo told his story to Zora Neale Hurston in 1927, he was the last survivor among the captives who founded Africatown, and was the last man alive who'd experienced the Middle Passage. Hurston lived in Mobile for several months and visited with Cudjo at his home multiple times a week when he was eighty-seven years old. They ate the melons and peaches she brought, visited with his grandchildren, and he told her of all he'd had, and all he had lost. To her profound credit, Neale took photographs and also filmed Cudjo with a windup film camera. In heavily patched pants and a blazer, the old man raises an ax and chops wood in the flickering black-and-white movie. He sits on his porch. He smiles. At eighty-seven he is spry and fit. Study his hands in both the film and the photos of him standing in the cemetery where his wife, six children, and most of his fellow captives were buried. The knuckles are enormous with rheumatoid arthritis, protruding at a forty-five-degree angle away from the top of the fingers. They testify to the decades he spent after emancipation making wooden roofing shingles at a sawmill in Mobile owned by his enslaver.

Cudjo tells his story to Hurston in fits and starts. He won't let her visit him every day, and never in the mornings. It is summertime on the Alabama coast when she visits, and he spends the cooler morning hours working the sprawling garden that surrounds his clapboard cabin. Talking is for the afternoon, he says, when it is too hot to work. Often, he cries as he speaks, sometimes from pleasant memories of his African youth, sometimes as the horrors he has seen overwhelm him. Some days, he won't talk about Africa at all. On Hurston's third visit, perhaps prompted by a watermelon she and Cudjo share on his porch, the old man begins to talk of his childhood. He describes lush tropical palm forests where he and his siblings would climb trees for coconuts and hunt for bananas, oranges, mangos, and pineapples by following the scent of the fruit on the breeze. In the garden, they grew yams as big as nail kegs and people made beer from banana mash. At one point, Hurston, ever the anthropologist, tries to redirect him, goading him to tell her the folk stories he grew up hearing. He gently refuses, telling her, "nexy time you come set wid me. Now I tell you 'bout Cudjo when he a boy back in de Affica."

He was born to the second of his father's three wives, who together had eighteen children. All three women lived in their own small houses surrounding their shared husband's home. The homes were made of mud. Several *Clotilda* survivors described to Roche how the houses were built, and similar techniques are still in evidence in Benin today. "First, a circular trench was dug and a wall of mud four feet high and a foot and a half thick was laid," he wrote. Once that dried, another four foot section was built atop the first, and then another on top of that, making for walls twelve feet high. Then a thatched roof was added on top of that, and coated in mud, making it watertight. The front door wasn't on hinges. Instead, it was propped in front of the doorway and moved aside to enter or leave. Cudjo's family compound was one of many in the village he lived in. The town itself was surrounded by a thick and high mud wall with eight gates. Cudjo frequently references the secret of the gates, which keep the town safe. While there were a number of tribes represented among the *Clotilda* captives, it appears most were members of Cudjo's community, which would have been quite large. Gabin Djimasse, who guided me around Benin, said that based on the surviving descriptions from Cudjo and other historical sources, he was most likely from an area called Bante, more urban than rural in nature. This fits with Sylviane Diouf's findings, which linked his African name, Kossula, to Bante, in the center of the modern nation of Benin. She further links him to a subset of the Yoruba people known as the Isha. Mentions of a market inside the walled city, as well as the fact that it was ruled by a king, mean it was an economic hub for the surrounding area, a trading center for the hundreds, or more likely thousands, living both inside and outside the protective enclosure. Other *Clotilda* captives were Dendi, Fon, and Atakoran, but it is only Cudjo's story that we have from beginning to end.

Cudjo stresses that his father was not a rich man, having just three wives and limited property. "Dey ain' got no ivory by de door," Cudjo says, explaining that elephant tusks outside the door denote the dwelling of a king or ruler. Even today, there are still elephants in Benin, along with lions, buffalo, and various antelope and gazelle species, which all would have been targets for Cudjo's spear. Though his father was not wealthy, Cudjo's grandfather was quite prosperous, and served as a minister to the king, who gave him a lot of land. He had "plenty" of wives, children, goats, and cows. He also had slaves. In one of the most poignant moments of his tale, Cudjo recalls his grandfather keeping his slaves in line by threatening to sell them to the Portuguese slave traders in Ouidah, the very city where Cudjo would soon find himself one among thousands of Africans offered up for sale. Cudjo tells Hurston how his grandfather dealt with the son of one of the people he enslaved who woke him from a nap. "Whoever tellee you dat de mouse kin walk 'cross de roof of de mighty?" his grandfather asks the child. "Where is dat Portuguese man? I swap you for tobacco!"

While he insists his grandfather never sold the people he owned in this fashion, the casual way Cudjo tells the story makes clear that owning other Africans was an accepted and normal part of life in his tribe. His grandfather's reference to Ouidah indicates the kidnapping raids and the slave markets of the Dahomeans were well known in the village, and explains both Cudjo's yearslong training as a warrior prior to his capture, and the importance of the wall and gates that surround and protect Cudjo's village.

He talks of his childhood and young adulthood as idyllic. His eighteen siblings were his playmates, wrestling, playing games, racing against each other, and passing through the initiation rituals and rites of adulthood together. Food was plentiful in his village, and only a modest amount of work was required to support a family. At "almost fifteen rainy seasons old," Cudjo begins his training as a warrior for his tribe with the other boys who have at least fourteen rainy seasons behind them. The earliest lessons are about stealth and concealment, learning how to walk in the bush and not reveal themselves to enemies or prey they are hunting. The young men accompany their elders on hunts that sometimes last days, or "two or three sleeps," in Cudjo's parlance. He learns to keep his bearings in the forest by breaking branches as he travels, and situating them so they point toward home. Then, by moving from one broken branch to another, he can retrace his steps even over dozens of miles. He describes traveling as "running," a reflection that his tribe, like many in Africa, was used to covering large distances at great speed. The teens practice with bow and arrow and spears, hunting game in the jungle. They learn the war song, which Hurston captured this way: "Ofu, ofu, tiggy, tiggy, tiggy, tiggy batim, ofu,

ofu, tiggy, tiggy, tiggy, tiggy, batim! Ofu batim en ko esse!" She translates this as:

> *When the day breaks the cock shall crow*
> *When the day breaks the cock shall crow*
> *When the day breaks the cock shall crow*
> *When someone crosses our roof we shall tear*
> *A nation down.*

Cudjo describes his king as peaceful, preparing soldiers for defense, not to attack his neighbors. The war training goes on for five years, until Cudjo is nineteen years old. By then, he says he has grown "tall and big. I kin run in de bush all day and not be tired." He has passed through some of the initiations required to become a man, but has several more to come before he will be considered an adult and a warrior. One rite of passage ritual occurs after he is seen following a pretty girl through the market. She wears gold bracelets from her hand to her elbow, which make a musical jingling Cudjo recalls fondly even sixty-seven years later. "She so pretty I follow her a little way, but I doan speak. We doan do that in Afficky. But I like her," Cudjo says. An older member of the tribe witnessed his pursuit and speaks to his father. "Your boy is about breakin' de corn. He is getting to be a man an' knows de secret of man. So put goats down or a cow an' let us fix a banquet for him." A banquet is organized, and Cudjo is brought to the initiation house. But before the feast begins, a strange noise rises in the woods. The men of the village send Cudjo into the forest to find the source. He dashes into the trees, but the noise is all around, sometimes a sort of roaring, sometimes a barking. First it is behind him, then in front, then far off to the side. He races through the palms in chase, but the noise is always just out of reach. "I never find it. De men are playing wid me." Eventually, they bring him into the initiation hall and show him the secret of the noise, a small, shaped piece of wood attached to a string of about six feet long that emits a sound when whirled around at great speed. Today, they are called bull roarers, and historically they were used widely in Africa, by Native Americans, and by Aborigines in Australia. Armed with this new secret, Cudjo begins his feast, with roasted meat and wine made from the fruits of the palm trees. His ear is pinched tightly by each man to teach him to keep secrets, including the secret of the noisemaker. Cudjo is given a peacock feather, another step in his initiation, and told he is now old enough to wear it in public. "In Americky soil I see plenty wimmins wear de peacock feather, but dey doan know what dey do. In Afficky soil a boy got to gettee plenty secrets inside dat he doan talk 'fo' he gittee de peacock feather."

On the question of wives, Cudjo says that a man marries his first wife, they have children, she takes care of them and tends to the home. But after a certain amount of time—seven years in his example—the first wife begins to look for a second wife for her husband. When she finds a suitable woman, the first wife approaches her and invites her to become wife number 2. Then the first wife and the prospective wife meet with the candidate's parents to seek permission for the union. If a match is agreeable to all parties, the husband makes payment to the woman's parents.

Here, haggling over the price comes into play. Cudjo explains that if the woman is the daughter of a wealthy man, her price will be much higher, "two of everything for her. Two cow, two sheep, two goat, chickens, yams, maybe gold." The rich woman

will have been "in de fat-house long time. Sometime two year."
In the "fat house," according to Cudjo's telling, the woman will
have been fed up to eight times a day, and the person in charge of
fattening the woman will lift her in and out of bed so she doesn't
lose weight from the exertion of getting up. "Man pay different
price for different girl. If she de daughter of a po' family, or she
been married before or somethin', he don't pay much for her."

In a moment all the more ominous because we know what
comes next, Cudjo describes the arrival of three men from Dahomey who ask to speak to the king of Cudjo's village. The
men warn Cudjo's king that Dahomey's King Glele is "Tenge
Makanfenkpar—a rock, the fingernail cannot scratch it," and a
"lion of lions." King Glele's emissaries demand half of the crops
raised by the village. When Cudjo's king refuses, the Dahomeans
warn that Glele will attack. Cudjo's king clearly felt his band of
warriors represented enough of a threat in their fortified compound that he felt safe resisting the slaving king of Dahomey.
But then, according to Cudjo, a traitor emerges. This traitor
sneaks off to Dahomey and trades the secret of the village gates
for riches, selling out his own people.

It was already late in the dry season, around the end of
March, when the Dahomean delegation visited Cudjo's town.
The barracoons at Ouidah were already nearly full thanks to
several raids that spring. But King Glele wasn't quite satisfied.
He wanted more prisoners to sell and to sacrifice in a big celebration to be held in honor of his late father, King Ghezo, who
died two years previously.

Even at 106 miles away, Cudjo's village was closer to Abomey—
the capital of Dahomey—than many of the Dahomeans' recent
targets. Perfect for one last quick raid. So the war party set out.

The Dahomean soldiers crept up and surrounded the walled village in the crepuscular hours before dawn. Thousands of men, armed with swords, spears, and guns, waited outside each of the eight gates that were supposed to protect the inhabitants. They would make sure no one would escape from within once the bloodletting started. Meanwhile, the shock troops, the warrior women of Dahomey, scaled the walls of the town with ladders and spread across the interior like spiders in the dark. Cudjo said he awoke to a great chopping sound and yelling as the invaders destroyed the main gate. As he emerged into the darkness outside his house to see the commotion, the flashing machetes of the Amazons were all about. One she-warrior was on top of his neighbor, sawing through his neck even as the front gates caved in. She twisted the head sharply when the flesh was cut away, breaking the spine so the head came away free in her hand. All around him, women were hacking the jawbones from people's faces, or stealing the whole head. The jawbones were coveted back in Dahomey, where they were used as ornaments on the handles of umbrellas and swords, according to Sir Richard Burton's account in *A Mission to Gelele*. The jaw "is taken with horrible cruelty; the muscles at each rampus are severed with a knife, and the jaw is torn out with the left hand from the yet living victim."

Cudjo says the killing came so fast that the elderly who tried to flee were caught as soon as they emerged from their homes. All around, headless bodies, young and old, poured blood into the streets. The air was filled with the iron stench of blood, and with screaming, from both the dying and the war cries of the Amazons marauding through the streets.

As he recounts the story sixty-seven years later from the

safety of his Alabama porch, Cudjo weeps and crosses his arms
over his chest; his mouth falls open and he mutters, "Oh Lord!
Lord!" at the memories. Like everyone else in the village still
alive, he ran for the gates, hoping to make it into the forest and
escape. All around, the killing continued. But the secret of the
gates was only that there were eight. The idea was that even
as an invader stormed the main gate, the populace could flee
through the smaller, more discreet gates and hide in the bush
until the invaders left. But the traitor had revealed this secret.
Cudjo found Dahomean soldiers at every gate, killing the old
and young indiscriminately as they approached, and capturing everyone of slaving age, from teenagers, including Cudjo,
to adults in their early thirties. As they bound his hands with a
cord woven from palm fronds, he sobbed and begged to be let
go to find his mother. He could see none of his relatives among
the captives. All were lost.

Even as the captives lay on the ground, hands bound and
with killing all around, things were about to become ever more
horrific for them. Cudjo told Hurston he witnessed the capture
of his king, who like his followers was snatched as he attempted
to flee through the same gate Cudjo had used. He was brought
before Dahomey's King Glele, who, along with his royal court,
waited out of harm's way as his warriors sacked the town. Glele
demanded to know why Cudjo's king thought his people could
resist Dahomey.

Then Glele looked at one of his soldiers and pointed at the
opposing monarch. An Amazon stepped forward and in one
quick swipe of the machete lopped off his head. Then she picked
it up, blood still gushing from the gaping neck, and handed it to
her king. Historical accounts report that the skulls of conquered

kings were preserved in the palace, usually set inside a hollowed-out gourd in a place of honor in the throne room. King Glele was reported to have the skulls of forty rulers after just three years as king, his three favorites highly polished and on display in court. That is likely what happened to the skull of Cudjo's king as well. The heads of the common people who fell, among them perhaps all of Cudjo's immediate family, were retained by the Amazons and male warriors alike as trophies. Cudjo speaks of this in perhaps the most horrifying part of his account.

Shortly after the attack, as the sun is rising, they begin the march back to Dahomey, several days away. Cudjo begs for his freedom, but says, "De soldiers say dey got no ears for cryin'." The soldiers are carrying the heads of everyone they killed in the town—with ropes running through both eyes or up the ripped open throat and out the mouth—tying them together on their belts. By custom, a Dahomean warrior could only brag of killing someone if they had the head as proof. "Some got two, three head dey carry wid dem to Dahomey." During the march, which Cudjo recounts as eight days spent walking, the Dahomeans stop at various villages where the residents offer corn and yams to feed the troops in the hopes of avoiding the fate of the thousands tied together in the slave coffle. At night, the bound slaves slept on the ground as best they could linked together by ropes. Cudjo said he cried throughout the ordeal. By the third day, the heads of the fallen begin to stink badly. The column stops and the Dahomeans build huge fires. The heads of the victims are set atop sharpened sticks and slowly smoked over the flames, cured to prevent further rot. The process takes nine days by Cudjo's count. "We got to set dere and see de heads of our people smokin' on de stick." It is a scene almost unbearable to imagine. After surviving a murderous rampage involving thousands of deaths, the survivors were forced to watch the faces of friends, relatives, and neighbors slowly withering and twisting into ghastly masks.

A few more days of marching and the slave coffle reaches Abomey, where Glele's palace is located. Cudjo tells Hurston that the palace is "made out of skull bones." His recollection comports with eyewitness reports from European visitors of the era. Skulls were set at regular intervals on spikes atop the fortified walls. The spikes even had small shelves beneath them designed to hold the jawbone in place with the rest of the skull. Thigh bones jutted irregularly from the mud brick by the gate, and the palace officials who came to meet the entourage carried sticks topped with skulls. The returning warriors, meanwhile, place the freshly smoked heads of Cudjo's people on top of tall sticks they hold high above the procession as they parade into town. There could be no mistake about Cudjo's future. It could not be more grim. The only question was whether his clan would be enslaved and sold, or ritually sacrificed during the king's tribute to his father. The captives are locked in a barracoon outside the king's palace in Abomey for three days while the king and his minions feast—singing, dancing, and beating on drums. While it is not mentioned by Cudjo, this feast almost certainly included numerous sacrifices. At its conclusion, Cudjo and the rest were shuffled back onto the slave road—a trail beaten by the passage of millions of feet from Abomey through the sandy red clay of the jungle to the slave port of Ouidah sixty miles away on the coast.

Several of the books and articles written about the *Clotilda* tell a story about an enormous pile of small stones that sits just inside the walls of a modern-day high school in Abomey. It is more than ten feet tall. According to these accounts, the pile is a sort of accounting system for recording all the souls bartered by Dahomey. Every captive that passed through the city on the way to the markets in Ouidah was supposedly forced to drop a stone onto the pile. Though the stones have never been counted, it is clear there are hundreds of thousands, perhaps millions.

The only problem with the story about the stone pile is that it is false, according to Gabin Djimasse, the history expert and tourism chief for the city of Abomey.

"There are no stones in Abomey. Look on the ground, you do not find stones here. This story is false. And the road to Ouidah is not connected to that school. The school is not on the slave route," Djimasse said. He says the stones were from a battle during the reign of King Ghezo. The tribe the Dahomeans were attacking lived in the north part of Benin, where it is rockier, and they planned a sneak attack, knocking an enormous stone wall over on top of the invading army, killing and injuring many of the Dahomeans. Ghezo had his soldiers each carry stones from the wall back to Abomey and stack them in a huge mound as a sort of memorial to those lost in the attack. The stones have been preserved in the pile because they are historic, Djimasse said, but they are not a tally of those who were sold. "People not from Benin tell this story in their books, and it is nice, but it does not make sense."

It would be convenient if the stone story were true, because it would give us a window into how many people were sold through Ouidah, which was one of the top three slave ports in the world, ranked just behind Bonny in Nigeria and Cabinda, Angola. But even if Cudjo and his companions were represented in the pile, and we could count all the people ever sold through Ouidah, it would still represent only a fraction of the human cost in Africa. This is because the dead they left behind in their various hometowns—the millions of people who were killed instead of being sold—would not be counted or remembered in the stone census.

This is one of the unfathomable and unknowable costs of the trade in humans—the staggering number of people murdered in their villages during the brutish raids. Also unfathomable are all the cultures and traditions lost forever as entire kingdoms like Cudjo's disappeared from the map at the point of a spear.

Chapter 5

BARRACOON

By the time Cudjo's group reached Ouidah, they had been prisoners for several weeks. The barracoon where they were locked up in the port city would be their home for the next three weeks. Forts built by the colonial powers served as prisons in Ouidah. The French, Dutch, Danish, Portuguese, and English all built forts in Ouidah specifically to enable the slave trade. Today, the last surviving barracoon houses a museum in the central building, with an area of five or six acres inside the huge encircling wall. The captives were held in pens built inside the confines of that wall. There may have been some areas for them to hide from the rain beneath a roof, but for the most part, it appears they were simply left exposed to the weather like herds of cattle. By climbing up the walls of the jail, Cudjo could see the Atlantic Ocean in the distance, as well as the *Clotilda*, riding the swells at anchor just beyond the breakers. The prisoners couldn't see the beach itself because a white house next to the barracoon blocked their view. The ocean and a sailing ship would have been new sights for tribespeople who lived far inland. Likewise with the sight of the white men who milled around in front of the white house. Cudjo said he had heard talk of white men growing up, but never laid eyes on one before. Food in the barracoon consisted of rice mush cooked in palm oil. By Foster's account, there were more than four thousand prisoners kept in groups in large pens. Cudjo said that each pen housed people from different kingdoms. Sometimes, the newly enslaved hollered back and forth to find out where other groups had come from. Cudjo's pen was stuffed with people from his town, including cousins and friends.

As he recounted the story to Hurston sixty-seven years on, Cudjo remembered that his nineteen-year-old self managed to play games with his fellow captives in the barracoon. As he explained it, everyone in the prison was young. The slavers had killed anyone approaching forty years old back in the village. Cudjo, at nineteen, was probably around the average age of the captives. According to some historic accounts, during part of their imprisonment the captives were tied by the wrist to large stakes embedded in the dirt floor of the barracoon, but this doesn't seem to concur with Cudjo's report of climbing the wall of the prison to stare at the ships on the horizon, or with playing games. It is possible the captives were bound in this fashion for their four-day stay in the barracoon at Abomey, but not for the three weeks spent in Ouidah. A month after their capture, Cudjo tells Hurston, "we not so sad now." Yet another hardship was soon to come as the survivors knew they were destined to be sold off and parted from their fellow townspeople, yet another round of loss and separation.

That moment arrived on May 23, 1860, when Foster strolled into the barracoon in the company of a Dahomean prince and an interpreter. The Bante captives were told to form circles, each containing ten men or women. Foster stepped into the middle of each circle and inspected the captives, checking their teeth, their feet, their skin, exactly as one would inspect a horse or cow before purchase, searching for signs of disease or infirmity. After careful consideration, Foster selected a man from a circle, then a woman from another, moving on until he reached the 125 agreed to with the prince. After the selection process, Foster left the barracoon and entered the adjacent white house. This is where the trade was finalized. The captives would be transported to the *Clotilda* the next morning, and Foster's gold would be delivered to the prince. For Foster, the transfer couldn't happen soon enough. The prince's delays had left him nervous, and he feared a double cross. The British often paid for information that led to the capture of a slaver, and a week's delay would certainly have allowed the Dahomeans time enough to alert the British to the *Clotilda*'s purpose anchored off Ouidah. It is easy to imagine a scenario where the Dahomeans collected Foster's gold in the morning, helped him load his captives, and then watched as the tipped-off anti-slaving squadron intercepted him before he'd even had a chance to weigh anchor and set sail.

Back in the barracoon, the guards told those selected they would be leaving in the morning. Extra food was provided for what Cudjo described as a big feast. But it was a sad affair with many tears. "We doan want to leave the rest of our people in de barracoon. We all lonesome for our home. We doan know what goin' become of us, we doan want to be put apart from one 'nother." In the morning, they were chained together and led out of the prison, saying goodbye for the last time ever to friends, parents, and siblings.

Cudjo told Roche of an incident that didn't make it into Hurston's book, but that meant he almost avoided the trip to America aboard the *Clotilda*. He said that as the group waited for Foster to finish paying in the white house, a Dahomean stole him from the coffle and stashed him under the building. Perhaps the thief made a habit of peeling off a slave or two from large transactions, either to sell or keep for himself. Either way, Cudjo was not liberated for long. According to his recollection, after hiding under the house for a time, while the rest of the group was led away, the sights and sounds of the nearby sea proved too much of a lure. The white house had obscured the view of the beach from the barracoon during his three weeks of captivity. He snuck out from his hiding place to peer over a fence at the ocean. "I wanta see what maka dat noise, an' how dat water worka—how it fell on shore an' went back again. I saw some of my people in a little boat and I holler to them. Then Captain Foster spied me." In the version he gave to Hurston, Cudjo never mentions being stolen or crawling from a hiding place. Instead, he says simply, "Dey almost leave me on de shore. But when I see my friend Keebe in de boat I want to go wid him. So I holler and dey turn around and takee me." It is a poignant moment, especially so if he volunteered himself to the slavers so he could stay close to his friends a little while longer rather than seize the chance to escape.

The Atlantic Ocean is clear and shallow along the wide beach at Ouidah, with a low, almost nonexistent dune line. A fringe of palms and papaya trees peters out about three hundred yards from the water's edge, making for a long, sun-blasted walk through the sand. The ocean would have been the most dramatic thing Cudjo saw on his walk toward captivity, and it is easy to understand his desire to see it with his own eyes. But the change in the surrounding landscape as the prisoners were marched from their rocky home near Bante, to the red clay world of Abomey and finally the sandy streets of Ouidah would have likewise been profound.

On the beach, the slaves were slowly ferried out to the *Clotilda* at anchor a mile and a half offshore. Their bonds were removed as they boarded the giant canoes manned by Kroo tribesmen. Cudjo derisively refers to the Kroo as "Many-costs," because of their reputation of working for whites as porters, and because of a long-standing West African joke that you could hire many Kroo for the "cost" of a single worker from another tribe. The crew threw the casks of rum and other trading goods overboard into the water for the Kroo to gather and ferry to shore. In a final humiliation before boarding the canoes, the Dahomean guards ripped what tattered clothes the prisoners were wearing from their bodies. Given that they had all been roused from sleep by the attack, it is likely none were fully clothed to begin with. And after a forced march that required sleeping in the dirt for several weeks, followed by nearly a month of captivity in the barracoon, both clothes and bodies would have been filthy.

When he was seventy-nine years old, Cudjo gave a newspaper interview and offered a brief insight into how he felt in the moment. He describes the events leading up to boarding the ship this way: "All of us that were left were taken to the coast and loaded into a big ship by white men, a sight we had never seen before. We were mighty scared, but we thought anything was better than death such as our brothers and sisters suffered, so [we] made the best of it and came peacefully with those strange white men. I was between 18 and 20 years old when they caught me."

As the captives were climbing up a rope ladder from the canoes to board the *Clotilda*, an alarming call came down from a man high up the mast in the rigging with a telescope. "Man aloft with glass sang out 'Sail Ho' steamer to leeward ten miles," Foster wrote. The captain noticed a series of black and white flags, which he knew to be distress signals, spread for miles down the coastline. Foster's suspicions about a double cross during his time on shore were suddenly manifest as two steamships emerged from behind a point about six miles south. On returning to his ship, Foster learned that a slave squadron vessel flying English colors had approached the *Clotilda* while he was ashore. The British had not searched *Clotilda* out of respect for the American flag, but being spied at anchor at one of the world's top three slave ports was not a good development. The captain climbed the rigging to study the ships with the telescope himself. If the steamers captured the ship as the prisoners were being loaded aboard, there would be no escape for him and his crew. Though only 75 of the agreed upon 125 captives were on board, Foster hollered down to heave anchor and raise the sails. The only hope was for the *Clotilda* to outrun the steamships. But instead of heeding the captain's order, the crew mutinied again. "The crew, thinking our capture inevitable, refused duty and wanted to take my boats from the vessel and go on shore," Foster recalled, explaining that trying to ride the ferocious surf in their tiny rowboats could only end in death. Even if they made it ashore, they'd be paddling right into the hands of the very people who had apparently double-crossed them and sold them out to the slave squadron ships. A fight ensued as the steamers grew larger on the horizon. In the account relayed by Meaher's son, as the crew attempted to lower the landing boats, the captain drew a pistol on them and forced them to raise sail.

As the crew reluctantly made ready to depart, two more canoes pulled alongside with another 35 slaves, including Cudjo, who was on board the last boat to make it to the *Clotilda*. He and the others were hurried aboard, put in leg irons, and forced into the hold as the ship began to make way with 110 captives. The fifteen souls left behind on the beach would have been worth $22,500 back home, or more than $600,000 in today's dollars. As *Clotilda*'s sails unfurled, the steamers changed course in an attempt to intercept her. But the *Clotilda*, flying all of her extra canvas, was running with the wind and making eleven knots within a few minutes, outpacing the slower steamships. Four hours into the voyage, both Africa and the slave squadron disappeared below the horizon.

So began the trip to America for the *Clotilda* captives—naked, terrified, and locked in the pitch-black of the ship's hold in groups of six or eight. For people who had never seen the ocean to suddenly find themselves bobbing up and down in a small ship on the open Atlantic was disorienting and frightening. The creaking of the ship's planking, the whine of wind through the rigging, and the flapping and luffing of the sails were all foreign. Cudjo remembers it this way: "I so skeered on de sea! De water, you unnerstand me, it makes so much noise! It growl lak de thousand beasts in de bush. De wind got so much voice on de water. Oh Lor'! Sometime de ship way up in de sky. Sometimes it way down in de bottom of de sea."

During the history of the Atlantic slave trade, it is likely that hundreds of thousands, perhaps millions, of people died of disease, seasickness, fear, or heartbreak before they made it across the ocean in what is famously known as the Middle Passage. Two people died in the close confines of the *Clotilda*'s hold. They were dumped overboard by the captors. This was a common occurrence on slave ships. Some of the largest boats in the trade with Brazil, which carried more than a thousand people at a time, could lose as many as a quarter of those trapped on board each voyage, due to massive overcrowding, disease, and limited food and water. For those stolen from their homes, the Middle Passage was mostly about surviving. Again and again in the records of the Slave Squadron, we find vivid and awful accounts of life aboard captured slavers.

"The negroes are packed below in as dense a mass as it is possible for human beings to be crowded; the space allotted them being in general about four feet high between decks, there, of course, can be but little ventilation given," wrote Lieutenant T. Augustus Craven, who commanded the steam-powered slave-ship hunter *Mohawk*, describing conditions aboard slavers he caught around Key West. "These unfortunate creatures are obliged to attend to the calls of nature in this place—tubs being provided for the purpose—and here they pass their days, their nights, amidst the most horridly offensive odors of which the mind can conceive, and this under the scorching heat of the tropical sun, without room for sleep; with scarcely space to die in; with daily allowance of food and water barely sufficient to keep them alive. The passage varies from forty to sixty days, and when it has much exceeded the shorter time disease has appeared in its most appalling forms, the provisions and water are nearly exhausted, and their sufferings are incredible."

Twelve days after the *Clotilda* left Ouidah, a man-of-war ship loomed on the horizon. Capture at this point, with a ship full of Africans, meant risking the gallows for captain and crew. When he was in his eighties, Cudjo Lewis told a newspaper reporter an anecdote that appears nowhere else in the *Clotilda* record. He said that when a ship appeared on the horizon, Captain Foster made preparations for dumping all of his captives overboard. If it is true, it likely occurred at this moment. The reporter who interviewed Cudjo captured the scene this way: "The whole consignment of slaves was driven on deck and manacled to the anchor chain stretched along the decks. A fast cruiser of one of the powers policing the middle passage to put down the slave trade had given chase. Had the cruiser overhauled the slaver, the chain would have been let go, carrying its helpless, shrieking burden overboard. This inhuman act would have destroyed evidence against the slaver's crew. It was frequently done." Indeed, there are a number of accounts of slave cargoes dispatched to the bottom of the sea in just such a fashion, so the slavers might escape prosecution.

Foster says the ship was saved from capture thanks to a heavy squall that arose suddenly, its high winds enabling *Clotilda* to outrun yet another pursuer. The next morning, the *Clotilda* caught the northeast trade winds and her pace picked up to fourteen knots per hour. Running a broad reach against a stiff wind—a nautical term for a favorable course that allows a ship to take full advantage of the breeze—Foster finally felt safe enough to bring his prisoners up on deck in groups so that they might walk around in the fresh air.

On top of all the horrors, and coping with so many crushing losses, there was the boredom. So it was a welcome moment when the captives were allowed onto the deck for the first time. "Cudjo suffer so in dat ship. . . . On de thirteenth day dey fetchee us on de deck. We so weak we ain' able to walk ourselves, so de crew take each one and walk 'round de deck till we git so we kin walk ourselves. . . . We lookee and lookee and lookee and lookee and we doan see nothin' but water. Where we come from we doan know. Where we going, we doan know." Topside, the prisoners were given their daily water allowance of one and a half pints. The water was sour, treated with vinegar to help ward off scurvy. Each group was allowed an hour topside, then made to wash the section of the ship where they were held. Manual bilge pumps in the hold would have moved the rancid wastewater overboard, making for a slightly more tolerable voyage through the Middle Passage than most captives experienced. Meals came twice a day. It seems likely that Foster, who would soon own ten of the people on board, took extra care to see that they arrived in Alabama healthy and well fed. The *Clotilda* also ended up carrying a lot of extra provisions. Meaher and Foster had hoped to buy as many as 170 people for their twenty-seven pounds of gold and packed accordingly when stocking the galley.

The old sailing captains always made use of well-known water currents, like the Gulf Stream, and dominant wind patterns, like the famous trade winds, to slingshot themselves toward their destination. By the evening of June 30, less than a month out from Ouidah, the *Clotilda* was already across the Atlantic, shooting through the gap in the reef around Abaco Island. These are treacherous waters, even today, and they almost claimed the *Clotilda*. Crossing the reef at twilight, the ship ran up on a sunken vessel, the wreckage just breaking the water's surface. The ship's lookout saw the wreck at the last moment before impact and sang out "hard a starboard!"—signaling the helmsman to swing the wheel hard to the right. The *Clotilda* passed within ten feet of the wreck, narrowly avoiding the same fate.

Entering the Caribbean Sea, Foster removed the extra rigging that had been installed to make speed across the Atlantic. They were just days away from Alabama at this point, and the extra rope and wood made *Clotilda* conspicuous. The big square-rigged sails were stowed and the extra timbers added to increase the height of the mast were taken down. The ship once again looked like a common schooner trading between Gulf Coast ports. The disguise was put to the test the very next morning when two men-of-war were spotted sailing nearby. Neither vessel altered course toward the *Clotilda*, which Foster steered northwest toward Mississippi. Once in the Gulf of Mexico, the captives were kept belowdecks to avoid discovery. "We been on de water seventy days and we spend some time layin' down in de ship till we tired, but many days we on de deck. Nobody ain' sick and nobody ain' dead. Cap'n Bill Foster a good man. He don't 'buse us and treat us mean on de ship," Cudjo told Hurston.

As they approached Mobile, the captain took a purposefully circuitous route, sailing right past Alabama and the twin forts that guarded the main entrance to Mobile Bay. He kept the ship far offshore as he passed, to ensure her sails wouldn't be spied by the lookouts at the forts or by the keeper of the Sand Island Lighthouse. Due to the curvature of the Earth, ships disappear below the horizon once they are about twelve miles offshore. Foster was making for Petit Bois Pass, which runs between Dauphin Island and Petit Bois Island, barrier islands each about seven miles off the coast. The pass is at the far west end of Dauphin Island, about eighteen miles from Fort Gaines, which sits on the extreme eastern tip of the island, guarding the main entrance to the port of Mobile. He knew no one at the fort would be able to spy *Clotilda* as she came ashore there. This was all part of the plan hatched before the voyage even began. Foster and Meaher agreed they would try to sneak the *Clotilda* into the Mississippi Sound and hide her at a place called Pointe aux Pins. The point is a marshy outcropping that juts out from the Alabama coast between two geographic features, Bayou La Batre and Grand Bay. As the English translation of its name suggests, "Point of Pines" features a dense forest of tall slash pine trees, which would have helped obscure the *Clotilda* from the view of any ships heading north up Mobile Bay.

The area was uninhabited except for a small outpost of fishermen who lived in rough cabins a little way up the bayou in an area known as San Souci, which translates as "without a care."

The plan called for Foster and the slaves to wait aboard the *Clotilda* for Meaher, who was supposed to be monitoring the rendezvous location for the ship's arrival. Meaher was to bring another vessel and take the captives up the bay, into the Mobile River and on to his waiting plantation. Meanwhile, Foster would sail the *Clotilda* to Mexico, have her thoroughly scrubbed to wash away the evidence of slaving, then rename the ship, change its rigging, and purchase fake papers clearing her for a cargo run to New Orleans. Unfortunately, while Foster was sailing to Africa, Meaher and the other conspirators had bragged of their caper to anyone who would listen. Meaher became convinced he was being watched by federal officials lying in wait for *Clotilda*. Not only was Meaher too scared to post a watch at the rendezvous point, as their plan called for, but the *Clotilda* made better time than expected on the return journey and was back in Alabama ahead of schedule.

While Foster claims in his journal that he passed through Petit Bois Pass on July 9, it is almost certain it was July 7, a Saturday. Cudjo remembered that the ship dropped anchor and stopped moving for the first time in the journey. The next morning, the crew brought a tree branch covered with green leaves to the captives to communicate that they were close to shore and had arrived at their destination. The slaves were told to stay quiet. Meanwhile, up on deck, Foster was having yet another showdown with a mutinous crew. After waiting all night and into Sunday morning for his partner in crime to arrive, per their plan, Foster realized he would have to go to Mobile and fetch Meaher to the ship. But the crew wasn't having it. They were now pirates in possession of a ship full of human contraband. It wouldn't matter to the authorities that none of them had known the true mission of the ship when they left port. The fact that they had sailed a ship full of kidnapped Africans across the ocean meant they were all eligible for the noose. The last thing the crew wanted was more time resting at anchor in American waters aboard the evidence of their crime.

"The mates and crew did not want me to leave the vessel until they were paid for the voyage and said they would kill me if I attempted to take the negroes ashore without their money," Foster wrote. The captain was allowed to leave the ship only after promising to return with the crew's wages. He rowed to shore and hiked to Bayou La Batre about two miles distant. There he rented a horse and buggy from a farmer for $25 to ride to Meaher's house north of Mobile, about twenty miles away.

On hearing that the cargo had landed, Tim Meaher sent one of his brothers to St. John's Church to pull his tugboat captain out of Sunday morning services. He ordered several of his steamboats to fire up their boilers to help collect the prisoners and hide the *Clotilda*. Instead of coal, Meaher burned huge slabs of bacon as fuel. Bacon burns hotter than coal, leading to a significant increase in speed.

While Foster returned the farmer's wagon, James Meaher and an enslaved Cherokee named James Dennison steamed on pork power toward Pointe aux Pins aboard the tugboat *Billy Jones*. Out of all the people the Meahers enslaved, Dennison was the most trusted. He had even been trained to pilot the family steamboats in the rivers. His Native American parents were enslaved in North Carolina. The Meahers bought him at the Mobile slave market after he'd been sold downriver and away from his family. Dennison and Meaher stopped in Bayou La Batre to pick up Foster and traveled the last mile from the bayou to the other side of the point.

But Foster was returning empty-handed. He had failed to get the crew's money from Meaher, who refused to honor the promise of double wages Foster had made the first time the crew mutinied on the way to Africa. The lack of money caused an immediate problem upon Foster's return. The crew thwarted every attempt to tie a tow rope from the *Billy Jones* to the *Clotilda*. They knew the people in the hold were worth $187,000 on shore, or about $6 million today. From the crew's perspective, the entire voyage had been a double cross from the moment they left the dock. They were unwittingly forced into piracy of the worst kind, had taken all the risk, and now the men responsible were refusing to pay them. Foster and James Meaher had no choice but to steam back up the bay to Mobile to get the cash, leaving their entire ploy vulnerable to discovery for the better part of a day. In Mobile, Timothy Meaher would only provide the originally promised wages, not the double pay. He sent his brother and Foster back with just $8,000 and told them he'd take care of the crew once they were on the big steamboat. Five toughs from the shipyard escorted Foster and the crew of the *Billy Jones* to make sure there was no trouble. They reached the ship at 9 p.m. The tug's throbbing and whistling steam engine was the first motor the Africans had ever heard. From down in the hold, they decided it sounded like a swarm of bees.

The masts had been removed from the *Clotilda* as she lay behind the trees of the point. The idea was to disguise her as a barge for the trip up the bay. A tug pulling a barge up the bay at night was much less conspicuous than a tug pulling a seagoing ship. Plus, a ship returning to port from overseas was legally required to report to the harbormaster on arrival. It was imperative that no one in the harbor know of her arrival. The lay of the land would provide some natural cover for this most perilous part of the journey. Both Fort Gaines and Fort Morgan face south, toward the Gulf, watching for attack from foreign navies. The *Billy Jones* towed the *Clotilda* east through the Mississippi Sound, hugging the shoreline of the mainland, which was separated from the barrier islands and the forts by about seven miles of open water. The moon was nearly full, casting a distressingly bright light on their activities, but it couldn't be helped. The tug made the run without lights, hoping the watchmen of the fort wouldn't spy them across so much open water. They passed through the bay without incident, a journey that would have taken about three hours with a ship in tow. The next challenge was getting past downtown Mobile and the port, which sits at the head of the bay on the Mobile River. The river was the main thoroughfare for everything shipped into or out of Alabama, and it cut through the heart of downtown. But it wasn't the only river that entered the top of the bay. In fact, the thirteen-mile-wide swamp that stretches east away from Mobile is now known as 5 Rivers as a tribute to the other rivers that dump into Mobile Bay through the same swamp. Meaher and Foster planned to steam right past the entrance of the port and tuck into the nearby Spanish River, which was much smaller and totally uninhabited. This route took them around the back side of Pinto Island, which was then heavily forested, shielding them from any prying eyes in Mobile. A few miles farther north, well past the port, the Spanish and the Mobile Rivers converged. From there, it would be a simple matter to transport the captives upriver to the plantations of the conspirators.

What happened next is subject to contradictory explanations from those involved. Some of those contradictions appear to have been intentional, designed to throw investigators off the trail of Meaher and the other perpetrators. Their disinformation campaign worked well, thwarting the discovery of the ship for 160 years.

For now, it is enough to know that the *Billy Jones* steamed into the Mobile River, met up with the *Czar*—a family steamboat carrying both Timothy and Burns Meaher—and headed two miles north into a swamp best described even today as a remote and haunted location. The shores are lined with a thick and marshy strand of bulrushes, wild rice, and cattails, chest-high and difficult to walk through. Hanging overhead, cypress and tupelo trees drip with stalactites of Spanish moss. The big moon would have made for eerie silhouettes that night, coal-black against its brightness. The rush of senses the Africans experienced as they climbed from the hold: the smothering embrace of the Alabama night, ninety degrees and dripping with humidity; the deafening roar of the swamp as hundreds of thousands of amorous insects, frogs, and birds sang out their desire to couple; and terror at being forced from the *Clotilda* onto the smoking and belching steamboat. Foster's widow relayed that the crew of the *Clotilda* mutinied one final time, after the prisoners had been moved onto the steamboat. The sailors refused to board another boat carrying the human contraband. Foster forced them off the *Clotilda* with a pistol in each hand, declaring, "hit the grit and never be seen in Southern waters again," according to his wife. The mates and crew would have learned of the original plan to sail the *Clotilda* to Mexico for refitting and a new name, as they would have been expected to sail her there. But they were probably unaware that Meaher and Foster had changed the plan and were going to burn the ship, precisely because the crew had proven so troublesome. Afraid the crew would talk, Meaher was going to make them disappear.

The reluctant crew finally joined Meaher and the captives on the *Czar*. The ship's furnace was stuffed with the hot burning slabs of bacon, and the race was on to catch up to Timothy Meaher's alibi, his ship the *Roger B. Taney*, already partway to Montgomery on its usual Sunday run. The *Taney*'s first mate left the dock with passengers and cargo at the regular departure time Sunday afternoon and set a leisurely pace. Dinner was not to be served until Meaher was on board. The passengers he ate with would become his alibi, proving he couldn't have been a part of a slave-trading operation that night on the river.

As the *Czar* sped away, Foster and a couple of men carried

seven cords of fatwood—heart pine laden with explosively flammable sap—onto the *Clotilda* and spread them around the ship. Before lighting the conflagration, Foster rescued the desk from his cabin, along with his chair and the ship's clock. Just before lighting the fire, he would have opened the valves in the bilge, letting water pour into the hold. The ship would have been sinking even as he lit it on fire. In his journal, he described the end of the *Clotilda*'s final voyage this way: "I transferred my slaves to a river steamboat and sent them up into the canebrake to hide them until further disposal. I then burned my schooner to the water's edge and sunk her."

Fueled by the fatwood, the fire would have been intense. The glow over the swamp would have been noticeable even from Mobile, about eight miles south. For Foster it was a bittersweet moment. He would complain for the rest of his life that the ship was worth much more than the ten people he was given for his role. That proved especially true when everyone was freed by the war just five years later.

First, the prisoners had to be quartered somewhere away from the prying eyes of the law. Conspirator John Dabney's plantation at a big river bend on the Tombigbee was conveniently on the way, and it was agreed that it would likely prove safer than hiding them on property owned by one of the Meahers, all located much closer to Mobile. The *Czar* pulled up to Dabney's pier at the base of the plantation's giant cotton slide, and the captives were led onto dry land for the first time in two months. The decision was made to keep them down by the river, away from the plantation house and slave quarters, so as to avoid detection by anyone on the plantation, including the 47 American-born people Dabney had enslaved, who would definitely have noticed and talked a lot about the sudden presence of 110 Africans in their midst.

Meanwhile, the *Czar* motored back downstream to the Tombigbee's confluence with the Alabama River, and then sped north up the Alabama for the rendezvous with the *Roger B. Taney*. Coming alongside the steamer, Meaher quickly moved the *Clotilda*'s eleven crewmen into a locked room on the ship's upper deck, away from the main salon. They were provided with whiskey and a few decks of cards and told to keep quiet. The main goal was to keep them away from the rest of the passengers on the boat. At 9:30 p.m., dinner was announced in the salon and Meaher assumed his place at the head of the table. In a newspaper interview in 1890 with the *St. Louis Globe-Democrat*, Meaher recounted how handily he comported himself. The reporter captured the scene this way: "When the captain took his seat at the head of the table his face wore a most nonchalant appearance, and gave forth not the slightest intimation that he had been engaged in other than the legitimate performance of his duties. He was plied with all manner of questions as to his whereabouts during the earlier hours of the trip, but to all of these interrogatories he made evasive replies and was wholly non-committal."

Meaher's son later said that his father told the passengers that a sick cook was to blame for the late dinner. He couldn't have cared less about his customers' inconvenience. By making them wait for their supper until he could join them, Meaher gained dozens of witnesses who would swear he'd dined with them on the steamboat, and couldn't possibly have been elsewhere smuggling people into the country.

On arrival in Montgomery, the *Clotilda* crew were taken directly to the train station and placed on a mail train headed for

New York. At this point, as they were being disappeared out of Alabama, they finally received their pay—but only the $700 they had originally been promised, not the double wages Foster guaranteed during their first mutiny in Porto Playa when *Clotilda*'s rudder was repaired. It is unknown whether the sailors complained, or were just glad to have escaped from the clutches of the men who'd forced them into piracy.

Captain Meaher steered the *Roger B. Taney* back to Mobile the next day and began bragging to friends about his bet.

Chapter 6

INTO THE
CANEBRAKE

The swamp around Mount Vernon would have been a wholly alien environment for the Africans. Tall and craggy cypress trees grow right out of the water along the banks, their limbs wearing a heavy drape of Spanish moss. Alligators are numerous, as are three species of venomous snake, bears, and, at that time, panthers. The forests are thunderingly loud night and day in July, with the voracious hum of thousands of insect species, frogs, and hundreds of kinds of birds.

Dabney's property was home to an almost impenetrable band of thick cane that lined the riverbanks and filled in most of the surrounding floodplain, which was where Meaher planned to hide the captives. Though they are almost unknown in Alabama today, dense canebrakes such as this used to crowd the banks of rivers throughout the state. It was one of the dominant ecosystem types along the rivers, but it has almost completely disappeared today. Thirty major dams have so altered the hydrology of the state's rivers—including when the rivers overflow into the floodplains, and for how long—that the water-loving canebrakes simply can't survive.

It was into such a thicket that the captives were led as they emerged from the steamboat. Imagine a forest of dense bamboo, the stems growing so closely together they shade out any other type of tree. American naturalist William Bartram, who named many of the plants in the South during his travels in the late 1700s, was particularly taken with the majesty of the canebrakes along this same stretch of the Tombigbee in 1775. He recounted that "the reeds or canes grow here thirty or forty feet high, and as thick as a man's arm, or three or four inches in diameter."

The captives were to remain in the swamp for their first eleven days in America, and were told not to speak above a whisper during their canebrake captivity, lest someone passing by on the river hear their foreign tongues. James Dennison, the enslaved riverboat pilot, was left to guard the captives with a few other people enslaved by Meaher. To keep them secret, Dennison moved the captives every day, from one section of the swamp to another.

None of the sources make mention of whether or how the captives were bound. It seems likely they were still chained in the small groups of eight as they had been on the ship, perhaps still by the neck. Of course the strange new world of the swamp probably helped police the group as well, as it can be a scary place. By the height of the summer in July, several species of spider have reached enormous size, with bodies the size of your thumb, and legs up to four inches long. Their webs are strung through the floodplain jungles in such number that it is almost impossible to avoid walking into them. The Africans would have recognized alligators, as Benin is home to a small crocodile species, but the West African crocs, which top out around seven feet long, are much smaller than American gators. The largest alligator ever captured was killed in 2014, on the Alabama River, just a few miles from the swamp where the captives were stashed. That animal was 15 feet, 9 inches long, and weighed 1,000 pounds. The gator had a whole deer in its belly, an animal that weighed 115 pounds. Swallowed in one gulp. Seeing a dangerous animal they were familiar with from home, but in far, far larger form, must have conjured fears in the captives about other threats lurking in the forests. And indeed there were: water moccasins, biting yellow flies, and swarms of mosquitoes—all threats to which they would have been exposed fully naked.

On the eleventh day, some old clothes were provided. It had taken a while to round up enough for 110 people, and by the time the captives received them, they were a welcome comfort. Meaher's houseboy, Noah Hart, described the clothes as "rags an' pieces er corn sack an' skins tied round day bodies." Still, clothing was one of the only things Cudjo mentioned when describing the first days in America to Hurston. Many of the survivors later spoke of the moment they were again able to put on clothes. The other thing he mentioned was the onslaught of the mosquitoes. In fact, he remembered it this way: "Dey keep us up de Alabama River and hide us in de swamp. But de mosquitoes dey so bad dey 'bout to eat us up, so dey took us to Cap'n Burns Meaher's place and vide us up."

Of course it was not out of concern over mosquito bites that the captives were removed from the swamp. Rather it was because Meaher and his conspirators had gotten wind of a plot by federal officials to confiscate the Africans and prosecute the Meahers and Dabney for illegal slaving. This seems an inevitable outcome, given the excitement in Mobile and indeed around the country concerning the arrival of the Africans. Recall that the news of the ship's departure for Africa had made national news shortly after she sailed. Just two days after her return, a news article appeared in a Georgia newspaper that, while it got the number of captives wrong, was accurate enough to include a telling detail: "The schooner *Clotilda*, with 124 Africans on board, arrived in Mobile Bay today, and a steamboat immediately took the negroes up the river." The newspaper I once worked for, the *Mobile Register*, hailed the *Clotilda*'s arrival with a congratulatory editorial: "Whoever conducted the affair has our congratulations on his or their success." It went on to argue for the smuggling of more captives, repeating the trope that it was for the Africans' own good, after all. "We take it that the trade is, to all intents and purposes, opened—why not? Why should not those who are in want of negro labor import it at a low cost, when they are civilizing and Christianizing a set of barbarians by the same course?" Within a week, more articles appeared in national publications, containing the name of the ship and the detail of a steamboat's involvement. Likewise, the story spread from newspaper to newspaper via telegraph, from California to Texas to New York.

Timothy Meaher was arrested first and brought before his close friend, U.S. Circuit Court Judge William G. Jones. Coincidentally, the year prior, Jones had played an outsize role in how the federal courts handled the cases related to the Africans illegally smuggled aboard the *Wanderer*, the ship that inspired Meaher to send the *Clotilda* to Africa in the first place. Judge

Jones's precedent-setting courtroom decision regarding the trial of Mobilian Horatio Gould—who was charged with purchasing Africans imported aboard the *Wanderer*—drew nationwide attention. In his decision in the Gould case, the judge effectively gutted the laws that outlawed the international slave trade. Jones ruled that Gould could not be tried under the federal antislavery laws based on a specious technicality, arguing that once an illegally imported person had "mingled with the inhabitants of the State," federal laws—including those that prohibited importation and sale of Africans in the first place—no longer applied to the captive. He ruled that only state courts had jurisdiction once an enslaved person arrived in the United States, and there were no state laws prohibiting the importation of captives from abroad.

That Judge Jones should have recused himself from hearing Meaher's case is obvious from one fact alone: the pair were close enough friends that Meaher had named a steamboat after the judge. Instead of recusing himself, however, Jones released Meaher from custody immediately on the basis of the captain's sworn statement that he was aboard the *Roger B. Taney* on its regular run up the river, and that dozens of witnesses who dined with him on board the boat could corroborate that fact. But Meaher's release by Judge Jones had likely been a foregone conclusion even before he was arrested, as Jones's sympathies aligned with Meaher's on the question of slavery. Within a year, at the outbreak of the Civil War, Jones would resign his federal post and sign on as one of the first district court judges in the Confederacy.

While there is no proof, I suspect Meaher received a tip from his friend Jones—perhaps in the judge's chambers after Meaher's release—suggesting that the U.S. District Court's enforcement officers were planning to head straight for Dabney's in pursuit of the *Clotilda* captives. There is a story Meaher often repeated in interviews about what happened next. It is a self-glorifying tale, still told by Meaher's descendants, that has him once again outwitting all pursuers, especially the federal agents chasing him. In Meaher's telling, he had received word that the feds had chartered the *Eclipse*, a steamboat, to take them upriver to collect the captives at John Dabney's plantation. With the *Eclipse* already preparing to leave, there was no time to get word to Dabney's or to move the prisoners, unless Meaher could find a way to stall the steamer. This came in the form of whiskey. Meaher dispatched an employee to buy several bottles and sneak them to the crew of the *Eclipse*, who were waiting at the dock for the federal agents and soldiers to show up. By the time the officers of the court appeared for the run upriver, supposedly the crew was so drunk they couldn't operate the ship. An entirely new crew had to be rounded up. Meanwhile, Meaher used the delay to stoke the engines of one of his boats once again with bacon sides and hurry upriver to Dabney's. The prisoners were quickly loaded up and moved to brother Burns's plantation, miles away, located on another river altogether. By the time the federal marshal's team reached Dabney's, all they could find were several abandoned campsites where the Africans had been quartered during their first week and a half in the canebrake.

At Burns's place, the captives slept under a roof for the first time, though it was just for a pole barn for wagons, a building with a roof but no walls. The same dreadful monotony ruled their lives there—up before dawn and disappeared into the swamp, where they were forced to remain until nightfall. When

Roche interviewed the last eight survivors decades later, they remembered that James Dennison and Noah Hart would lead them with hand gestures and "a shooing sound—such as you would drive chickens or geese."

The captives remembered being overwhelmed with sadness and grief during this time. In the preceding two months, they had been roused from their beds at the point of spear and gun, watched as their siblings, parents, grandparents, friends, and leaders were killed, then locked in an internment camp for weeks. After weeks in the pen, their coming fate unknown, they were sold to the first white man they'd ever seen and loaded onto the first ship they'd ever seen, which was floating on the first ocean they'd ever seen. Then forty-five days spent naked and chained in the dark hold of a ship. When they finally escaped the confines of the ship, it was only to find themselves still chained but wandering naked through a dense jungle in an alien landscape. Their new reality was to be herded like livestock from place to place by people they could neither understand nor communicate with.

With the ruse of the *Eclipse* successfully behind them, the word was put out to the conspirators to meet at a secret location to divvy up the loot. Dennison, the Cherokee pilot, loaded the men, women, and children of the *Clotilda* onto another steamboat and delivered them to the site, where the captives would soon undergo another heartbreaking separation. Males and females were divided and made to stand in two long rows. They had been captives for about three months at this point, first in the barracoon, then six weeks on the ship and now two weeks marched daily through a muddy swamp, still with no chance to bathe, their new clothes nothing but rags to begin with. We know some of them, such as Sally "Redoshi" Smith, were just children, as young as twelve. The buyers—who included the Meaher brothers, John Dabney, and a few other, unidentified, men—circulated among them, examining bodies, teeth, and feet. Before any were sold, the Meahers and Captain Foster took turns making their selections. The best accounting from the various sources suggests that Timothy Meaher took thirty-two, evenly divided between men and women, while Burns Meaher took twenty, Foster got sixteen, and James Meaher got eight, including Cudjo. The final thirty-four were sold to slave dealers from Montgomery to help cover the costs of the voyage. They would have been worth more than a half million dollars in today's currency. It is not known what happened to most of the final thirty-four, but a number of them, including Sally "Redoshi" Smith, ended up at points north, mostly in a place called Bogue Chitto, near Selma. As they were parted, Cudjo said, "we very sorry to be parted from one 'nother. We cry for home . . . we cain help but cry. So we sing."

As the group sold to the slave dealers were marched off to their new lives, the slave dealer herding them suddenly ushered his coffle of Africans off the road and hid them in the bushes. A string of wagons from a traveling circus was coming, and the dealer didn't want his foreign charges discovered. The captives said they were forced to face away from the road, perhaps to hide their facial scarifications and tattoos. As the circus passed, an elephant trumpeted, an unmistakable sound to anyone who has ever heard it. This was especially true for a group of people just removed from a country where elephants were so common that a depiction of an elephant in a crown graced the royal flag of King Glele, the man responsible for selling them to the Americans. As the survivors recounted the story to Roche decades later, the captives began hollering, "Ele! Ele!"—meaning home—and then "Argenacou," the Fon word for "elephant." Alas, the elephant was as much a stranger and a captive as the Africans. It may well have been offering a lament for its homeland, just as the *Clotilda* captives continued to do.

"Our grief so heavy look lak we cain stand it. I think maybe I die in my sleep when I dream about my mama," Cudjo told Roche.

Shortly after the *Clotilda* passengers were divided up, a series of letters from the U.S. Attorney of the Southern District of Alabama were sent to Washington, D.C. Federal summonses followed quickly, on July 27, 1860, issued for Burns Meaher, John Dabney, and Captain William Foster. This was eighteen days after the ship arrived, and about a week after the prisoners had been divided and sold. The federal documents are all handwritten in longhand. The court records for the case are a testament to the rapid acceleration of government bureaucracy in the 1800s, with pages and pages of legal text copied over and over when really all that was needed was a single paragraph that could have covered all of the accused. For Burns Meaher, the tight cursive script of the summons states: "Against Burns Meaher, that one hundred and three negroes were imported or brought to the United States from a foreign kingdom, place, or country, with intent to hold, sell, or dispose of said negroes or slaves, or to hold them to service or labor; and that the said Burns Meaher holds the negroes afore said." The papers state that Burns had 25 men, 25 women, 25 boys, and 25 girls, making for a total of 100. Dabney's summons is identical in its details, except for suggesting he had 40 of the captives. Together the men are charged with holding 140 Africans, out of a supposed total of just 103. While the numbers don't add up or reflect how many prisoners Burns and Dabney actually got, the summonses show that the federal officers knew, even at this early date, that the group had been split up among the conspirators, and they show the feds knew who the perpetrators were.

Interestingly, the summons for Dabney and the Meahers were issued on July 27, 1860, but not served for five months, until December 17, 1860. There is no explanation in the records for the delay in serving the men. This delay seems suspicious because the whereabouts of all the *Clotilda* players were well known, save the crew of sailors that had been disappeared on the train heading north. It would have been a simple matter to serve the summonses to the Meahers, Dabney, and Foster promptly, rather than months later. But the orders to serve them had to come through Judge Jones's court. It seems a safe bet that the Meaher family's long friendship with Judge Jones was responsible for the laconic pace. In any case, the result of the summonses was unambiguous. In the "Final Record" for the cases against the men, court officer C. M. Godbold stated, "The within mentioned negroes not found in my district, 20th Dec. 1860." With no Africans, the cases against the Meahers and Dabney were dismissed.

Foster's case, on the other hand, was a little more complicated. It was clear and irrefutable that he had returned with cargo from a foreign port without registering with port officials in the United States or paying proper duty and taxes for the cargo. Not only did he not check in, as required, but he was suddenly unable to account for the whereabouts of his large and very valuable ship. For Foster, the charge meant a $1,000 fine, equal to $32,000 today. But he never had to pay it. After several continuances and delays, his day in court was going to be Friday, April 12, 1861, but that date just happened to coincide with the opening battle of the Civil War. Federal courts across the South were disbanded as the judges, Jones included, resigned and were appointed as district judges for the Confederacy. Foster's case is mentioned twice in federal court records from 1866, the year after the war ended. It appears there may have been some interest in prosecuting him then, but the trail goes cold. There are no records indicating he ever paid the fine.

In the end, not only was no one hung for the *Clotilda*'s illegal slaving run, as Meaher had predicted a year prior on his steamboat, no one was ever convicted of a single crime.

In fact, the only person ever hung for slaving, Nathaniel Gordon, captain of the *Erie*, was captured just three weeks after the *Clotilda* arrived safely back in Alabama in July of 1860. Gordon was caught in the Caribbean with 897 slaves locked in the hold. He was executed in 1862, after Abraham Lincoln became the first president to refuse to pardon a convicted slaver. At Gordon's trial, Judge W. D. Shipman handed down a death sentence, quoting the Bible and warning Gordon of the eternal fate that awaited him for his great crime: "Do not attempt to hide its enormity from yourself; think of the cruelty and wickedness of seizing nearly a thousand fellow beings, who never did you harm, and thrusting them beneath the decks of a small ship, beneath a burning tropical sun, to die of disease and suffocation, or be transported to distant lands, and be consigned, they and their posterity, to a fate far more cruel than death." It is a safe bet that Meaher and Foster both followed Gordon's trial with more than a little relief at their narrow escape from a similar end.

Chapter 7

FIVE YEARS A SLAVE

Within days of arriving at the plantations where they would spend their captivity, the Africans demonstrated two traits central to their survival in the coming years: they stuck together, and they fought back.

The group was able to remain connected, despite being split between four plantations, thanks to the Meaher family steamboat fleet. Each brother contributed some of his slaves to serve on the boats, and the boats made regular stops at the three Meaher plantations as well as Dabney's. News within the group traveled quickly up- and downriver. Even the people who were not from Bante had at four months been a part of the group long enough to have formed friendships and tight bonds since meeting in the barracoon and enduring the Middle Passage together.

Much of what we know about the Africans' first days in Mobile comes from an 1893 interview with Noah Hart, who was enslaved as Timothy Meaher's houseboy and was one of his most trusted servants. Hart was privy to many things no one else witnessed, such as the moment Foster showed up on a lathered horse from Pointe aux Pins to announce the arrival of the ship, and the first time the Africans made clear they would not tolerate harsh punishment from their new enslavers.

That moment came inside the Meaher house, where Captain Tim's wife, Mary, had taken a shine to one of the African girls who was soft-spoken and pretty. Mary wanted the girl to work in the house instead of the fields, so she assigned Aunt Polly, her hired cook, to teach the teenager light housework and to help in the kitchen. Aunt Polly became frustrated teaching the girl how to sweep and slapped her in the side of the head. Noah said the African girl put her hand up to her face and "stan' lookin' lak she wuz done lost her senses." Aunt Polly began backing away from the girl, toward the staircase.

"All of a suddent, de gal thowe back her head an' give one screech. Never in all my life I hear er soun' lak dat gal made," Noah said, describing it as a combination of a wailing calf and a wildcat in the darkness. He said it raised goosebumps the size of potatoes on his arms. It also brought the rest of the Africans running, men and women. They came from the cotton fields, the cane fields, and the rice fields far away by the creek. They came carrying the shovels and tools they'd been working with, calling back to the woman in the house with a noise as "ungodly as de screech of de gal herself." The Africans charged into the house as Polly and Mary Meaher retreated to an upstairs bedroom and locked themselves in. The Africans beat on the bedroom door, looking so terrifying that Noah "thought dey wuz gwine to kill eve'body." After a few minutes, Mary Meaher stepped out of the bedroom and stared the Africans down. Noah was told to try and calm them. After a few minutes exchanging pantomimes, the Africans returned to the fields. Aunt Polly quit and went to work for someone in Mobile. Noah said, "nobody didn't touch one er dem Affikins no more."

Cudjo told Hurston a similar story about another uprising on Timothy Meaher's plantation, also caused by early efforts to control the Africans through application of corporal punishment. Meaher's overseer berated one of the African women working in a field with a group of her fellow prisoners. The overseer hit the woman with a whip. The Africans charged en masse.

"One man try whippee one my country women and dey all jump on him and takee de whip 'way from him and lashee him did it. He doan never try whip Affican women no mo'," Cudjo told Hurston.

One of the most unusual things about the *Clotilda* group is that they remained together after their capture. Many of them were from the same village and had grown up together, or were related. Their bonds to each other were lifelong and made stronger through shared hardship. We know several of the men, including Cudjo and his friend Keeby, trained as warriors before they were captured, and were skilled with weapons. They did not hesitate to protect their own in this new land, even from those in authority. This effect was compounded precisely because they remained together as a large and formidable group.

Noah Hart's first introduction to the Africans came the day fifty of them were moved from Burns's plantation downriver to Grub Swamp, near the homes of Tim and James Meaher and

Captain Foster, along Chickasabogue Creek. The Africans were still sleeping rough, outdoors and at the mercy of the elements, as they had been for their first two weeks in America. Meaher sent Noah to feed Cudjo and the others cornbread and meat the day they arrived at Grub Swamp.

"Hit wuz jess turrible. Dey wuz wanderin' around lak crazy pussons, skeered at ebberyting: half naked, an' 'most starved ter der death, fer dey couldn't skacely eat none er our wittals," Noah recalled. "Dey stayed dare in de swamp four days, us er feedin' 'em, before ole Marse dast bring 'em to de plantation."

When the fifty people in Grub Swamp were moved to their new homes, Cudjo ended up at James Meaher's, where he and the others were made to sleep underneath the house, outdoors on a brick floor. Like many old plantation houses, James's was raised up about six feet off the ground, built on top of brick pillars in the hope of gathering more breeze through the windows in the main living quarters. This open-air space beneath the house provided protection from rain for the captives, but that was all. The Africans' accommodations never changed at James's, no matter the season. They were given blankets, but never enough to be warm, according to Cudjo, and left to fend for themselves against rain, winter weather, and summer heat with no walls. Mobile is a subtropical climate, with nights regularly above ninety degrees in the summer, and often below freezing in the winter. Fleas, ticks, and flies are everywhere. In my experience visiting old plantations and antebellum houses in Mobile and across the South, this living situation for Cudjo's group was unusual. Slave quarters, primitive and rough, were common everywhere, except, apparently, at James Meaher's house. Still, Cudjo regarded himself lucky to have ended up with

James, rather than one of his brothers. By Cudjo's reckoning, Burns was the most brutal of the brothers when it came to how he managed the people he enslaved, followed by Tim.

"Cap'n Jim, he a good man. He not lak his brother, Cap'n Tim. He doan want his folks knock and beat all de time. He see my shoes gittee raggedy, you know, and he say, 'Cudjo, if dat de best shoes you got, I gittee you some mo'!'" This was a marked contrast to Burns, who bought the Africans he enslaved one set of shoes in five years. The people on his plantation were in the fields working before the sun rose and still at it as the sun set. Burns and Tim both employed overseers to keep those they enslaved in line.

Cudjo used the word "astonished" to explain what he and his countrymen felt the first time they saw a mule pulling a plow, never having imagined such a labor-saving partnership between man and beast. But they also complained at how hard they were forced to work, much harder than they ever did at home. "But we doan grieve 'bout dat. We cry 'cause we slave."

Everyone and everything seemed so strange to the Africans. They tried to talk to the American-born Black people they encountered on the plantations, but couldn't bridge the language gap. Often, the Americans made fun of the Africans, including for the fact that they arrived naked. This remained a source of shame for the descendants of the Africans, even one hundred years later. Cudjo and others spoke often of their disappointment with their American brethren for ostracizing them. "When we at de plantation on Sunday we so glad we ain' gotten no work to do. So we dance lak in de Afficky soil. De American colored folks, you unnerstand me, dey say we savage and den dey laugh at us, doan come say nothin' to us."

Most of the women were put to work in the fields, which they were accustomed to from their previous life. On the Meahers' plantations, cotton, corn, sugarcane, and rice were grown at an industrial scale. Other crops, such as collards, beans, peas, and tomatoes, were cultivated in gardens for consumption by the many mouths on the plantations, which already had at least five dozen enslaved people working on them before the arrival of the *Clotilda*. The captives complained for the rest of their lives about how much harder it was to farm in the Alabama dirt, compared to their homeland, where they had grown yams, beans, black-eyed peas, okra, and corn. They also cultivated palm trees for their nuts, which they used to make cooking oil, or fermented to make beer. Pineapples and bananas had been imported to Dahomey more than one hundred years earlier, through the slave trade, and grew wild there. Back home, growing giant yams was as simple as burying an eye from a potato in a hill of dirt. "We go way, we come back, push, dig de dirt—great beeg yam like keg, nail keg. We cut off vine with little piece of yam and cover it up again. Another beeg yam. Whole family couldn't eat at one time. For seven years don't need no new seed, it keep making yams." But in America, growing crops was "work, work, work." The biggest difference between the region of Benin the captives were from and Mobile comes down to one thing: winter. Both locations feature fertile soils and abundant rainfall. But the temperature in Benin seldom drops below seventy degrees at any point in the year, day or night. The things the Africans planted grew year-round in their lush climate, whereas crops planted in Alabama died every winter and had to be restarted from seeds.

Once the Civil War began, about nine months after they arrived, most of the Africans started living at Magazine Point, near the Meahers' plantations, but also close to the shipyard, the wharf, and the sawmill. Many of the men on the different plantations worked in these Meaher family businesses, so members of the group saw each other frequently. But Cudjo was among the unfortunate souls who ended up working on the riverboats.

The lot of the enslaved on a steamboat was a notoriously hard one. Rather than spend money on coal, which had only recently been discovered in Alabama, the Meahers ran their boats on wood cut from the riverbanks. Workers on shore would do the cutting, and the boat men, like Cudjo, would run up the riverbanks and bluffs and tote the logs down, a process known as "wooding." In old paintings of the steamboat days, you invariably see the lower deck of the boat stocked with cords of carefully split and stacked firewood. But Cudjo's descriptions reveal that the artists' renderings were more fanciful than real. Instead of toting carefully chopped firewood, the slaves were hauling sections of tree trunks as large as they could carry. At some landings, where there was enough space along the riverbank, the trunks would be heaped close to the water. But at most, where the edge of the water gave way immediately to steep bluffs, the men would race to the top of the cliff and throw the logs down the hillside, letting gravity carry them toward the boat. The logs were cut in five-foot chunks, the maximum size that would fit in the furnace that fired the ship's boilers.

Sixty-seven years later, during an interview with Hurston, Cudjo listed twenty-one of the landings the steamboats called at along the Mobile and Alabama Rivers, in the exact order they occur moving upstream. During five years working the boats, he would have stopped at each spot hundreds of times. Every time the boat stopped at a landing, the overseer, "de whippin' boss, he go down de gangplank and standee on de ground. De whip stickee in his belt. . . . He cut you wid de whip if you ain' run fast 'nough to please him. If you doan git a big load, he hitee you too."

William Howard Russell, an English journalist, traveled aboard Timothy Meaher's *Southern Republic* in 1861, ten months after the *Clotilda* arrived. The journalist made a study of a young boy working on board and recounted the scene in his diary. "A boy of some twelve years of age, stout, fat, nearly naked . . . his color was jet black, his wool close as felt, his cheeks were marked with regular parallel scars, and his teeth very white, looked as if they had been filed to a point, his belly was slightly protuberant, and his chest was marked with tracings of tattoo marks."

Captain Meaher saw Russell's interest in the young man. By this time, the story of the *Clotilda* and its illicit cargo was well known, having been published in newspapers around the nation. These accounts included Meaher's rumored involvement. Russell describes Meaher as "a character—perhaps a good one . . . with a gray eye full of cunning and of some humor, strongly marked features and a very Celtic mouth of the Kerry type." He also describes Meaher as a storyteller who "favored me with some wonderful yarns, which I hope he was not foolish enough to think I believed." This last was almost certainly a reference to the story recounted below.

In this version, Meaher makes a show of demonstrating to Russell that the men and boys working on his boat could never have come from Africa. "Wall now! You think them niggers I've aboard came from Africa! I'll show you. Just come up here Bully!" Meaher called to the young man, so clearly different from the American-born enslaved people Russell had grown accustomed to in his travels. With fifty years since the widespread importation of Africans, for a person to have been born in Africa would have meant he or she was approaching seventy, unless they were imported illegally. The captain made a show of asking Bully where he was from.

"Me born Sout Karoliner, sar!"

"There, you see he wasn't taken from Africa," Meaher smiled. "I've got a lot of these black South Carolina niggers aboard."

Russell inquired about the scars on his face.

"Oh them? Wall it's a way them nigger women has of marking their children to know them." The captain explained the tattoos as remnants of smallpox scars. And the filed teeth, "Bully done that himself, for greater ease of biting his vittels."

This encounter marks the first appearance of any of the *Clotilda* captives in print, in this case while they were still enslaved, just months after they arrived in Mobile.

"Are you happy Bully? Show how you're happy," Meaher coached. The boy rubbed his belly, grinned broadly, and said, "Yummy! Yummy! Plenty belly full."

Later, by torchlight on the lower cargo deck, the enslaved deckhands danced to a fiddle and banjo accompaniment for the pleasure of the passengers, "with immense gravity and great effusion of sudor [sweat], shuffled and cut and heeled and buckled to each other with an overwhelming solemnity." Cudjo may very well have been one of the dancers. As his captives danced, Meaher, tipsy and spitting tobacco juice, remarked, "Just look at them, how they're enjoying it; they're the happiest people on the face of the Airth."

Russell's description of the work Cudjo and the other enslaved deckhands performed suggested otherwise.

"The negroes half-naked leaped ashore, and rushing at the piles of firewood, tossed them on board to feed the engine, which, all uncovered and open to the lower deck, lighted up the darkness by the glare from the stoke-holes, which cried forever, 'Give, give!' As the negroes ceaselessly thrust the pine beams into their hungry maws."

The hard and dangerous work on a steamboat didn't end. While underway, Cudjo and the others took turns working the levers of the ship's heavy manual bilge pumps, which had to be operated constantly to keep the steamers afloat, because the wooden vessels leaked badly. They had to keep the boiler fire stoked with logs at all times. In between landings to load wood, they would try to grab an hour of sleep on top of the cotton stacked on the open lower deck. Cudjo said his years aboard the boats was the most miserable time in his life. "Oh, Lor'! Oh, Lor'! Five year and de six months I slave. I workee so hard!"

The life of the steamboat crews was made more difficult because Alabama's rivers are subject to great fluctuations in flow and depth according to the season, something still true today, but much more dramatic in the era before thirty large dams were erected to help control flooding. In the summer and fall, the rivers were at their low ebb, with exposed banks and shallow depths. Meanwhile in the winter and spring, the rivers were overflowing, and flooding the surrounding forests. The difference in water level between spring floods and summer flow could be as much as fifty feet. This meant that steamboats generally tied up to trees along the banks, or held their place in the current against a shoreline by running the engine, turning the giant paddle wheel on each side of the boat just enough to hold steady. It was impossible to construct docks that could be used both when the river was high and when it was low, and at many landings the "dock" was little more than a muddy hill that ended at the water's edge.

This meant plantation owners had to come up with ingenious ways to load their most precious cargo, cotton, onto the steamboats that would carry it to market in Mobile. The cotton bales coming through the port of Mobile averaged 504 pounds, according to shipping records from Liverpool in 1850. At some landings, planters built rail tracks down the incline to the river, and workers would manually crank a windlass to lower carts full of cotton or other goods down to the boats. But most plantations and cotton warehouses employed a wooden structure like a giant playground slide. The bales would be placed at the top of the slide and given a push, sending them careening downhill, often for hundreds of feet, to the deck of the steamer waiting below. Frederick Law Olmsted, designer of Central Park, traveled Alabama's rivers by steamboat in 1853, and witnessed cotton being loaded via slide. His trip, made while he served as a correspondent for the *New York Times*, and written about in his book *The Cotton Kingdom*, helped establish him as one of the most prominent abolitionist voices in the country.

"There was something truly Western in the direct, reckless way in which the boat was loaded. A strong gang-plank placed at right angles to the slide-way, a bale of cotton was let slide from the top, and coming down with fearful velocity, on striking the gang-plank, it would rebound up and out on to the boat, against a barrier of bales previously arranged to receive it. The moment it struck this barricade, it would be dashed at by two or three men, and jerked out of the way, and others would roll it to its place for the voyage, on the tiers aft. The mate, standing near the bottom of the slide, as soon as the men had removed one bale to what he thought a safe distance, would shout to those aloft, and down would come another. Not infrequently, a bale would not strike fairly on its end, and would rebound off, diagonally, overboard; or would be thrown up with such force as to go over the barricade, breaking stanchions and railings, and scattering the passengers on the berth deck."

Russell described his trip downriver this way: "The river, the scenery, and the scenes were just the same as yesterday's— high banks, cotton slides, wooding stations, cane brakes—and a very miserable negro population, if the species of women and children at the landings fairly represented the mass of the slaves. . . . Those condemned to work in the open fields must suffer exceedingly."

Once the Africans settled in, Noah Hart, the houseboy, said they were "powerful easy critters; didn't lak no roughnes' an' shoutin'." They'd work all day, then "at night dey would gedder in one er dey cabins an' sing an' laugh an' play 'mongst themselves." In this quote, we learn that Tim Meaher provided traditional slave quarters for his Africans, and that they didn't mix with enslaved Americans. They always stood out, apart, Noah recalled. "Dey wuzn't lak us 'Merican niggers at all. Dey wuz mo' blacker an' straighter an' bigger dan us; an' somehow dey seem mo' fiercer, although dey never did fool wid us nor squabble 'mongst deyselves."

Noah said the Africans put special stock in the arrival of the new moon every month. The group would meet in the woods surrounding the plantation as the barely visible moon rose, and make crowns for themselves out of bay leaves. "When the little young moon is jes' tremblin' on de pine tree tops, dey digs a hole, an' all lays down an' whispers somethin' in it; den dey each puts one leaf in de hole an' kyvers it up, an' all jumps an' dances on top er it."

Sylviane Diouf, who describes herself as an "Africanist" because of her interest in the history of the continent as it relates to the African diaspora, explored this and several of the other rituals Noah observed the Africans perform. They are tied to tribes in the northwest Atakora region of Benin, around the Atakora Mountains. This seems to fit what one of the Africans told an interviewer in 1890 when she described her homeland as "A'tarco." This is several days' walk from the Bante region where Cudjo and most of the group lived before capture. The moon ceremony was a chance to say goodbye to problems and hardships, and ask for better days to come in the new month.

To have Noah Hart, an enslaved African-American, providing firsthand observations of the assimilation process for newly arrived Africans is exceptionally rare, Diouf said. Most of what we know regarding slavery in America comes from the nineteenth century and is about people who were born on Southern plantations. Those few, scant firsthand observations of newly arrived Africans from the years prior to 1808, when importation was banned, were mostly written by white people. Diouf said it is clear that Noah's observations are not made up, or heavily embellished, because he is accurately describing customs that existed among different cultures in West Africa. The historian was able to link the few words Noah could still remember in the 1890s to specific places and tribes.

Noah witnessed a burial performed by the group at Tim

Meaher's in the Atakora style, which calls for the body to be buried in a standing position. A deep, narrow hole was dug, and then filled partially with bark sliced from oak trees. The entire body was covered in strips of bark, which were tied down with cuttings from saplings. The bark-wrapped body was carried to the grave and then completely buried with slice after slice of bark. The grave was then covered with dirt. Once the dirt was packed down, the group formed a circle around it and crossed their arms over their own bodies, then grabbed a hand of the person on each side of them, until all were connected.

"Fust de swing de left foot over twice, all swingin' togedder; den de right foot over to de left, all turnin' de same way, an' den begins to sing de most ongodlest kind er song, lak cryin' an' yet lak crazy pussons. An here dey go, dancin' an' singin' wid de tear drops runnin' down dey cheeks. . . . I can't tell what made it so pitiful, but hit sho wuz."

We know that several of the *Clotilda* women were married after their arrival. Some of the Africans chose to partner up together, such as Gumpa—the member of the Dahomean court given to Foster—who had a child with fellow *Clotilda* passenger Josephine while they were enslaved. But there were also forced marriages for some after their arrival in Mobile. Given that half of the fifty-five female captives were described as "girls" and half as "women" by various observers, it seems likely many were pressed into marriages at young ages, which was standard practice on plantations.

We have new insight into the forced marriage of one of the *Clotilda* passengers. In an authoritative research paper published in 2019, historian Hannah Dorman finally connected the dots linking a brief mention of "Sally Smith" in Zora Neale

Hurston's archives and letters to a Selma woman who pops up several times in the historical record. Dorman figured out that the woman, Sally "Redoshi" Smith, was part of the group that Meaher sold to the slave dealers from Montgomery. She lived two years longer than Cudjo, until 1936, which makes her the last known survivor of the *Clotilda*. Remarkably, we also have film footage of her, meaning she and Cudjo are the only African-born enslaved people ever captured on film. The footage of her was filmed for a government documentary released in 1938, after her death, ostensibly aimed at African-American farmers and titled *The Negro Farmer: Extension Work for Better Farming and Better Living*. She is on-screen for just eighteen seconds, and though her lips are moving we cannot hear what she is saying. But she is animated, smiling below a shock of white hair and wrapped in a quilt on the porch of her home. For her entire life, Redoshi remained in the one-room slave cabin on the plantation where she had been enslaved, including the seventy-two years she was free.

Hurston actually met Redoshi during her travels. Not only met her, but interviewed her. It seems certain that Cudjo introduced the pair, as he was in touch with Redoshi until his death. We don't know why Hurston never presented Redoshi's story to the public, and she doesn't share her reasoning in a letter to poet Langston Hughes in July of 1928: "Oh! almost forgot. Found another one of the original Africans, older than Cudjoe about 200 miles up state on the Tombigbee River. She is most delightful, but no one will ever know about her but us. She is a better talker than Cudjoe."

Redoshi was also interviewed by Civil Rights icon Amelia Boynton Robinson and appears in her memoir *Bridge Across*

Jordan. Robinson's account of Redoshi's marriage has the ring of truth, compared to an article written in the *Montgomery Advertiser* in 1932. The Alabama journalist who wrote the newspaper piece was in the thrall of the daughter of Redoshi's former enslaver, "a gracious Southern lady," whose family owned a bank in town. We are told that this version of Redoshi's story has been "confirmed" by the family. In this sanitized and curated chronicle, instead of noting that on arrival in Alabama Redoshi was forced into a slave marriage at just twelve years old, the article fancifully describes her as a "dark, supple princess of the Tarkars" who was both married and twenty-five years old when she was captured.

The truth, as Redoshi recounted to Robinson, was darker. "I was 12 years old and he was a man from another tribe who had a family in Africa. I couldn't understand his talk and he couldn't understand me. They put us on block together and sold us for man and wife." Meeting Redoshi was a pivotal moment for Robinson, then a young African-American activist living in Selma, who would rise to national prominence two decades later as one of the organizers of the Civil Rights movement in that city. It was at her home that she, Martin Luther King, and other leaders gathered to plan the Selma to Montgomery march that led to the Bloody Sunday confrontation as protesters crossed the Edmund Pettus Bridge. Robinson was beaten unconscious in the march, and an image of her limp and bloodied body ran on newspaper front pages across the country.

We know another of the *Clotilda* captives, Kanko, was "married" to James Dennison, the enslaved Cherokee riverboat pilot the Meahers assigned to lead the Africans through the swamp during their first two weeks in the country. The union, ordered by Burns Meaher, was made over Kanko's objections in June of 1861, about eleven months after their arrival. In a memoir about the couple, Kanko's granddaughter, Mable Dennison, writes that "their owners or someone performed a wedding ceremony for the two of them for the propagation of slavery. Jim's wife, [Kanko], refused to have any intimate contact with her husband, Jim, for she believed that they were not truly married according to their way of life." Cudjo spoke extensively to Hurston about the courtship rituals of his people. Kanko's parents would normally have been intimately involved in arranging a marriage for her, and protecting her from her husband or his family if things did not go well. It is unsurprising she bucked against this marriage to Dennison, especially as it put her in a bed with one of her captor's most important servants. This act of defiance, refusing to consummate the marriage, was an early clue regarding Kanko's personality. She would act in similar fashion throughout her life, flouting conventions and sticking to her convictions, as would James.

This shared trait came to the fore for the young couple in 1864. Unlike many in the ranks of the enslaved, who struggled for information about the war, James was well up on current events thanks to his position as a riverboat pilot. He frequently traveled downriver to Mobile for supplies for the plantation. He knew the South was losing, and that if the Confederacy was defeated, he'd be a free man. Freedom would be an especially exciting proposition for a man who knew how to captain a steamboat, a highly coveted skill. James knew he could make a good living if he could gain his freedom. He would likely have interacted with some of the hundreds of free blacks who'd lived in Mobile before the war. Temptation was at hand for James after the Battle of Mobile Bay in the summer—where Union admiral David Farragut famously uttered, "Damn the torpedoes! Full steam ahead!" By August, both Fort Gaines and Fort Morgan at the mouth of the bay were in Union hands. This meant freedom was forty miles downriver at the bottom of Mobile Bay. If he could just make it there.

James plotted an escape, and planned to enlist in the Union Army if he could make it to Fort Morgan. He knew the rivers well and could easily make the run down the bay. If he sailed down the same route through the Spanish River used to bring the *Clotilda* in, he could avoid the port of Mobile altogether and likely escape detection. He included a few others on the plantation in his plan: his aunt, his new bride Kanko, and—according to his granddaughter—some cousins or siblings. They planned to leave on a Saturday night. The Meahers did not make them work on Sunday morning, so their disappearance might go unnoticed a little while longer that way. When it came time to depart, a man who was supposed to join in the escape failed to show up. He had betrayed the group and warned Burns Meaher of their departure. The group was quickly chased down by riders on horseback who shouted at them and waved guns as they followed along on the riverbank. Other plantation owners joined the chase. The escape was a failure. We do not know what punishment befell the group for the runaway attempt. Only how tempting it must have been to try again with freedom so close.

But their official captivity was about to end with the looming defeat of the South in the war.

As the Union forces closed in on the South, Timothy Meaher saw an opportunity and turned into a war profiteer. More specifically, he became a blockade runner, which dovetails perfectly with everything known about him—that he liked to back up his convictions with reckless action, that he was keen for an adventure, and that if there was money to be made, he wanted in. As a plantation owner who had enslaved more than twenty people, Meaher was exempt from being drafted into the Confederate Army. Rather than fight on the battlefield, he chose to embrace one of the most lucrative occupations available during the war years and built two specially designed ships to accomplish the mission, the *Grey Jacket*—the name a signal of his allegiance with the Confederacy, whose soldiers wore gray jackets—and its sister ship, the *Red Gauntlet*.

Blockade runners were built for evading the Union ships then patrolling Confederate ports on the Atlantic and the Gulf as part of a massive naval blockade designed to cripple the rebel economy. The blockade's aim was to cut the South off from the markets of Europe, which typically purchased nearly all of the cotton coming out of the Confederate states. In Mobile, the cotton trade amounted to about $38 million a year in 1860. Only New York and New Orleans had more trade than Mobile. With the Union blockade in effect, not only could less and less cotton make it out of the country, but no weaponry or gunpowder could make it into the country to equip the Confederate Army. Of course it wasn't just weaponry that was in short supply in the South due to the blockade. The wealthy suddenly found themselves cut off from everything Europe and New York had to offer, including wine, fine clothing, and other luxury goods.

This made blockade running exceptionally lucrative. A single round-trip could often cover the entire construction cost of the ship, and provide a generous profit for the daring captain to boot. To be a blockade runner quickly became synonymous with being a swashbuckling adventurer. Rhett Butler, Clark Gable's character in the film version of Margaret Mitchell's *Gone with the Wind*, made his fictional fortune as a blockade runner. In real life, blockade running was dangerous. By the war's end, the Union had captured more than 1,000 blockade runners, and sunk 355 of them. Historians calculated the likelihood of being caught at one in ten in 1861, when the blockade first began. But by 1864, about one in three blockade runners were captured.

We know of Meaher's work as a blockade runner because he got caught on New Year's Eve, 1863. By that time, Mobile was the last Confederate port still open, and Meaher and a few other captains had successfully completed more than two hundred trips into or out of Mobile despite the blockade. That was thanks largely to the twin forts guarding the mouth of Mobile Bay, the same forts Captain Foster had sought to avoid when returning with the *Clotilda*. Confederate forces took both Fort Morgan and Fort Gaines within days of the start of hostilities in 1861, which allowed them to keep the Union blockade miles offshore, away from the mouth of the bay. This gave the blockade runners in Mobile a better chance at evading capture than those in the other port cities. For Meaher, there couldn't have been a more lucrative opportunity. His home port was the last hope for the Confederacy, and the rebel government was paying handsomely for his services.

The *Grey Jacket* was designed to be a high-speed greyhound of oceangoing steam power. Her hold was ten feet deep and could carry 420 tons of cargo. She sported two engines to maximize her speed. According to the record of Meaher's capture, he tried to run the blockade during a tempestuous and stormy night carrying a full load of Confederate cotton, turpentine, and rosin. He was bound for Havana, Cuba, where arrangements had been made to trade the cotton. To understand the stakes, the ship could carry 1,680 bales of cotton, each weighing five hundred pounds. With cotton at $1.80 a pound due to scarcity at the height of the war in 1864, the *Grey Jacket*'s cargo was worth $1.5 million, or almost $25 million in today's currency. Under his agreement with the Confederacy, a copy of which he had in his cabin on board the ship, Meaher was to receive half the value of the cargo upon delivery in Havana. For the return trip, he was to fill half the ship with weapons, gunpowder, and other supplies for the Confederacy. The other half was his to fill with liquor, fine clothes, or whatever other commodities he could sell for profit in Mobile. The chase lasted twenty-four hours before the *Grey Jacket* was captured forty-one miles offshore by the Union gunboat *Kennebec*, whose captain, Lieutenant Commander McCann, was well taken with Meaher's sleek ship. The navy's action report says she was caught when her engines gave out, "after a long chase in a gale and very heavy cross sea. This steamer is loaded with cotton, entirely new, and Lieutenant-Commander McCann says that she is one of the most perfect sea boats he ever saw. She will make an excellent gunboat, and at trifling expense, and I trust may be taken by the government for that purpose."

The ship and her cargo were sailed to New Orleans, which the Union controlled. The U.S. Navy incident reports note that the *Grey Jacket* was actively dumping cotton overboard throughout the pursuit, in an attempt to lighten its load. When her engines broke down and navy officers boarded, they found five hundred bales still on board. The captain who captured the *Grey Jacket* recognized Meaher's name from the news, and included this detail in his official report: "The master and supposed owner, Meaher, a wealthy and influential man of Mobile, is sent to New Orleans in the prize, as are all the papers." Suddenly, three and a half years after escaping prosecution for illegal slaving, Meaher found himself a prisoner on his own boat, being delivered into the hands of the enemy.

Meaher apparently spent the next eight months in New Orleans, appearing for various court hearings. It didn't look good. The only reason he had surrendered was because his engines failed. He had clearly left the port without authorization and in violation of the federal blockade. Unfortunately for him, he was caught with a copy of the agreement to deliver the load of cotton to Havana for the Confederate government. He also had letters of introduction to Spanish traders in Cuba. Despite this damning evidence, Meaher swore in a new affidavit in August that he was actually running away from the Confederacy with a load of his own cotton, planning to betray the Confederate government. The court record states that Meaher attempted to "set up an entirely new state of facts" compared to his previous sworn statement. "He never sympathized with nor gave any aid to the rebellion. The steamer was built to enable him to get away with as much as possible of his property. He did not take his family with him, lest it might excite suspicion and defeat his object."

His first mate told a different story after they were captured, confirming that they were headed to Havana to sell cotton for the Confederacy. Ultimately, Meaher fought the case all the way to the U.S. Supreme Court, where it was heard in 1866. Unfortunately for Meaher, his hero, Roger B. Taney, died in 1864, and the new chief justice, Salmon Chase, was not as friendly to the cause of slavery and its sympathizers, who had just been defeated. The justices found the case "had no redeeming feature" and concluded "the vessel and cargo were properly condemned as enemy property and for breach of the blockade." In the end, after selling the cargo and confiscating the ship, the federal government netted about $400,000 on the deal.

By the time Meaher returned to Mobile, late in 1864, many of the men enslaved by his family had been commandeered by the Confederate Army for months to help build a giant network of earthen breastworks to surround the city for its defense. The project involved thousands of laborers, and the results were extensive, snaking through swamps and across river valleys. I often stumble onto sections of the old trenches while walking in the woods of south Alabama. Given the remote and swampy places I find the old fortifications, it must have been incredibly grueling to build them in the heat of the Alabama summertime. They consist of a trench about three feet deep with a hill of dirt in front of it about two feet high. The idea was to protect most of a soldier's body as he aimed at the enemy, with only the soldier's head and arms above the breast-high wall.

In the end, the redoubts didn't matter. Once Fort Gaines and Fort Morgan were captured and a complete blockade was enforced across the mouth of the bay, the squeeze was on for the entire Confederacy. Food was tight. Both plantation owners and the people they enslaved were hungry, and reduced to burning rice to make a coffee subsitute, sweetening it with molasses because there was no sugar. "Dat doan tastee so good," Cudjo remembered. To keep the Africans fed James Meaher was forced to slaughter some of his hogs, a meat typically considered too valuable to be wasted on the enslaved. The end was coming for the Confederacy. Highlighting the importance of the transatlantic trade coming through Mobile, the war was over just months after the Union Army captured the port. Unable to get goods in or out of Mobile, the Confederacy was simply starved of income and gunpowder.

The last battle of the war was fought around the abandoned city of Blakeley, just on the other side of the swamp from the Meahers' sawmill and shipyard at Magazine Point. You could hear the booming cannons, which thundered for several days, from Meaher's front porch, softening up the Confederate lines before the inevitable Union assault.

Sixteen thousand Union troops, including five thousand men in all African-American United States Colored Troops infantry regiments, fought four thousand Confederates for seven days. In the final battle, the African-American infantry companies joined together, forming the entire right flank of the Union forces. The African-American troops, comprised of the formerly enslaved and free men alike, suffered the highest casualties at Blakeley, but also won the final, decisive battle.

The United States Colored Troops charged the rebel lines at 5 p.m., as a Confederate gunboat began shelling their position. When they were one hundred yards from the breastworks, showers of musket balls began raining down on them, fired from cannons behind the rebel lines. They suffered heavy casualties, with seven of the eleven officers for the colored troops either killed or wounded in the fusillade. It began to look like the rebels might flank their position and trap them. Knowing that if they were captured, they would most likely be killed, rather than made prisoners like white soldiers, the men "concluded the best thing to be done was to fight it out. Then the men fixed bayonets, and some were heard, with clenched teeth, to say they would die sooner than surrender or retreat." Writing about the role of the colored troops in the battle years later, Brigadier General Christopher Columbus Andrews said "greater gallantry than was shown by officers and men could hardly be desired. The latter were burning with an impulse to do honor to their race, and rushed forward with intense enthusiasm, in face of a terrible fire." (Until recently, the spot where the African-American units wiped out the last Confederate position of the war was not included in Blakeley State Park, which preserves much of the battlefield. This most important piece sat just outside the park boundaries and had been owned by the Meaher family for decades, used primarily as a place to hunt ducks. It was purchased and added to the park in 2020.)

The fall of Blakeley is considered the last major battle of the Civil War, and meant the city of Mobile was defenseless. Though it was unknown in the city at the time, the war had actually ended a few hours earlier on April 9, with Robert E. Lee's surrender at Appomatox at 4 p.m. But word of the surrender wouldn't reach Mobile until April 12.

That morning found Cudjo and the rest of the slave crew waiting aboard James Meaher's steamboat at the downtown wharf, ready for the regular Wednesday run to Montgomery. But the captain was nowhere to be seen. Unbeknownst to Cudjo and the rest, the Meaher brothers had left the day before, steaming toward Selma in a flotilla of nine boats to help the Confederate Army escape upriver with as much weaponry as possible after they were routed at Blakeley. The *Southern Republic* and the blockade runner the *Red Gauntlet* were both part of the convoy, which dropped mines in the Mobile River to prevent Union ships from following.

The Union troops overran Mobile with little to no resistance. Though the steamboat dock where Cudjo spent the day was in the heart of downtown, he makes no mention of the chaos that engulfed Mobile as the Confederate cavalry marched out of town just ahead of an arriving column of Union soldiers. This is remarkable, because the Confederates ignited a cotton warehouse along the wharf, causing considerable panic and smoke, and the citizenry engaged in a daylong riot, looting government warehouses for food that had been rationed. "The tide in the different thoroughfares set in one direction, converging toward the government warehouses on Water Street. . . . All day long, like a colony of ants, men, women, and children were rushing through the streets in jealous fear of not getting their share."

For Cudjo, the fall of the city was nothing compared to the other news he was to receive that day. Still waiting hours later, Cudjo watched a group of Union soldiers walk toward the wharf where the steamboat was tied up and start eating mulberries off a tree by the water. When the soldiers saw Cudjo and the rest of the crew sitting idly on the boat, they called out and told them that the war was over. Cudjo remembered the soldiers saying, "'You free, you doan b'long to nobody no mo'.' Oh, Lor'! I so glad. We astee de soldiers where we goin'? Dey say dey doan know. Dey told us to go where we feel lak goin', we ain' no mo' slave."

In his book on the history of the Mobile River, city historian John Sledge quotes a tantalizing tidbit in a letter written by an angry Mobilian who witnessed the riots the day the city fell. It appears to give us another clue about the reaction of Cudjo and his fellow deckhands, who had spent their day waiting at the city wharf at the foot of Government Street. "At about 4 o'clock the advance of the Yankee Army reached the city at the same time one of their boats arrived at the foot of Govt. Street. As soon as the negroes and puerile white people saw the boat at the wharf they rushed down the street shouting and hurrahing. . . . Soon the deck was crowded with 'gemmin of African 'scent and their white livered brethren." Though he never mentioned the moment in any of his interviews, perhaps Cudjo and his fellow Africans had a bit of a celebration at the wharf with the Union soldiers who'd notified them of their liberation.

Ultimately, the Africans gathered their few belongings off the boat and walked back to the plantation. Their owners were nowhere to be seen, still headed upriver toward the Confederate Armory at Selma. The emancipated Africans already knew they'd have to come up with new places to live. "We cain stay wid de folks what own us no mo'. Derefo' where we goin' live, we doan know," said Cudjo, summing up the thoughts of four million newly freed men and women scattered across the country confronting the same reality. They were free, but they were also homeless and unemployed. The Africans decided those were worries for another day. The first thing they did as free men since their kidnapping five years before was make a big drum out of a log and "beat it lak in de Affica soil."

Chapter 8

AN AFRICAN TOWN

*E*ven with their new freedom, the *Clotilda* captives were still imprisoned. They were trapped in a faraway land, removed from families and all they had known—desperate to return home, but unable to figure out how to accomplish the task. The Africans had no resources, and no support system other than relationships they had built with each other in the days since they left the barracoons of Dahomey. Together, battling through hostility showered on them by both white and Black Americans, the Africans fought to make a place for themselves, and fought against every effort to oppress them anew in the Reconstruction era.

For the *Clotilda* captives, the desire to return to Africa was the ultimate example of the dream deferred. As they worked toward their shared goal of making a home in their new country, they chose to remain outside of American society, going so far as to set up a community where they controlled everything, even the laws they lived under. Yet despite this desire to be apart, they found themselves repeatedly and dramatically involved in the current events of the day, pushing the boundaries of their new freedom. They boldly confronted their former enslavers and demanded a form of reparations, fought for their right to vote, successfully sued one of the nation's largest railroad companies, built a school for their children because the whites wouldn't give them one, started the area's first church, and created the first and only community in the nation started by enslaved Africans. They suffered through racial violence, murder, disease, and betrayal by people they trusted. All of this in what was then the nation's most intensely racist state, where the very wheels of government continually sought new ways to suppress them. But the Africans did not shrink and hide away among themselves. They fought back. Of course, they had branded themselves as fighters from the start, from the moment they stole the overseer's whip and lashed him with it in Meaher's field. Everything that happened after that was just a continuation of that first impulse—to fight, fight for their lives, their rights, their future, and their children.

The first move for the Africans on Burns Meaher's plantation forty miles upriver was to rejoin the fifty plus Africans who had been enslaved by the Meahers and Foster in Mobile. We know something about their journey from a violently racist article published in *Confederate Veteran* magazine decades after the war. It was written by a soldier who was on board one of the boats as Timothy Meaher retreated with the flotilla to Selma. The piece describes how the vanquished rebel soldiers tormented the newly freed people they encountered floating downriver toward Mobile in pirogues or on homemade rafts. In one instance, soldiers pulled a freedman from his dugout canoe and whipped him aboard the steamboat. Heading downriver would have been the lot of the twenty Africans who lived upriver at Burns Meaher's plantation as they tried to rejoin the larger group at Magazine Point. At least the first part of their journey must have occurred by boat, as it was impossible to reach Mobile from the plantation without crossing the Tombigbee River. Floating downstream to Mobile would have been the easiest way to make the forty-mile trip, as the river would have carried them all the way to their destination, door-to-door service from one Meaher riverfront property to another.

In all likelihood, the group was led downriver by James Dennison, the Native American riverboat pilot married to Kanko. But if he did lead them, Dennison wasn't with them long once they arrived at Magazine Point. On April 19, he left behind his African wife and their son to join the army. He enlisted in the 47th Infantry of the United States Colored Troops, one of the units that had helped win the final battle at Blakeley ten days prior. He signed up for a three-year hitch. The only known picture of James was taken at this time, in his new uniform. He is twenty-five, a handsome, dark-skinned man with piercing, deep-set eyes. His hair, usually worn in two long braids, was cut short for his entry into the Union Army. He would only serve about a year before being discharged. In the biography written by his granddaughter, she reports that he tended livestock in the army, and "contracted rheumatism, diarrhea, and fever from exposure and drinking the unwholesome water of the rivers and swamps due to his army affiliation."

Meanwhile, all of the newly free Black Americans seemed on the move. Numerous accounts following the South's surrender describe a sudden exodus of the freed, some searching for loved ones in other places, some looking for work, and some just trying to put as much distance as possible between themselves and places they desperately wanted to leave behind.

The Africans wanted to move as well, back to Africa. In their first days of freedom, they set their goal as raising enough money to hire a ship to carry them home. They agreed that the Meahers and Captain Foster should use one of their boats and return them where they'd found them five years before, but knew that even asking the Meahers was a lost cause. "We think we save money and buy de ticket ourselves. So we tell de women, 'Now we all want to go back home. Somebody tell us it take lot of money to keer us back, in de Affica soil. Derefo' we got to work hard and save de money. You must help too. You see fine clothes, you must not wish for dem.' De women tell us dey do all dey kin to get back in dey country, and dey tellee us, 'You see fine clothes, don't you wish for dem neither.'" Of course after five years in the rough-hewn slave clothes they'd been provided, fine clothes would have been a modest wish. It's likely they were in something close to rags by the war's end, even though they'd been provided new clothes on arrival five years earlier. The privations of the blockade era would not have encouraged many of the enslavers to worry over their prisoners' garments.

Most of the men quickly found work with the railroad, a gunpowder factory, or at the Meahers' sawmill for $1 a day. Cudjo would work at the mill until 1902, mostly chopping down trees and making wooden shingles, while Pollee Allen, one of Cudjo's next-door neighbors, would spend his days stacking fresh-cut lumber. Others from the *Clotilda*, including Charlie Lewis, went to work as gravediggers for the funeral home owned by Emma

Roche's father when the author was a child. This established the connection between Roche and the *Clotilda* survivors that led to her book *Historic Sketches of the South*, which was the first and most definitive account of the *Clotilda* saga, and included interviews with the last eight survivors. According to local lore in Africatown, during this time the newly reassembled *Clotilda* passengers lived outdoors for a few weeks on a forested hummock along the Mobile River. Before long, they were renting accommodations at a railroad section house, typically used to house rail workers while they worked on a "section" of railroad. Then they rented several cabins, though it is unclear from whom. The men went to work, mostly at businesses associated with the Meahers, while the women embraced the same work many of them would have been doing if they'd never been stolen from Africa: growing vegetables to sell.

"Dey raise de garden and put de basket on de head and go in de Mobile and sell vegetable," Cudjo recounted, describing the way Africans still carry heavy loads today, on top of their heads. In this fashion, African Town and its residents became well known in Mobile. It was a three-mile walk to Mobile, a short stroll by African standards, and mention of the women walking to town with their vegetable baskets balanced on their heads appeared in the press. Importing other traditions from their African home villages, the women swept their yards first thing in the morning, and cooked what they grew to sell in hot lunches along the roadside or to the men working in the mills. In the evenings, the men worked crafting African-style baskets from reeds and green branches, which the women also sold. No one was idle as they moved toward their collective goal of returning home.

In *The Story of the Negro*, Booker T. Washington spoke of his personal worries as Reconstruction began regarding how African-Americans just released from enslavement would fit into society. "It did not seem possible that a people who yesterday were slaves could be transformed within a few days into citizens capable of making laws for the government of the state or the government of the nation."

And yet this is precisely what the Africans set about doing as soon as they were free. Almost immediately, in an extraordinary act of self-governance, the group began to build a community for themselves ruled by the social strictures and systems they had grown up with in their native lands.

"We see we ain' got no ruler. Nobody to be de father to de rest. We ain' got no king neither no chief lak in de Affica. We doan try get no king 'cause nobody among us ain' born no king. Dey tell us nobody doan have no king in 'Merica soil. Derefo' we make Gumpa de head. He a nobleman back in Dahomey. We ain' mad wid him 'cause de king of Dahomey 'stroy our king and sell us to de white man. He didn't do nothin' 'ginst us."

It's a magnanimous position for the group to take regarding Gumpa. After all, he had been a senior member of King Glele's court, a part of the governing class of the warmongering kingdom that had stolen their freedom and killed their relatives. However, they had been through a lot together, with Gumpa suffering alongside them for five years. He was as much a victim of Glele as they were, similarly snatched from his homeland and family. The pathos of his one-sentence summary of his fate, "My people sold me and your people bought me," is inescapable. Unlike his fellow shipmates, he wasn't captured in war by a rival king to sell for gold. He was given away on a whim as a gift to a slave trader. The shock and misery of that event must have stayed with him always—one moment standing in Glele's court as a trusted adviser, the next shackled and led to the barracoons, knowing he would never see his wife, children, friends, or homeland again.

He was considered a man of noble birth, and one of the oldest among the group, both facts that in and of themselves would typically lead Africans reared in tribal cultures to pick him as their leader. Even after five years in America, Cudjo was just twenty-four. Many of the others were even younger than he was. Several captured as boys and girls were only seventeen at the Civil War's end. Most, like Cudjo, had never finished the initiations required in their cultures to pass into adulthood. Their desire to immediately re-create a form of government familiar to all of them—with a respected elder in charge and laws everyone agrees to obey—speaks to their powerful instinct to build a society apart from the Americans, white or Black. For the Africans, reassembling a piece of their homeland by living together as a village was a way to reclaim their identity and power. They created a place beyond the insults and ostracizing of Mobile society. They created a place where they could be and, more important, feel African. Unlike the American Black people, who had been born into slavery and never knew freedom or citizenship, the Africans had only been captive for five years. Most of them were from Bante, a large market town. Their families back home had been sophisticated businesspeople, accustomed to buying, selling, trading, and the experiences of earning money and owning land. In essence, unlike their newly emancipated American counterparts, the Africans already knew how to be free. Meeting at night after work, the group chose leaders and established rules, and then selected punishments for any of their number who violated those rules. In *Barracoon*, Cudjo speaks at great length about the system of justice among his people. When it came to adherence to the laws, there were no exceptions made for the wealthy or influential. And the punishments were severe, often involving a slow and agonizing death in a public place in the center of town. Cudjo said the harsh consequences of theft, murder, and other crimes meant rule-breaking was rare. He said a person could leave a bag with money or other valuables somewhere in the community and know with confidence that it would be sitting there, unmolested, when the owner returned to retrieve it. This was the model for Africatown's earliest governance. With Gumpa serving in the traditional role of king, even without the title, two others of the group—Jaybee and Ossa Keeby—were chosen as judges who would serve as a sort of tribunal for community disputes. The entire group collectively created laws governing "how to behave ourselves," Cudjo said. If someone broke one of the laws, or a disagreement arose among members of the community, a meeting was called for the evening, usually at one of the judges' homes. The entire group would assemble as a sort of Greek chorus, to watch over the proceedings. The final punishment was up to the judges, with the group collectively supervising the deliberations to make sure the decisions were just. This system, putting the rule of the town in the hands of carefully supervised judges, would serve the community well. Even with original leader Gumpa long dead, the remaining members of the group still governed themselves in the same fashion fifty years after their arrival. "As old as they are, if Charlie [who became chief after Gumpa died] told them they could not do a thing, no matter how strong the desire, they would not disobey," Roche wrote.

There were rules against hurting anyone, stealing, and getting drunk, among other stipulations. The Africans would come to be known as strict disciplinarians. If a person was caught stealing, Cudjo "terminated his relationship with you," remembered John Randolph, a man who grew up in Africatown before the last of the Africans died. "Their moral standards were way beyond those being displayed by our current generation."

Cudjo himself recalls: "When we speak to a man whut do wrong de next time he do dat, we whip him." There are no accounts of anyone receiving whippings or other punishments in any of the historical texts or interviews with the *Clotilda* survivors. But Cudjo suggests the group was particularly intolerant of drunks.

"When we see a man drunk we say, 'Dere go de slave whut beat his master.' Dat mean he buy de whiskey. It belong to him and he oughter rule it, but it done got control of him," he said.

One of the Africans' first communal decisions was to ask Timothy Meaher to give them a piece of his land around Magazine Point so they could build houses. He had plenty of land, they reasoned, some of it purchased with the money they had made for him through five years of free labor. They appointed Cudjo to talk with Meaher. His chance to approach Timothy came when the old captain came strolling through a section of forest where Cudjo was chopping trees for the mill. Meaher sat down on a felled log and started whittling on a stick. The conversation occurred where the elementary school in Africatown stands today.

Telling the story sixty years later, Cudjo told Hurston that his emotions overwhelmed him as he asked Meaher, his former captor, to turn over part of his plantation to the Africans.

Describing the scene in detail, Cudjo said he stopped working altogether as he fought back tears and tried to speak.

When Meaher finally realized he no longer heard the fall of Cudjo's ax against a tree, the captain looked up from his whittling to see his former prisoner fighting back tears.

"Cudjo, what makes you so sad?" Meaher asked.

"Cap'n Tim, I grieve for my home."

"But you got a good home, Cudjo," Meaher said, referring to the cabins the Africans had rented from the railroad.

"Cudjo doan want it 'cause it ain' home. Cap'n Tim, you brought us from our country where we had lan'. You made us slave. Now dey make us free but we ain' got no country and we ain' got no lan'! Why doan you give us piece dis land so we kin buildee ourself a home."

Meaher leapt to his feet and thundered at his former slave. In Roche's telling, she says Cudjo imitated Meaher in dramatic fashion, suddenly speaking like a character out of the King James Bible the African loved so dearly in his later years.

"Thou fool! Thinkest thou I will give you property upon property? You do not belong to me now," Meaher said, adding that he had treated the Africans well and owed them nothing now that they were free.

Coming just weeks after the end of the Civil War, this moment was likely the first instance of freed slaves anywhere in the nation demanding reparations from their former masters. While it did not go well, asking Meaher to replace what he had stolen from them was the first instinct for the *Clotilda* captives. It fit with the style of justice brought from their home villages, and reflected their sense that owning land was the highest priority. This was their moment of self-determination, the moment they decided they would fight back and demand their due, even if it was risky.

When the fledgling community met to discuss the failed negotiations with Meaher, they decided they would quit saving for passage back to Africa and start saving to buy land so they could re-create their homeland here. It's possible the decision came down to realizing how difficult it was going to be to raise the tens of thousands of dollars it would take to get eighty people back to Africa. At best, it would take years and years to save enough money. Meanwhile, many of them had young children who needed homes immediately. It's also possible that even in these early days the Africans had begun to worry there might not be anything left to go home to. Most knew the life they remembered had been largely destroyed when they were captured, their friends and family either murdered or sold into slavery and shipped to parts unknown. And if they did go back, what was to stop the Dahomeans from capturing them all over again? Ironically, America was now the one place they knew where they were safe from being captured and enslaved the way they had been five years earlier.

Living on cornbread and molasses, the group members worked hard and saved. When they weren't at their jobs, they made baskets, farmed their small plots, and hunted in the swamps around Hog Bayou. In a year's time, they had enough to buy a parcel from the Meahers.

"Dey doan take off one five cent from de price for us. But we pay it all and take de lan'," Cudjo said. They divided the land—which consisted of low, rolling hills, a creek, and some swampy bottomland—into small parcels, about two acres per family. The Africans then worked together as a group to clear the new properties of the dense Alabama underbrush and build houses for each other—small, simple wood frame cabins with brick chimneys and hearths. The lumber would have come from Meaher's mill. In some of the houses, the chimneys were connected to two fireplaces, each facing into a different room. The bricks were homemade. Cudjo and some of the others had learned how to make bricks during enslavement. Cudjo said he was one of the last to have his house built because he was one of the last to marry.

"We call our village Affican Town. We say dat 'cause we want to go back in de Affica soil and we see we cain go. Derefo' we make Affica where dey fetch us. . . . We here and we got to stay."

A plat map from the 1920s shows that Cudjo and Gumpa were next-door neighbors, each sitting on about two acres, with Pollee Allen and Ossa Keeby a stone's throw away. This meant that four of the central leaders in Africatown's earliest days were next-door neighbors. Meaher's plantation butted up to the new parcels. The Africans would remain lifelong neighbors with the man who'd enslaved them, until Timothy's death in 1892. When Cudjo finally built his house, he erected a fence around his property and put in eight gates as a nod to his native village. The next purchase was made by a group that had been enslaved on Thomas Buford's plantation, about a ten-minute walk through the woods from the property bought from Meaher. Included among the group with Charlie Lewis, his wife, and several other *Clotilda* couples was an American-born couple who had also been enslaved on the Buford plantation. Horace and Matilda Ely were the first non-Africans invited to live in African Town. They would not be the last. This group split up the seven-acre parcel, which was about a half mile away from the property purchased from Meaher. It has come to be known as "Lewis Quarters," and the eight neat and tidy homes in the neighborhood are still inhabited today by descendants of the Africans. More of the group bought two- and three-acre parcels from the Meahers and other sellers, centered around the first purchases.

In their expansive gardens, which encompassed most of each family's property, the Africans grew a mix of American crops and several West African plants they were familiar with, such as black-eyed peas and okra, which had become common crops in the South. The produce was sold in town by the women, mirroring the native cultures of the *Clotilda* captives, where women run the markets and sell the produce even today. Cudjo's family was known to grow corn, beans, scuppernongs (a grape native to the American South), and sweet potatoes. There are stories of children being chased by Cudjo for stealing peaches from his trees. Pollee, living a few hundred yards from Cudjo, grew peanuts, cantaloupes, pears, plums, garlic, and okra.

The men also hunted and fished for their families, and likely sold some of their catch in the markets along Mobile's wharves. They carved dugout canoes in a style still seen on the water in Benin today to access the network of rivers and floodplain forests surrounding their village, which are still home to abundant animal populations. Cudjo was said to be expert at trapping raccoons, opossums, and other animals using techniques he'd learned in Africa. It is possible and even likely that the *Clotilda* captives owned and used guns for hunting by this point, though there is no mention of it.

As they started buying property and interacting with the government and organizations like the Freedmen's Bureau, the Africans, like all newly emancipated Black people, had to formalize their names, and come up with both a first and a last name. They needed full names to become U.S. citizens, which they accomplished in 1868, less than three years after they were freed. And they needed names so they could vote, which they tried to do for the first, and perhaps only, time in 1874, in one of the most contentious elections in U.S. history, marred by racial violence across the South. It was a bold and dangerous step, and required much persistence on the part of the Africans. They told the story to Roche in great detail.

It began when Timothy Meaher showed up in the village and began lobbying the Africans to vote the Democratic ticket in the upcoming national election instead of for the Republican Party of the day, Lincoln's party. We can glimpse where Meaher's heart lay in the Democratic Party platform for Pike County, Alabama, in 1874. The platform advocated "social ostracism of all those who act, sympathize or side with the negro Republican party. . . . Henceforth we will hold all such persons as enemies of our race, and we will not in the future have intercourse with them in any of the social relations of life."

A group of Republicans visited the Africans after Meaher had, and promised "great rewards" would come from voting Republican. Among those rewards was passage of a federal civil rights bill that would guarantee African-Americans the right to use public transportation, hotels, and restaurants. I suspect that James Dennison, and other American-born Blacks in the Africans' orbit, were the visiting Republicans mentioned. The position of the Democratic Party in Alabama was hardly a secret, and blacks overwhelmingly voted Republican throughout the South. One of the consequences of this sudden voting power was a backlash that took the form of the White League, a sort of paramilitary white supremacist organization aligned with the Democrats that had multiple chapters in Alabama. On Election Day in 1874, the group attacked two polling places in Barbour County, about a hundred miles from Mobile. The population in the remote area was dominated by freed Black people, who outnumbered whites two to one, and had repeatedly voted for Republicans by overwhelming margins. In the attack, the White League killed seven people waiting to vote Republican, injured seventy more, and scared more than a thousand people from the polling place. While the Africans couldn't know of the day's events as they walked to their polling station, a White League sympathizer sought to similarly disenfranchise them.

When Cudjo, Pollee Allen, and Charlie Lewis arrived at the polling place closest to their homes, they found Meaher waiting. He pointed them out to the poll workers.

"See those Africans? Don't let them vote. They are not of this country," Meaher sneered. They were turned away by election officials on Meaher's word, even though they had become citizens. So they headed to another nearby polling place. Meaher, on a horse, beat them there and thwarted them again. This happened a third time, prompting the Africans to pray to God for help. As the Africans headed away from this latest encounter, they resolved to outsmart Meaher. Instead of heading to the next closest polling place, they headed to Mobile, where there were too many polling places for Meaher to guard all at once. Choosing one on St. Francis Street, just around the corner from the now closed slave markets on Royal Street, they each shelled out a day's worth of wages to pay the $1 poll tax and voted Republican. The Civil Rights Act of 1875 passed the following year, granting all races equal access to public transportation, hotels, and restaurants.

As for the surnames the group chose for their American identities, it was common at the time for people who had been enslaved to adopt the names of their enslavers. None of the Africans chose this route. There are no explanations directly from them for this in any of the interviews or articles about the group, but we can safely assume that the last thing they wanted to do was link themselves to their enslavers with something as important as a name. In their native cultures, names carried special meaning, and often provided details about their families, where they lived, or their tribe.

Cudjo picked up the last name Lewis at this time. It was not his first choice. At first, he tried to approximate Western-style names by adding his father's name—O-lo-loo-ay—as his last name. "But it too long for de people to call it. It too crooked lak Kossula. So dey call me Cudjo Lewis," he told Hurston.

During my time in Benin, I heard a new and compelling theory on how Kossula ended up with the name Cudjo—which means "one who is born on Monday" in Fon. An important detail for this discussion is that Cudjo could neither read nor write. The spelling of his name as we know it today comes to us from newspaper articles and books written by Americans, not because Cudjo himself spelled it that way. While it is possible he was born on a Monday and chose this new name for himself when he arrived in Mobile, Cudjo is not much easier to pronounce than Kossula for Americans. His Majesty Dada Daagbo Hounon Houna II Guely, the spiritual leader of Benin's native Vodun religion, said he believes the name may have had more significance. He said this seemed especially likely to him given the numerous historical accounts that describe Cudjo as being well known for reciting African parables.

"Cudjo is the son which is born on Monday, that's what this name means in our language. As we break it down though, Cu is death. Jo is liberation. Together it means death is gone, or free from death, or born again. It is possible he said his name was Cu Jo, but there was a problem with the translation a century ago. If I say 'Cu Jo' it is different than 'Cudjo,'" Guely explained. "I think maybe he was talking about himself with that name. Kossula in his homeland was dead. But he still lived, in a new life. He was Cu Jo, dead and reborn."

A few of the other Africans, such as Ossa Keeby, never took American names. But most of the shipmates adopted American names at this time. In fact, for most of the *Clotilda*'s passengers, we know only their adopted American names.

Emma Roche interviewed eight surviving members of the tribe who provided both their African and American names. In a touching moment, the survivors ask Roche to call them by their African names in her book, hoping "in some way these names might drift back to their native home, where some might remember them." Cudjo's wife Abila adopted the name Celia; Ar-Zuma adopted Livingston; Jaba adopted Jaybee or Jabez; Abache adopted Clara Turner; Shamba adopted Wigfall; Kupollee adopted Pollee Allen; Monabee adopted Katie Cooper; and Oluale adopted Charlie Lewis. It does not appear that Cudjo and Charlie were related, despite the shared last name. Cudjo was quoted several times saying all of his kin died during the raid, and he never says Charlie was a relative in any of his numerous interviews. Still, some descendants of the men in Africatown today insist they were related and refer to them as Uncle Charlie and Uncle Cudjo. When it comes to the offspring born in the United States, many of the Africans gave their children both American names, to use when they were out in the world, and African names, which they used at home.

"They would have an African name for us, and my name was Jo-ko," said Eva Allen Jones, one of Pollee Allen's ten children, born in 1894, thirty-four years after the *Clotilda* arrived. She knew Cudjo, Ossa Keeby, Gumpa, and the rest for decades in her youth. At the time of her death in 1993, she was one of the last direct links to the original *Clotilda* group. She expressed re-morse that she did not learn her parents' native tongue, but said the children were embarrassed by the language and their African names. "We didn't recognize those names. We didn't want kids laughing at us for calling those names. But in our homes, we had our names and they'd call Jo-Ko and never call me Eva."

Cudjo was one of the last of the bunch to marry. He'd spent much of his five years of enslavement on the steamboat running up and down the river, away from the rest of the group, where he might have found a wife. Everyone else who came from his town was married and had children. He was lonely. "I ain' got nobody," he lamented. He had his eye on Celia. She wasn't mar-ried yet either. One day, Cudjo told her he'd like to marry her. She asked if he thought he could take care of her.

"Yeah, I kin work for you. I ain' goin' to beat you," he prom-ised. "I didn't say no more. We got married one month after we 'gree 'tween ourselves. We didn't have no wedding."

Shortly after their union, the pair decided to convert to Christianity. Free George, who befriended the Africans and tried to help them assimilate soon after their arrival, had been qui-etly encouraging them to find Jesus since their earliest days. Free George himself had been enslaved until a free woman fell in love with him and bought his freedom with money she earned as a cook. During visits to the plantation, he convinced the Africans to quit dancing on Sundays, even if they wouldn't come to church.

"Free George, he come to us and tell us not to dance on Sunday. Den he tell us whut Sunday is. We doan know whut it is before. Nobody in Afficky soil doan tell us 'bout no Sunday. Den we doan dance no mo on de Sunday," Cudjo said, with no apparent bitterness. "Free George come help us all de time. De colored folks whut born here, dey pick at us all de time and call us ig'nant savage. But Free George de best friend de Aficans got. He tell us we ought gittee de religion and join de church."

The Africans fervently embraced Christianity, but they did not want to attend one of the established churches in the area. Cudjo said they didn't want to "mixee wid de other folks what laught at us." Too many of the members of those churches mocked the Africans for the way they spoke and the habits that identified them as foreigners. Instead, the Africans decided to build themselves a church where they could worship without scorn. The first version of the church was a brush arbor in a clearing next to Cudjo's house. In time, they built a classic wooden church with a steeple and bell and called it the Old Landmark Baptist Church. Today, the sturdy brick edifice of the Union Baptist Church sits on the same spot. About a hundred yards away stands a brick chimney that used to be attached to Gumpa's house. It is the last structure built by the Africans that is still standing. Cudjo's land lay in between the church and Gumpa's chimney. The decision to adopt a new religion must have been emotional for the Africans, many of whom had been vetted in some version of Benin's native Vodun religion, which centers on various animal spirits and a reverence for nature and ancestors. While it is clear they never fully abandoned their old ways, their commitment to Christianity was serious, and the Africans and their children were baptized just down the hill from the church, in Three Mile Creek. Cudjo served as a sexton at the church until his death, and Roche remarks that during her interviews, Pollee's "constant companion is a small, much worn New Testament."

"I don't know of no other place they went for enjoyment but the house of prayer. They'd have service there every Wednesday night, every Friday night, and every Sunday night. On Sunday morning, 4 o'clock we went to a prayer meeting, it was black dark. We stayed until sunrise. Called that sunrise meeting," recalled Eva Allen Jones of her childhood in the early 1900s. Jones was one of the last children born to one of the original founders. "After sunrise, we came back home, ate our breakfast and 9 o'clock we went to Sunday school. We stay until 11 o'clock service, and after that was over, we went home and ate our dinner. At 3 o'clock that bell ring, we went back to church. Went home, ate our supper, at 7 o'clock we was right back in church."

Cudjo and Celia had their first child ten months after their marriage and had five more in short succession, for a total of five boys and one girl. The other couples in the village also had many children. Soon it was time for a school for the children, something unknown in their villages back home, and unknown for most Blacks across the South at the time. The first classes were held in the newly constructed church, but before long, the community built a schoolhouse on land donated by several of the *Clotilda* families.

"We Afficans try raise our chillun right. When dey say we ign'ant we go together and build de schoolhouse. . . . We Afficky men doan wait lak de other colored people till de white folks git-tee ready to build us a school. We build one for ourself."

Cudjo's statement, "We build one for ourself," sums up the ascendance of the Africans in the years after they were freed. They were not going it alone like most people who were newly emancipated and left vulnerable to the machinations of a white population growing more hostile toward them by the year. Instead, the Africans' decision to band together, govern themselves, and share resources and labor elevated them. Within a few years of gaining their freedom, they were living in houses they built themselves, worshipping in a church they built themselves, sending their kids to a school they built themselves, and doing it all in a village they built themselves—a village where they had significantly more autonomy than most who had been freed by the Civil War.

By the 1880s, the children of the *Clotilda* passengers began to marry and build small houses in the community, often on their parents' parcels. American-born Black people were attracted by the growing reputation of African Town, a place not ruled by whites, and began moving to the area. By then, popularly known as "Plateau" because it was built at the top of a slight hill above the river, the town was far enough from Mobile at about three miles that the land was cheap, especially so because the peninsula the town was on was surrounded on three sides by swampland. Meanwhile, the death of Timothy Meaher in 1892 reminded the nation of the story of the *Clotilda* and kindled new interest into what had become of her passengers. Obituaries in the *Mobile Daily Advertiser and Register*, the *New York Times*, and papers all over the nation, described Meaher as "the venerable steamboat man" and "swashbuckling." But most of the ink in every obituary was spent telling the story of the *Clotilda* and the creation of Africatown. Many of the obituaries included descriptions of the settlement, such as this from the hometown *Daily Advertiser and Register*: "They mix very little with other negroes and preserve many of their native customs, using their native language, speaking English with difficulty and being ruled by a queen of their own choosing. They enjoy a high reputation for honesty and industry."

While it is unclear where the local paper got the notion that Africatown was ruled by a queen, the renewed interest directly inspired Alabama poet and author Mary McNeil Scott to visit Africatown for the first time, where she interviewed Noah Hart, whose recollections have proven invaluable. Scott's eight novels, published under the pen name Sidney McCall, were well received in their day, and her poetry, often centering on flowers, was published in newspapers across the country. The article under consideration here, titled "Affika Town," was also published widely. It includes the only interview conducted with Noah Hart, who as Timothy Meaher's houseboy had a front-row seat to the *Clotilda* story. Scott wrote the breezy feature after her "pretty New York cousin," came to town and asked to visit "an African Village near here. I have heard it spoken of so often."

It is fascinating that a New Yorker had not only heard of the settlement, but had heard of it often, in 1893. Scott allows that while "the natives sometimes bring vegetables in to sell, I have never thought of going to see them." Chastised by her cousin for not showing her this obvious point of interest during a tour of Mobile, Scott says, "Come, we will be two Mrs. Sheldons, and start even now to penetrate Africa." This last is a reference to

May French Sheldon, who famously led an expedition through Kenya in 1891, "without the assistance or companionship of white or black men or women above the rank of servitors." Sheldon's trip was inspired by family friend Henry Morton Stanley of "Dr. Livingstone, I presume" fame. At the height of the Victorian era, Americans were fascinated by Africa, and Sheldon was the toast of the world by 1893, after a lecture tour and the publication of her travel accounts. One of the primary reasons she gives for her journey was "having ever flouted in my face the supercilious edict that it was outside the limitation of woman's legitimate province."

It was blind luck, according to Scott, that their carriage driver for their trip "to penetrate Africa," ended up being Noah Hart, by then an old man. He was recommended by her houseboy, who said Noah was "'bout de onliest driver what knows de way." The resulting article is one of the only sources with any information about the *Clotilda* captives' first days as slaves, and of Meaher's early efforts to hide the arrival of the ship from the government. The article is also unique for the vivid picture it paints of African Town, circa 1893. Scott's first question for Noah was whether he thought two women would be safe going to the community. "Pufficly safe, pufficly safe, Miss," he responded.

As the carriage approached the settlement Noah warned the ladies, "You mustn't spec ter see nothin' noway oncommon, ladies. You know de Affikins lives jes erbout lak 'Merican niggers now." As they reached the top of a hill, "down through the valley and up on the slope of the hill beyond were dotted little cabins. Sometimes two or three would be huddled together; then again one would stand out far from the rest. Each had its little patch of flower garden, its clambering vines and its vegetable garden of potatoes, corn, tobacco and watermelons. As we jogged on past dilapidated fences and unattractive cabins, we came to one rather worse than the others, where a bent old woman, with a head as white as snow, was hoeing among the melon vines."

Noah attempted to draw the woman into conversation, offering to buy melons from her garden. This was almost certainly a woman named Zuma, by then a widow and something of a hermit. Roche's description of her, though unkind with its descriptions of "many pounds of superfluous flesh," may be accurate: "she sits for the most part silent and brooding in her squalid hut. . . . Brooding, she is pathetic; aroused and speaking of home, she is tragic." Roche said her English was barely intelligible compared to her shipmates'.

"She walked slowly toward us, with her keen eyes fixed on our faces; but some feet inside of her rickety gate she stopped, and no amount of wheedling brought her a step nearer. I suppose that she had 'sized us up,' and made up her mind that we had called for curiosity rather than melons, and her dignity was therefore offended," wrote Scott. It is telling that sightseers were common enough for Zuma to recognize one when she saw them, and that she stared at them with enough menace for Scott to register that the woman was offended by the objectifying attention.

Henry Romeyn, an army captain, visited the village a few years after Mary McNeil Scott, perhaps drawn by her article. At the time, he was told that about forty of the original Africans remained. He found that "about thirty small houses are scattered irregularly over an area of forty or fifty acres; many of them quite comfortable structures, compared with ordinary cabins of the country." When he visited the group at church, he said they "were fully as well dressed as are the majority of laboring people white or black, in their locality; and most of them had in their appearance and surrounding, an air of substantial physical well-being none too common in the laboring class in that section of the country."

Perhaps Romeyn's most prescient comment was "Any romance connected with them is fast fading away, and with the passing of the original members of the colony from the scenes of action, it will have ceased to exist, and their descendants will be merged into the ordinary colored inhabitants of the section where they reside." After more than three decades in Alabama, that very thing had already started to happen in Africatown, as the founders began to die off, and more of their children married American-born Blacks.

We can see that this loss of Africanness had already begun in some measure by the time Noah Hart took Mary McNeil Scott to visit "Affiky Town." From the interview with Hart, we know that when the Africans first arrived, they danced frequently to express both sorrow and joy. We know they performed African-style burials. We know they continued ceremonies surrounding the new moon and the arrival of new children, the worship of weather events such as thunderstorms. What we don't know is precisely when those things disappeared. Cudjo hints at it when discussing the death of his first child in 1893. "We Christian people now, so we put our baby in de coffin and dey take her in de church, and everybody come look down in her face. Dey sing, 'Shall We Meet Beyond De River.' I been a member of de church a long time now, and I know de words of de song wid my mouth, but my heart it doan know dat. Derefo' I sing inside me, 'O todo ah wah n-law yah-lee, owrran k-nee ra ra k-nee ro ro.'"

Thirty-three years after he arrived in Mobile, Cudjo is

censoring himself, keeping the African death chant he grew up with locked in his heart while singing an American version out loud.

Cudjo's only daughter died in August of 1893 at the age of fifteen. In coastal Alabama, July and August are high time for mosquitoes, due to the very tropical wet season, with daily thunderstorms most afternoons. From Cudjo's description of the teenager taking to her bed and slowly withering despite various prescriptions from a doctor, it sounds like she may have succumbed to either yellow fever or malaria. Both remained widespread in Mobile into the 1920s, until window screens became common.

Cudjo lamented the first time "death find where my door is. But we from cross de water know dat he come in de ship wid us. . . . Her mama take it so hard. I try tellee her not to cry, but I cry too." In Bante, a Yoruba family would have buried their daughter under the hard-packed dirt floor of the home, or under the entranceway of the house. It was a way of keeping the dead close, where they could still be loved and safe from harm. We know from Noah Hart's firsthand account that when the Africans arrived, they buried their dead using traditional African methods. Burying the teenager in the new cemetery next to their church was hard for Cudjo and his wife, even though they could see the grave from their porch. But it had to be done, he said, because they had become Christians, and that's what Christians did. "We bury her in de family lot. She lookee so lonesome out dere by herself—she such a li'l girl," Cudjo said. He quickly built a fence around her grave so she would have protection out in the lonely cemetery. His wife would often sit by the grave.

During the coming years, death and hardship would remain

frequent visitors for Cudjo's family. They would encounter voter intimidation, racial violence, prison, and murder, even at the hands of law enforcement. By the 1890s, Alabama led the nation in lynchings, with 177 documented cases in the decade. The state steadily passed a series of ever more regressive state constitutions, each taking a little more freedom away from African-Americans. The constitution adopted in 1901, and still in force today—with many modifications forced by the federal civil rights laws—was designed specifically to disenfranchise them. John Knox, an Alabama lawyer who led the Constitutional Convention where the document was drafted, confessed as much during the convention. "If we would have white supremacy, we must establish it by law, not by force or fraud," Knox said. He blamed the "inferior intelligence and moral failings" of the state's nonwhite population. As he explained in his opening remarks at the convention, whites should rule because "there is in the white man an inherited capacity of government, which is wholly wanting in the Negro. Before the art of reading and writing was known, the ancestors of the Anglo-Saxon had established an orderly system of government. . . . The Negro on the other hand, is descended from a race of lowest in intelligence and moral perceptions of all the races of men."

The constitution as adopted established a requirement for residency in order to vote, along with a poll tax of $1.50 a year, the ability to read and write in English, and personal property worth at least $300 or the ownership of at least forty acres of land. The effects of the new constitution were immediate and profound. In 1900, there were 181,000 African-Americans registered to vote in the state. In 1903, there were just 5,000. The residents of African Town were among those who lost out.

The Lewis clan's experiences in the decades before and after 1890 mirrored what African-Americans faced across the South after emancipation. Several of the major incidents revolved around Cudjo's boys, five in all. Cudjo said the children of American-born Blacks called his children cannibals, ignorant savages, and kin to monkeys. These were all insults that would be hurled at African-Americans for the next hundred years, no matter where they were born. Cudjo said his boys had no choice but to defend themselves against the attacks. The words hurt their feelings, so they fought, and fought hard. Though it is left unsaid, it is a safe bet that Cudjo taught his children—including his youngest son and namesake, Cudjo Jr.—to defend themselves with the techniques he'd learned during his five years of training as a warrior.

"When dey whip de other boys, dey folks come to our house and tellee us, 'Yo' boys mighty bad Cudjo. We 'fraid they goin' kill somebody,'" Cudjo recalled. Dealing with the angry parents of kids who'd been beaten up, he likened his sons to rattlesnakes. "If you bother wid him, he bite you. If you know de snake killee you, why you bother wid him? Same way wid my boys." But the parents kept coming. "All de time, 'Aleck dis, Jimmy dat, Poe-lee dis an' t'other. David a bad boy. Cudjo fightee my son.' Nobody never say whut dey do to de Afficky savages."

This pattern of violence continued as the boys became adults. Son Cudjo Jr. became the owner of a grocery store, a prosperous and prominent occupation for an African-American in Alabama at the turn of the century. He was well regarded by both Blacks and whites in the community. For reasons unknown, he killed a man in 1899, Gilbert Thomas, who may have been his brother-in-law. Earlier in the same year, Cudjo Jr. had married a woman named Louisa Thomas, though it is unclear if she was related to Gilbert, the murdered man. Any police reports that may have existed describing the murder have long since disappeared, and neither Cudjo Sr. nor any of the Africans ever spoke of it. We know that Cudjo Jr. was convicted of manslaughter and sentenced to five years in the state prison. During that time, he was enrolled in Alabama's notorious convict leasing system.

This system came into existence in 1875 when the state faced a serious cash shortage. Alabama decided at that point to rent its prisoners to railroads, coal mine owners, and other heavy industry. The arrangement proved so profitable for the state, which simply handed the prisoners over to industry and let the companies feed and house them, that by 1883 a new arrangement had been made. Nearly all of the state's inmates were leased to three coal mining companies for a few dollars a month per prisoner. A Convict Bureau document from 1900 describes Cudjo Jr. as a second-class prisoner at Pratt Mines, earning the state $10 per month from the mining company for his labor. As a second-class prisoner, Cudjo Jr. was expected to dig three tons of coal a day from rock seams deep underground. Prisoners who didn't meet their quota were subject to forty to fifty lashes with a wide leather strap. The shackled miners were carried underground each morning, riding into the bowels of the Earth in mining carts, on the narrow-gauge tram system used to haul the coal to the surface. Equipped with picks, sledgehammers, and iron wedges to pry chunks of coal loose, the men worked by the light of tiny oil lanterns fastened to leather straps they wore around their heads. When Cudjo Jr. wasn't underground, he was kept chained with two hundred other prisoners in a crowded bunkhouse where tuberculosis and other diseases were rampant.

Thirty percent of the prisoners died each year. The system would continue until 1928 and is infamous for the abuses heaped on convicts. In 1900—the year Cudjo Jr. was imprisoned—the state reaped $400,000 from the program, the equivalent of about $13 million today. Conditions for the inmates were horrific. They worked twelve-hour days underground in unventilated mines, where they were choked on coal dust and were vulnerable to tunnel collapses, explosions, faulty elevators, and asphyxiation by pockets of deadly hydrogen sulfide gas, not to mention the whippings and other tortures documented at the mines.

Cudjo Jr.'s story was an unusual one. After a lobbying campaign involving law enforcement officers and community leaders, Black and white, he received a pardon from the governor after just one year underground. In the petition for the pardon, which was supported by ten of the twelve jurors who'd convicted Cudjo Jr. of manslaughter, his lawyer writes, "The present Sheriff tells me Lewis is a good negro, that he was of great service to the officers of the law in the apprehension of criminals and was always a peaceful, law-abiding citizen in every respect." Other documents reveal that Cudjo Jr. served as an informer for the sheriff, helping "him and his deputies in ferreting out crime and arresting criminals of his own race." Those documents also describe Gilbert Thomas, the man Cudjo Jr. killed, as "a desperate, dangerous, turbulent and blood-thirsty scoundrel whose taking off was an unspeakable blessing to the community in which he lived. He was a perambulating arsenal of homicidal fury and destruction." A letter included in the pardon petition was signed by some of Mobile's most prominent citizens, including the sheriff. The first signature on the letter is that of Augustine Meaher, son of Timothy Meaher.

Cudjo Jr.'s reprieve was as brief as it was rare. Two years later, in 1902, he was shot through the throat by an African-American sheriff's deputy. He lingered in bed for two days at the Lewis home, his breath wheezing through a gaping hole in his neck. "His mama never leave him. She lookee at his face and tellee him, 'Put whip to yo' horse, baby,'" Cudjo remembered. "I pray so hard, but he die. I so sad I wish I could die in place of my Cudjo. Maybe I doan pray right, you unnerstand me, 'cause he die while I was prayin' dat de Lor' spare my boy life."

Though she did not include the story in *Barracoon*, Zora Neale Hurston's notes included a description of what she believed happened, which she acknowledged was sketchy at best. Of one fact she was certain: "The community in general feared the Lewis boys." Her sources said there had been multiple fights between Cudjo's sons and another group in the community spread over months. This led up to a bloody confrontation on July 28, 1902. One man was shot to death and another suffered a grievous knife wound. "Young Cudjo was said to have done both the cutting and the shooting when set upon by some of his enemies." Hurston's notes suggest a sheriff's deputy had been trying to arrest Cudjo for three weeks, but was afraid of the confrontation. Unable to catch him off guard, the deputy hid behind the butcher's wagon when the butcher arrived to deliver meat. As Cudjo Jr. stepped out from his shop to settle with the butcher, the deputy shot him from his hiding place. There are no records of an arrest warrant or a charge against the younger Cudjo, and his father went to his grave believing his son had been murdered.

"He say he de law, but he doan come 'rest him. If my boy done something wrong, it his place come 'rest him lak a man. If he mad wid my Cudjo 'bout something, den he ought come fight him face to face lak a man. He have words wid my boy, but he skeered face him," Cudjo said. "Dis man, he hidin' hisself in de back of de wagon an' shootee my boy. . . . he make out he skeered my boy goin' shoot him and shootee my boy down in de store."

The deputy became the pastor of a church in the area, but never apologized to Cudjo for killing his son. Not long after the death of his second child, Cudjo himself had been badly injured when he was hit by a train while driving his buckboard wagon to Mobile to buy beans to plant in his garden in 1902. He was flung from the wagon, and his horse ran away. A white woman was among those who came to his aid at the scene and made sure he was taken to a doctor's office. Cudjo was bedridden for fourteen days, and given morphine to dull the pain of broken ribs and other injuries. The woman sent a basket of food and then came to visit Cudjo at his home, connecting him to a lawyer and urging him to sue the railroad. The woman's identity remains a mystery, though I suspect she was Emma Roche, who first captured the Africans' story for history. Roche's family was a prominent one in Mobile. Her father was a Confederate war hero and a prosperous funeral director, and the family mansion, which also housed the Roche mortuary business, still sits on Government Street, where Cudjo was hit by the train. Emma traveled broadly in her early years and studied at an art school in Manhattan. Her family had interacted with several of the Africans who worked for her father for years, and they knew the Africans' unique history before Cudjo's accident. When she spoke to him in the aftermath, she would have recognized his accent and linked him to Gumpa and the others employed as gravediggers. It seems likely that this was when she and Cudjo struck up the close friendship that would last the rest of their lives.

For an illiterate African to go up against the behemoth L&N Railroad was unusual, especially with a lawsuit for $5,000. The railroad's lawyer blamed Cudjo for not noticing the train before it hit him, but the jury was not moved by this argument, as multiple witnesses testified that the train never blew its whistle or rang its bell before barreling through the downtown intersection where Cudjo was hit. They had him remove his clothes in court to display his injuries, and a doctor testified that he was crippled for life and wouldn't be able to work at the mill any longer. In a surprise verdict, he was awarded $650, but his white lawyer, a member of Mobile's society set, kept stalling when Cudjo asked for the money. Within a year, the attorney died of yellow fever, and Cudjo never received a dime of his settlement. The congregation of the Old Landmark Baptist Church named Cudjo sexton, or caretaker.

Just a few months later, Gumpa, who had been the leader of the village for three decades, was also hit by a train. He succumbed to his injuries within a week, leading the group to elevate Charlie Lewis to the role of leader.

Death became a frequent visitor at Cudjo's house in 1905. David, the second youngest son, told his parents one afternoon he was headed to Mobile to pick up some shirts he'd had laundered. Hours later, he was found dead on the railroad tracks five miles in the opposite direction from where he had said he was going. He had been beheaded. When neighbors carried the body to Cudjo's house on an old window shutter, he refused to believe it was his son because the head was missing. Then someone walked up carrying a box with David's head in it. Celia began wailing. Cudjo reached inside his son's shirt and felt for the scarification marks they had put on his chest when he was a baby. Once he felt them, he knew it was his son. Cudjo leapt from the porch and raced into the forest, finally tripping and falling on his face. Some of "those who had come across de water come to find me" and brought him home. Three of Cudjo and Celia's children were now buried in the cemetery by his home. His son Pollee, named after Pollee Allen, was furious. One brother had been murdered by the deputy, and now another found dead in mysterious circumstances along the railroad tracks. His father had been hit by a train, only to have the court-ordered settlement stolen by his white lawyer. Pollee told his parents he wanted to move to Africa.

A few weeks later, he said he was going fishing in the creek down the hill from the house. Cudjo and the others kept dugout canoes they had made in the African way on the creekbank. He never came home. Cudjo told Hurston he hoped Pollee had decided to run away to Africa, but he was afraid someone had killed him too. "So many de folks dey hate my boy 'cause he lak his brothers. Dey doan let nobody 'buse dem lak dey dogs. Maybe he in de Afficky soil lak somebody say. Po' Cudjo lonesome for him, but Cudjo doan know."

Then in November, Cudjo's son Jimmy came home for work and said he didn't feel well. A doctor was called, but Jimmy was dead within two days. He died holding Cudjo's hand. Five of the Lewis children were now buried in the little cemetery on the hill. Only their oldest child, Aleck, was still alive, living next door to his parents with his wife and children. "I good to my chillun!" Cudjo said. "I want dey company, but looky lak dey lonesome for one 'nother. So dey hurry go sleep together in de graveyard."

Three years passed, just Cudjo and Celia living in their little cabin. "De house was full, but now it empty. We old folks now and we know we ain' going have no mo' chillun. We so lonesome, but we know we cain gittee back de dead. When de spit goes from de mouf, it doan come back. When de earth eats, it doan give back." One night Celia woke Cudjo to tell him she'd had a dream that their children were cold. When they were little, he said, she would often get up in the night to check on them and make sure they had enough quilts to keep warm. The next morning, she asked him to accompany her to the graveyard to check on the children. Cudjo said he would, but then disappeared to go clean the church, hoping she'd forget about visiting the cemetery, because he knew it would upset her. When he came outside, he spied her on the hillside moving among the graves. "I see Seely goin' from one her chillun grave to de other, lak she cover dem up wid mo' quilts." A week later she died and was buried alongside her children. A month after that, her oldest son, Aleck, died, in December of 1908, also under mysterious circumstances. Cudjo's last child took his place with the others on the hillside.

"Den I jes lak I come from de Afficky soil," Cudjo told Hurston, meaning both alone and lonesome. "I got nobody but de daughter-in-law, Mary, and de grandchillun."

It may have been the death of Cudjo's wife that brought Roche back into his orbit, or maybe she'd been a regular presence for the six years since the train accident. She describes the scene at Cudjo's home the Sunday after his wife was buried. The last of the Africans gathered together and told stories about their homeland, chattering quietly in their native language, and

Cudjo made a parable about his wife's death, explaining she got off the train they were riding unexpectedly. "She say, 'Goodbye, Cudjo. I hate to leave you.' But she git off," leaving him "still journeying on."

He was bereft. "Oh Lor'! Lor'! De wife she de eyes to de man's soul. How kin I see now, when I ain' gottee de eyes no mo'?" The gathering of the elders was repeated the following Sunday, again at Cudjo's home. Roche says the last of the *Clotilda* captives met this way every Sunday, either at Cudjo's, Pollee's, or Abache's. They gathered to speak their native language with the last of their kind, talking and taking care of one another. "I appreciate my countrymen dey come see me when dey know I lonely."

When he sits with Roche in these later years, she finds him warm and quick with a laugh. "The old man is cheerful—even merry—possessing a keen sense of humor and a lively imagination. To appreciate him fully he must be surprised at his home. There he will be found probably working in his garden barefooted, trousers rolled up above his knees; his costume clean but a marvelous piece of patchwork, even the old derby upon his head a much mended one." Roche does not mean insult when she remarks on his clothes. Cudjo loved to sew. He did all of the family's mending at night after work. This harkens back to life in Bante, and in the Yoruba culture, where sewing is traditionally a man's job. I witnessed as much as I traveled around modern-day Benin. In small storefronts, under shady trees, even in mud huts, I saw men hunched over old-fashioned sewing machines turning out dresses and men's suits.

Cudjo summed up his loneliness by explaining that God gave people six limbs so they could live: two hands, two feet, and two eyes. "I say dey cut off de feet, he got hands to 'fend hisself. Dey cut off de hands he wiggle out de way when he see danger come. But when he lose de eye, den he can't see nothin' come upon him. He finish. My boys is my feet. My daughter is my hands. My wife she my eye. She left, Cudjo finished."

Age sixty-seven, suddenly on his own, his injuries from the train accident meant he could no longer handle farming the large tracts of land he'd accumulated around his home. He sold off the first piece shortly after his wife's death, and slowly parted with other pieces to replace his lost income. He spent the next twenty-seven years awash in his loneliness, his only source of joy being his grandchildren and then great-grandchildren, who were constant companions. They read the Bible to him, and he grew sugarcane in his small garden so he'd always have something sweet to give them.

A photograph of him sitting by the fire in his home around this time shows walls made of pine planks gone dark with age and soot. One wall is covered in newsprint used as wallpaper. Three photographs hang on the wall, one is of a couple, perhaps Cudjo and his beloved wife. Three straw hats, each looking fairly new and in the boater style popular in the 1920s, hang on nails. Around the fireplace, crumpled wads of newspaper are shoved in cracks between the wood walls and the stones of the hearth. A few spiderwebs are visible against the dark wood planking. A kerosene lamp and a windup clock are perched on the cluttered mantel. Several large iron pots are stacked on the hearth, indicating Cudjo cooks over the fire, rather than on a woodstove. A wicker rocking chair is heaped with clothes and paper bags.

While Cudjo's cabin was primitive, Africatown was not. Rising alongside several other Black-governed communities around the country, it became a magnet, pulling in African-Americans from all over Alabama and beyond. Some of these largest African-American communities advertised themselves in nation-wide publications, attempting to draw residents. In advertisements in various publications Boley, Oklahoma, billed itself as a "progressive negro town," with schools, churches, and a business district. Mound Bayou, Mississippi, bragged that with its newspaper, telephone system, and electric lights, it provided all the amenities of a modern country town for "a man with brains and vision."

For Africatown, news coverage surrounding the death of Timothy Meaher and subsequent visits by Booker T. Washington and other celebrities of the day did the advertising. *The Negro Yearbook and Annual Encyclopedia of the Negro* put out every year by the Tuskegee Institute documented the community's rise. In 1912, it was listed as one of thirty towns nationwide that were governed by Blacks, with a population of two hundred, though in the listing the town is called Plateau. By 1921, just nine years later, the population had grown to fifteen hundred, making it the fourth largest African-American-governed community in the nation.

The fast growth—from the few dozen families that founded the town and were its first residents to a community where American-born Blacks far outnumbered the original African inhabitants—meant that the longtime system of governance, with a leader and judges chosen from among the original Africans, simply disappeared under the weight of the burgeoning population. The remaining Africans, fewer than ten by 1921, did not hold significant influence over the hundreds of new families. They were treated as respected elders by the community, but not so respected that the newcomers agreed to live under the community rules established at the town's founding, or abide by decisions rendered by the trio of old men whom the original Africans still followed as their leaders.

As the last Africans moved into old age, their children and grandchildren continued to work for the Meahers at the mill and shipyard, and farm the properties their parents were leaving behind.

Photographs of the scenes along Mobile's waterfront at the time show not much had changed from the Civil War days: stacks of lumber waiting to be shipped out, warehouses stuffed with bales of cotton, huge quantities of South American bananas being unloaded onto the wharves, and a lot of African-American laborers doing the work. Since Timothy's death in 1892, the Meahers' various businesses had expanded, and the mill and timber business were still major employers for the growing population of Africatown. Augustine Meaher, Timothy's son, now ruled his father's empire, though the original plantation house had long since burned down.

When the third schoolhouse built by the Africans since 1880 burned down under mysterious circumstances in the mid-1920s, the community turned to a program started by Booker T. Washington that provided grants to schools for African-Americans. In 1927, the school started by the Africans, then known as the "Plateau Normal and Industrial Institute for the Education of the Head, Heart and Hands of the Colored Youth," received a grant from the Rosenwald Fund to build a new, much larger school, with ten classrooms and living quarters for ten teachers. The fund was the brainchild of Booker T. Washington and Julius Rosenwald, the CEO of Sears, Roebuck and Co. The pair met in Chicago in 1911, after Rosenwald attended a speech by

Washington. Rosenwald, whose fortune would have ranked him as a billionaire by today's standards, was looking for a philanthropic cause to answer what he believed were "the special duties that capitalists and men of wealth owed to society." Rosenwald provided an endowment for Washington's Tuskegee Institute and embraced Washington's dream of funding schools across the South to teach what the educator described as "industrial education."

"The minute it was seen that through industrial education the Negro youth was not only studying chemistry, but also how to apply the knowledge of chemistry to the enrichment of the soil, or to cooking, or to dairying, and that the student was being taught not only geometry and physics, but their application to blacksmithing, brickmaking, farming, and what not, then there began to appear for the first time a common bond between the two races."

The first six schools the pair funded—thanks to a $25,000 grant from Rosenwald—were built in rural Alabama hamlets in 1914. By 1932, the fund had spent $28 million to construct 4,977 schools across the South, and 217 houses or dormitories for the teachers, including the ten teachers in Africatown. Washington was dead by the time the Africatown school received its grant of $4,800. The money allowed the school to significantly expand and saw it renamed Mobile County Training School. In Alabama, the phrase "training school" meant a high school for Blacks. The new Africatown school, built on the spot where Cudjo asked Timothy Meaher to give the Africans some land, was the first and only high school for African-Americans in all of Mobile, and the first one to receive official certification by the state of Alabama. Of the five thousand schools built with

Rosenwald grants, only the school in Africatown is still open and teaching students.

Meanwhile, one of the most consequential changes to Africatown since its founding occurred right outside Cudjo's front door the same year when he and several of his shipmates were compelled to sell some of their land to the city of Mobile for the construction of a road. The road bisected the properties of many of the *Clotilda* families, and was attached to a new drawbridge built in 1927 that crossed the Mobile River and landed right in the heart of Africatown. Its creation was coupled with construction of an earthen berm laid all the way across the top of Mobile Bay's marshy estuary for a new road. It connected Mobile for the first time by road to the growing cities on the other side of Mobile Bay, including Daphne, Spanish Fort, and Fairhope. Previously, the only way across the bay was an eight-mile boat ride. More important than connecting these local communities, the bridge was also part of U.S. 90, then the only highway that ran along the Gulf Coast, connecting Alabama to Florida, Mississippi, Louisiana, and beyond. The bridge was a big deal for the city of Mobile. It meant visiting the city no longer required making a long detour far out of the way for people traveling along the coast. Instead, the coastal highway now came through the city. Everyone heading through Mobile on the new highway had to drive right through Africatown on the newly paved road, passing within a few yards of the homes of Cudjo and Africatown's other original leaders, as well as the community's church and the cemetery. The road also crossed the swampy areas that had always isolated the peninsula that Africatown and the Meaher properties sat on, meaning the trip to Mobile was suddenly much faster. This would change Africatown in a profound way:

the community situated out on the end of a peninsula was instantly transformed from the equivalent of a cul-de-sac—a road that leads nowhere else—to a crossroads connected to places far and wide.

The change also meant the Meahers' extensive waterfront holdings along the Mobile River were suddenly accessible to major industry. Within two years of the bridge's installation, Augustine "Gus" Meaher, grandson of Timothy, made a deal that made his family even richer, and would set Africatown's course for decades. He leased about a hundred acres along the riverfront to International Paper Company to build what would become one of the largest paper mills in the world, and the company's global headquarters. The factory was built within shouting distance of people's houses in Africatown.

As construction on the mill began, Zora Neale Hurston visited Cudjo for a last time in 1928. By the time the smokestacks of the new factory emerged above the tops of his fruit trees, Cudjo was the last African living in African Town. Hurston asked to take his picture, which Cudjo agreed to, but only after he changed clothes. He emerged from the house wearing his best suit, but no shoes. Hurston asked why. "I want to look lak I in Affica, 'cause dat where I want to be."

All of his shipmates had passed away within the last few years. He and Redoshi, who lived a few hours away by train, were known to have continued visiting each other after all the other *Clotilda* captives had died. She would have been the last person Cudjo spoke to in his native tongue, probably in 1932. In these last years, he was visited frequently by reporters. One remembered that "the present of a dime or two-bits would refresh his memory regarding the past." His celebrity was such that a New York promoter offered a generous sum for Cudjo to appear as the star attraction in a vaudeville review in the city. At that point, he had lived in his one-room cabin for seventy-five years, and only spent two nights away from it in all that time. He had no interest in seeing New York or leaving his house or the graveyard out front where his wife, children, and shipmates were buried. Cudjo had never learned to read and write. For the last twenty-seven years of his life, night would close in on the old man mending pants by lamplight, nothing to keep his memories at bay but the dozens of Bible verses he had memorized. He spoke openly to everyone he encountered about the awful loneliness he felt in these last years, including in several public events put on in Mobile where Cudjo told his story and spoke and sang in his native tongue in packed auditoriums. He would fall to tears recounting the story of his capture and the destruction of his village, or his worry over his son Pollee, whose body was never found.

"After he was too weak to be about, when I called to see him the doors and windows would be closed tight," Roche wrote in an obituary for the Mobile newspaper. "Opening a door, I'd call, 'Cudjo,' and out of the gloom a low moan and a 'Thank God' would answer me."

The last time Roche called on her old friend, shortly before he died at ninety-four, an old, one-eyed man was helping care for him. His widowed daughter-in-law Mary and her children, who still lived in a house Cudjo and the Africans had helped his son Aleck build on the property three decades earlier, brought him food. Roche's arrival brought tears to his eyes as he raised his head toward the heavens and exclaimed, "Lord! God! I thank Thee, that I see her once again." His mind remained keen until the end, but his worn body was scarcely up to sitting in a rocking chair. Since his conversion to Christianity in 1869, Cudjo would point to the sky and say that when he died, "I want to go yonder." His last words to Roche as she left his house for the final time were, "When they tell you Cudjo is dead say 'No! Cudjo is not dead—he has gone to heaven to rest.'"

The last of the Africatown settlers went yonder on July 26, 1935. He was buried in the hillside graveyard just beyond his front door, next to his wife, children, and shipmates.

Chapter 9

AFRICATOWN–
THE FALL

*I*f Cudjo and the rest of the survivors had lived a little
longer, into the 1940s and '50s, they would have witnessed an almost unbelievable growth spurt for their
African Town. The growth continued unabated into the 1970s.
The original population of about thirty people blossomed into
a community of twelve thousand people, its shady streets and
rolling hills lined with tidy wood-frame and brick houses and
home to a vibrant commercial district. Building on the foundation the Africans left behind—a community of tight-knit,
multigeneration families centered around a growing church and
school—Africatown continued to serve as a model of autonomy
for Black people around the nation.

It would not last forever. By the time Eva Allen, the last
child born to an African parent, passed away in 1992, Africatown had fallen to blight, decay, and abandonment. The demise

is intimately tied to the same forces that propelled the town's rise—the gigantic factories looming over the neighborhood, and the bridge over the Mobile River.

The first paper mill represented the vanguard of a rapid industrialization that would soon transform Mobile's waterfront and especially Africatown. Within a few years, federal grants created the Alabama State Docks, which led to the construction of three major shipyards (including one practically in Africatown) and an Alcoa aluminum plant. By 1940, there were thousands of new jobs either in or right around Africatown, including at a sausage factory, another paper mill, and a second sawmill, Gulf Lumber, which opened up right next to Lewis Quarters. Hundreds of men in the community walked to work at the factories, all of which were so close that residents could hear the whistles at the plants signaling shift changes from their bedrooms. The community now had two of the biggest attractants for Alabama's African-American population—plenty of jobs and a place their children could go to high school.

World War II meant even more jobs as Mobile's shipyards began repairing battle-wounded warships and cranking out liberty ships to supply the troops overseas. Barbershops, movie theaters, butchers, pharmacies, a hotel, and several nightclubs sprang up in a new commercial district along Africatown's main roads. By the end of the war, houses and space in the high school were in short supply. Families moved into the hundreds of new houses being built all around the original Africatown core as soon as the paint on the new walls was dry.

The Meaher family were major players in this burgeoning real estate market, erecting more than five hundred shotgun-style houses between 1880 and 1950, making the Meahers one of Africatown's largest landlords. The houses rented for $1 a week. Each had three rooms, with no running water or plumbing, but they did come with a water pump that pulled from the shallow aquifer running below Africatown.

Running water and electricity were common in Mobile by the late 1920s. But even through the 1950s, Africatown remained a place apart. The community sat outside the legal control and tax jurisdiction of both Mobile and Prichard, a larger community just north of Africatown. The two main roads that ran through Africatown, Bay Bridge Road and Telegraph Road, were paved. But in the sprawling residential neighborhoods surrounding it, the roads were dirt, and neither running water nor indoor plumbing would arrive until 1960. In some measure in the intervening years, Africatown as a community existed outside of the heavy weight of segregation oppressing African-Americans living in Mobile and other Alabama towns. People in their seventies and eighties today describe the Africatown of their childhood as a strangely idyllic world that, for a time, seemed far removed from the racial strife rending the south.

The blinking lights of a nightclub with a flashing sign advertising live entertainment signaled arrival in Africatown for travelers coming over the bridge. The Black-owned club was integrated, welcoming truckers and wayfarers both white and Black at night. The Williams Motel was next door, where it still stands today. After passing the modest cabins of the first settlers, which stood hard against the highway's right-of-way, visitors came upon the empire of Clifton Adams, whose parents were among the first wave of American-born Blacks to move to Africatown in the 1880s. Adams was one of Africatown's most successful early entrepreneurs. His rise mirrored that of many in the community. His first job was driving a logging truck delivering trees to the mill. In his spare time, he grew vegetables to sell at the market, as the original African settlers had done. That led to his grocery store, which funded the construction of a movie theater called the Show, and a restaurant, a barbershop, and cleaners. Adams also built more than forty shotgun houses available for rent. His family says he was friends with Augustine Meaher, Timothy Meaher's son, who gave Adams permission to use a sprawling property and house located on the Mobile River, where the Adams clan would picnic and hold family reunions.

Plentiful jobs with good pay meant Africatown's families were middle class, with time for leisure. Going fishing was as simple as walking a few minutes to Three Mile Creek, Hog Bayou, or the Mobile River. Redfish, speckled trout, mullet, flounder, bass, bream, and blue crabs could be caught year-round, from the bank or from a rowboat for rent at one of the fish camps just over the new bridge. Game was plentiful in the swamp surrounding Hog Bayou.

"That's where the residents went to hunt. It was just across the street. That's how Hog Bayou got its name. It was full of game. You could literally walk across the street, kill a hog, kill a deer. Drag it back home, cut it up, keep what you wanted, and give the rest away to your neighbors," said Joe Womack, who hunted the bayou with his grandfather and Henry Williams, both of whom grew up in Africatown while the Africans were still alive. "We used to do a lot of crabbing. We'd take a washtub, catch a mess of crabs, and take 'em home to Momma. She'd make crab gumbo. If we weren't playing sports, we'd be out there fishing and crabbing."

Sports, particularly baseball, took on an outsize importance in Africatown. In addition to the teams for the school, each neighborhood and sometimes each street fielded its own baseball team, complete with uniforms. By the 1950s, kids coming out of Africatown's baseball leagues were earning college scholarships, and often a chance to try out for the major leagues. In the 1960s, there were six men on Major League Baseball teams who grew up playing against each other on the Mobile County Technical School's baseball diamond, a stunning feat for the tiny community. Two of Africatown's sons, Cleon Jones and Tommie Agee, were stars on the World Series–winning New York Mets of 1969 known as the "Miracle Mets." Cleon made the game-winning catch that clinched the championship for New York. All of Africatown crowded around radios during the game and erupted in cheers when they heard their hometown hero had won the game.

Just beyond the outfield fence on the school baseball field sits the Africatown Community Garden, covering about eight acres. Decades ago, residents appealed to the Alabama Power utility company for permission to farm in the company's right-of-way, beneath a web of transmission lines carrying tens of thousands of volts of electricity to the industrial corridor along the river. The area has been farmed continuously by Africatown residents going back at least seventy years, and is still the largest community garden in Alabama. For most of that time, pollution from the paper mills fell right on the corn, snap peas, butter beans, squash, okra, tomatoes, sugarcane, and collards growing in the rich dirt. Most often, it came in the form of a light dusting of an ashy material that sometimes puffed out of the towering smokestacks at the paper mills, drifting to the ground like falling snow. The dust was caustic enough that residents had to wash their cars every day to keep the paint from peeling off.

"There was little white stuff, then there was brown stuff that looked like rodent droppings. It would just fall from the sky. My momma bought a blue Plymouth and it ended up being gray within a year and a half," said Garry Lumbers, a great-great-grandson of Cudjo Lewis, who grew up in Cudjo's house in the 1960s and '70s. "The employees made good money. That's how all these brick homes got put in the community. Most of the employees had new cars, and they worried over them. They used to line up to run them through the car wash every day when they got off the shift."

To stop complaints from the community, International Paper installed a free car wash on the edge of its property and allowed anyone to use it.

"The stuff on the cars, your car would be brown with the fallout. People would come from all over town for the free car wash. My daddy used to use the car wash extensively," said Darron Patterson. "It was right there on Papermill Road. Everybody was just worried about getting it off their cars, or getting the laundry in off the line before it got stained. Nobody thought about what the stuff might be doing to us."

Residents complained, but because they came from an African-American community in rigidly segregated Alabama, no one in a position of power listened to the complaints. The Meahers had long ago ensured that property they owned along the river was zoned industrial. After all, their original businesses included what was then one of the largest sawmills in the South and a shipyard, and their land had been used industrially for a century. Properties the family controlled are now covered in oil storage tank farms, paper mills, and various other heavy-polluting industries. At the time, the community didn't have any real legal standing as a municipality. It was unincorporated, and amounted to a sort of no-man's-land between the nearby cities of Prichard and Mobile. The control the Africans had exerted in the early days did not have the force of law; rather, the residents had simply agreed to abide by the rules the group set. The lack of formal recognition meant the community could not fight back when officials demanded their land for the bridge, or when the Meahers leased the parcels butting up to their properties to the paper company, even in the 1920s considered one of the most polluting industries on the planet. Once Africatown's business district was in full swing during the postwar boom of the 1950s, both Mobile and Prichard began to covet the tax revenue from the busy commercial district, and they moved to incorporate the area in 1960. Prichard offered to provide water and sewer service to Africatown, an attractive pitch in a community where people still drank from wells and used outhouses. But Mobile's offer proved more attractive still, as it included the water and sewer, but also a promise to pave the streets.

"I remember my grandfather telling everyone to vote for Mobile," Womack said. "When they ran plumbing, people had running water for the first time. My grandmother was so excited."

Agreeing to incorporation cut both ways. Residents got water and paved roads, but Mobile gained new control over zoning and thus what industries could be sited in the neighborhood. In 1965, the City of Mobile tore down more of the oldest neighborhoods in Africatown, more than one hundred homes, to build a public housing project on forty-two acres. They named it after Josephine Allen, who had started a school for African-Americans in Mobile, and was married to the son of Pollee Allen, one of Africatown's leaders. That housing project, like much of Africatown, is now abandoned.

Speak to people who grew up in Africatown during its heyday and you hear the same story: It was idyllic, but then something happened. Or rather a lot of things happened in quick succession.

By the 1980s, Africatown had begun a spiraling descent just as epic as its growth spurt. Many of the businesses were gone, because many people were gone. When Clifton Adams, the early entrepreneur, died in the 1970s, the family chose to shut down his movie theater, restaurant, and grocery empire because no one wanted to run it. It wasn't financially viable anymore. The end of segregation played a role. After 1965, people in Africatown could shop anywhere they wanted. Cars had become common in the community, and the larger markets and department stores of Mobile's downtown shopping district were just a three-minute ride away. Likewise, desegregation meant African-Americans were no longer confined to living near the few schools available to the Black population. People started moving out, to other parts of Mobile, or to several small African-American towns that surround Africatown, places where you couldn't smell the overpowering stench from the paper mills. Contributing to the problem was a sudden dearth of housing when the Meaher clan decided to get out of the house rental business in 1967, after building more than five hundred rental houses in Africatown since the 1880s. Residents say the family simply moved people out and bulldozed the houses, destroying much of the area's longtime housing stock.

The family began knocking down the shotgun houses that were the closest to the paper mills in the early 1930s, to make way as the mills underwent successive waves of expansion. But hundreds more houses owned by the Meaher family remained available for rent in Africatown until the arrival of the water and sewer service. Augustine Meaher, Jr., Timothy Meaher's grandson, revealed the family's priorities when he told a newspaper reporter in 1967 that he planned to knock down nearly all of the remaining shotgun houses because the utility upgrades made the houses more valuable, thus increasing the family's tax burden. He warned that most of the tenants couldn't afford to pay a water bill on top of their $4-a-month rent. "Besides," he said, "people have lived perfectly happy and healthy for years without running water and sewers." Of his African-American tenants, Meaher said, "He don't need garbage service. . . . He don't need a bathtub—he'll probably store food in it. Wouldn't know how to use it."

Sitting in his twenty-sixth-floor office in downtown Mobile, Meaher closed the interview on a magnanimous note. "We'll probably leave a few [houses] there for the old darkies that worked for us," he tells the reporter, adding that he has come to regret not charging these former employees rent. "The government has softened them up in their old age these days. With those old age pensions you can't get them to work as hard anymore."

It is unclear what the Meaher family income from rental property was in 1967 when Augustine said he had to bulldoze the houses to save on his Alabama property taxes, which are historically among the lowest in the nation. By all accounts, the family has been fabulously wealthy since Timothy Meaher's day. Timothy's son was was described as a multimillionaire in newspaper articles as early as 1905. The real estate assets controlled by his great-grandsons—Robert, Joseph, and Augustine Meaher—were valued at $35 million in court documents in 2012.

"People in houses next to giant plants and facilities are a problem because they complain and they watch what you are doing. When you drive around Africatown today and see all these big chunks of woods in the neighborhoods near the factories, that was all houses owned by the Meahers," said Womack, the former Marine turned community activist. "Everywhere you see a vacant lot, there used to be a house there. There wasn't a vacant lot in Africatown when I grew up. When the Meahers decided to get out of the rental business, they just bulldozed all those houses."

Destroying so many houses stands out among the heap of many injustices committed by the Meaher family, according to Africatown's old guard. The Meahers still own 260 acres of land in the heart of Africatown, nearly all of it vacant since the shotgun houses were destroyed fifty years ago.

"I ain't got no feelings about the Meahers. They all right with me far as the ship. The only thing I got against the Meahers, there wasn't nothing but houses down in there," said LeBaron Barnes, pointing toward a city block overgrown with an unruly forest of skinny trees and scrubby bushes just past his own house. Like his father before him, LeBaron plows the community garden as a service to his neighbors. Much of the land around the garden is still owned by the Meaher family, and once included dozens of houses. LeBaron's aunts, uncles, and cousins lived all around him, in houses that are long gone. "It wasn't nothing but houses all around there. That school, it was houses, all that way, there was houses. Where the factories are, that was all houses. Over there where those warehouses are, that was all houses. Those

The author holds the first piece of the *Clotilda* to see the light of day in 160 years, discovered on April 9, 2018, in the Mobile River.

The *Clotilda* was burned and scuttled in this remote stretch of swamp deep in the Mobile-Tensaw Delta after the 110 captives aboard were transferred to one of Timothy Meaher's steamboats.

This chimney, made of homemade bricks, is the last structure still standing that was built by Africatown's first settlers. Many of the original cabins built by the Africans were torn down by the city of Mobile in 1992 to build the highway.

4

buggy to take me to Mobile. there I got a Steam Tug to tow Schr up Spanish river into the Ala. river. at "Twelve Mile Island" I transferd my Slaves to a river Steamboat. and sent them up into the canebrake to hide them until further disposal. I then burned my Schr. to the waters edge and sunk her.

This page from Captain William Foster's handwritten account of the *Clotilda*'s voyage provided the clue that led the author to the wreck at Twelve Mile Island.

5

Forty thousand people live in Ganvie, a village five miles from shore in the middle of Lake Nokoué, where the houses are built on stilts. Their ancestors left shore in 1704 to escape capture by the Dahomeans.

King Sagbadjou Glele is the last living grandson of the man who captured and sold the *Clotilda* captives. He still holds court at the palace in Abomey used by his ancestors. Its walls were once festooned with the bones Cudjo recalled seeing as the slave coffle passed by on the way to the barracoon.

Seh-Dong-Hong-Beh was a leader of Dahomey's all-female Amazon warriors. Drawn by British navy officer Commander Frederick Forbes during a visit to Dahomey in 1851, she is depicted with various weapons and holding the still dripping head of a male victim.

Five empty chairs covered in packages and clothes pushed against the spiderweb-covered wall of Cudjo's one-room cabin highlight his loneliness. His wife and children had been dead for decades.

Steamboat captain Timothy Meaher was seventy-three when this photo was taken in 1886. He paid for the *Clotilda*'s voyage. Though the trip cost close to $1 million in today's currency, Meaher died extremely wealthy.

William Foster sailed the *Clotilda* to Africa and negotiated with the Dahomeans for the *Clotilda* captives. He died bitter that Timothy Meaher received credit for bringing in the last load of enslaved Africans to America, though Meaher remained safely behind in Alabama.

This is a detail from the wall surrounding one of dozens of slavery memorials in Ouidah, once one of the world's three largest slave ports.

Cudjo grew sugarcane in his garden so he'd have something sweet to give his twin great-granddaughters, Mary and Martha, who lived in a house on his property.

On their way to the barracoons, prisoners were made to walk around this tree in Ouidah three times. This ensured that after death, their spirits would return to the homeland they were being stolen from.

Benin is not hiding from its past. There are statues honoring the lost victims of enslavement located all over the country, particularly in Abomey and Ouidah.

The *Clotilda* captives walked down this road, the old slave route, from the palace in Abomey through sixty miles of jungle to Ouidah, on the coast.

A woman sells her wares from a boat, traveling through the labyrinth of canals in the floating city of Ganvie, home to 40,000 people living in houses on stilts. The village was settled in 1704, five miles from land, in an effort to escape the warriors of Dahomey.

A museum dedicated to the Dahomeans kings is now housed in King Glele's palace, seen here. The bas-relief designs inlaid in the pillars are made of mud from anthills mixed with palm oil and stained with plant and mineral pigments. Much of the Dahomeans art in the palace was stolen by France after it conquered Dahomey in 1892.

Lorna Woods points to the grave of her ancestor Charlie Lewis, who arrived on the *Clotilda* and served as Africatown's second leader. Woods has worked for decades trying to keep the *Clotilda* story alive.

Dada Daagbo Hounon Houna II Guely, the leader of Benin's native Vodun religion, performed a Vodun rite aboard the author's boat above the wreck of the *Clotilda*, asking those sold into slavery to forgive the people of Benin.

20

Darron Patterson and Garry Lumbers, descendants of Pollee and Cudjo Lewis, with Mike Foster, a descendant of Captain Foster, who bought the *Clotilda* captives in Ouidah, together on the author's boat at the spot where the *Clotilda* was burned. This was the first time descendants of both sides of the *Clotilda* story were together at Twelve Mile Island since the night the ship was burned.

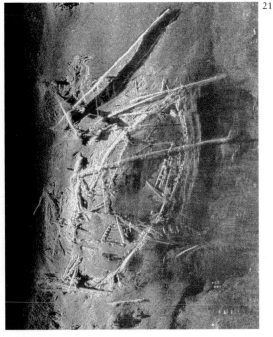

21

This sonar image was captured May 21, 2021, three years after the ship was found. Logs and other debris have collected on the ship, but the image makes clear the hull remains intact and has filled with mud. The heavy layer of mud has likely preserved items in the ship's hold, where the captives were held for nearly two months.

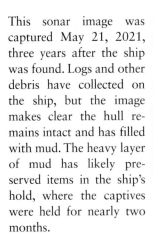

woods, that was all houses. It was so many people that are gone. We had everything then. We had movie theaters, stores, barbershops, service stations. We had everything around here. Now, we ain't got nothing. We don't even have a corner store. . . . People are saying they want to come back, but there's nothing to come back to. They tore down all the houses."

More and more, the children born in the sixties and seventies chose not to stay in Africatown. They had been well educated at the community school and left to find opportunities beyond the paper mills, chemical factories, shipyards, and state dock facilities that surround Africatown. When older Africatown residents died, their children and relatives living in other places often abandoned the homes left behind, letting weeds grow, roofs cave in, and taxes go unpaid. The economic downturn of the Reagan years hit Africatown hard. So did crack cocaine. The community's population dropped from about twelve thousand to two thousand.

"When the crack epidemic happened, it was bad here. I mean people that I knew, teachers at Mobile County Training School, and Whitley Elementary School, you'd see teachers on crack," said Lamar Howard, who runs a food truck and a T-shirt business. "We used to have swim instructors at the pool, you wouldn't see it at first, but then they started changing. The neighborhood, to be honest with you, the neighborhood wasn't bad. I mean they were selling crack, and it was bad that they were doing that, but it was like it gave an economic boost to the community when there wasn't much else. People had more money. They were able to live. . . . It was a way of survival for some people, because there were no jobs. The ones who smoked it, they're the ones who took the loss on it. And most of them were white folks driving into Africatown just to buy crack."

The decline accelerated in the nineties, especially with the creation of a new high-rise bridge, designed to be tall enough to allow oceangoing ships to pass beneath its span. The old two-lane Cochrane drawbridge built in 1927 was worn-out by 1990, and city and highway department officials wanted to replace it with a huge modern bridge that would take its two-lane capacity to four lanes, something Africatown residents had resisted for years due to traffic issues. The city promised to rebrand the bridge, and they built it over community objection. It was a disastrous decision.

The new bridge was part of a master plan to build a ring road around Mobile and facilitate the movement of 18-wheelers loaded with imported goods as they left the state docks. Three years after the bridge was finished, Interstate 165 was completed. The elevated highway is just two miles long, three lanes each way. For much of its length, it runs along the edge of Africatown—or rather *above* the edge of Africatown—and its construction meant the destruction of many more houses. The road connects the Alabama State Docks—one of the top ten busiest ports in the nation—with Interstate 65, which runs north toward Atlanta and Birmingham, and with the bridge and I-10, which runs west all the way to California. Bay Bridge Road, built in 1927 on land purchased from Cudjo and Gumpa and Pollee Allen, had been a two-lane affair. It ran in between the original churchyard and the founders' cemetery. Fifty-five years later, officials once again claimed huge swaths of the land originally purchased by Africatown's founders in the 1800s. The new version of Bay Bridge Road built in 1991 is a five-lane highway, heavily trafficked by 18-wheelers from the port and a lot of the traffic headed to and from Florida's beaches. In fact, any trucks hauling hazardous materials on Interstate 10, one of the nation's busiest roads, are required to leave the interstate as they approach Mobile and travel through the heart of Africatown instead in order to protect downtown Mobile from a possible chemical accident.

"There were lots of houses where they planned to put the new road, and those people did not want to leave those houses. They took them with eminent domain," Womack said. "The sad thing, those people whose houses they took, most of them were direct descendants. That's why they lived there by the church and the graveyard. They were on property that the original people bought, like Cudjo, Pollee Allen, Gumpa. We lost a lot of the original places they lived when they built the bridge."

Indeed, Cudjo's house, built in the 1860s by the *Clotilda*'s passengers, was among those torn down. Today, on a grassy lot about twenty feet back from the edge of the new highway stands the chimney from the house that belonged to Gumpa, who had been Cudjo's next-door neighbor. It is the last remnant of the original houses built in Africatown by the *Clotilda* captives. There are no signs to tell you what it is, or fences to protect it. The bricks are small and rough, probably homemade, most likely by Cudjo or his son, who had both learned how to make bricks. The chimney has a fireplace on each side, designed to heat both sides of a two-room cabin. It is so close to the road that if it were to topple over, some of the bricks might land in the very highway that permanently split the community in half and buried the founders' properties under miles of asphalt.

For years, the community couldn't even get a traffic light installed on the highway so they could get from the church to the cemetery on the other side for funerals. The highway made

Africatown a broken community, separating its three main neighborhoods from each other for the first time since the town was founded.

"The neighborhoods have become totally separate places now. Nobody is going to allow children to walk to school across a five-lane highway. That cut off all socialization between the neighborhoods," said Tori Adams, a local judge whose family has a long history in Africatown. "There were families where the kids could no longer get to their grandmother's house even though they could see it across the highway."

Jason Lewis, now a master chief in the U.S. Navy, was a child growing up in the Josephine Allen housing project in Africatown's old Happy Hill neighborhood in the eighties and nineties, when crack and then the new high-rise bridge came in. For two years, he's been leading a team of dozens of navy sailors, from Naval Air Station Pensacola an hour away in Florida, who volunteer weekends to help clean up Africatown. Many of his friends from the housing project are dead, shot while still in their teens. The life he describes was bleak, both in the project and in the rest of the community. The desolation seen today— the vacant lots, crumbling houses, abandoned cars, and empty storefronts—is how Africatown has looked his entire life. There were no stores his mother could walk to for groceries, no gas stations or convenience stores where kids could buy a candy bar or a Coke. His grandmother was one of two "candy ladies" in town, who sold cans of soda, potato chips, and candy bars out of their homes. Africatown had become so violent and poor that it was abandoned by everyone. Not even inner city stalwarts like Circle K or 7-Eleven dared to set up shop.

The most insidious of the destructive forces behind Africatown's demise involves the paper mills, which were at the heart of a billion-dollar lawsuit filed by residents. After seventy years as the main employers of Africatown's residents, both mills shut down in 2000. Suddenly, nearly two thousand jobs disappeared, along with the perpetual and noxious stench associated with paper making. But the job losses were just a scratch on the surface compared to the real, almost invisible damage the mills had inflicted.

To fully understand the story, we must step back in time to the 1980s, to a time when environmental laws in Alabama were essentially meaningless. Today, Alabama ranks last in the nation for what it spends to protect the environment, and is widely regarded by industry trade groups as the most permissive state in the country when it comes to setting or enforcing pollution limits. Back in the eighties and nineties, things were much worse. James Warr, who was the head of the Alabama Department of Environmental Management from its inception in the 1980s until the early 2000s, was opposed to vigorous application of environmental regulations for businesses. He was an odd fit for the head of an environmental agency tasked with regulating polluters, but I believe that is precisely why he was chosen—to ensure that the Clean Air Act and Clean Water Act didn't slow industrial production in Alabama. I was an environment reporter for the Mobile newspaper for eighteen years, beginning in 2000, and had numerous interactions with Warr and his agency. During an interview in 2003, Warr told me that the federal Superfund law was illegal and he had no intention of enforcing it or adding new sites in Alabama to the list. At the time, I was writing about McIntosh, Alabama, an African-American community north of Africatown where I'd discovered that the dirt roads had been paved with mercury waste, which had been given to the town as a "gift" by a chlorine plant located there. The EPA-led Superfund cleanup of the factory had only included the area inside the chemical plant's fence. Federal inspectors never even tested the houses for mercury exposure, or the people whose yards butted up to the fence. More importantly, regulators missed the strange salty covering on the town's main roads, as well as in the schoolyard playground and along the edges of the high school baseball field, which turned out to be intensely high in mercury. The only comparison I could find for similarly contaminated land was in California's gold mining country. Residents wanted the company to clean it all up. Warr resisted and refused to order any action. His complaint: It was unfair to punish companies and make them pay to clean up pollution they caused in the past if no one had warned them at the time that what they were doing was illegal or dangerous.

This is the regulatory attitude that prevailed for decades. During that time, from 1929 to 2000, the Africatown factories, one owned by International Paper and one by Scott Paper and then Kimberly-Clark, were among the most productive paper mills on Earth, producing paper and pollution for all those years. Imagine living in a community where people tried to wash their cars every day so the ash falling from the sky wouldn't eat the paint off so quickly. The ash didn't fall all the time. But when it did, it was dramatic.

"I can remember growing up, ash falling from the sky like snow in July. You'd be eating a sandwich at school and you'd have to brush that ash off the sandwich while you were eating it," said Joe Womack, the ex-Marine major, speaking at a U.S. Human Rights Network hearing in 2014 about environmental injustice in Africatown. Womack started a nonprofit called C.H.E.S.S.—which stands for Clean, Healthy, Educated, Safe, and Sustainable Community—to combat the presence of industry in Africatown. "If you were out playing ball and the ash started to fall, you knew you'd have to run home and help your mother take the clothes off the line because she'd have to wash them again and she washed them by hand. Nobody had to tell you. You knew to run and help her take those clothes off the line because it happened all the time. There was a lot of pollution. Ten years ago, we had to bury my younger sister at forty. She had lung disease from the chlorine."

There are few exposure scenarios in the United States that put people closer to the smokestacks than the situation in Africatown. For decades, homes were butted up to the fences around the factories, though most of the closest houses had been torn down by the Meaher family by the time the factories finally closed.

"Was it a terrible odor? Shoot yeah! Terrible odor. You couldn't get away from it. Most people didn't have any air-conditioning, so there was no getting away from it. It was an awful odor. You could smell it in downtown Mobile, but not like in Africatown," remembered Womack. "IP sitting right across the street from people's houses. Had those two giant smokestacks blowing soot, ash, and everything else. They utilized dioxin in those big tanks to make that paper. That causes cancer."

EPA began issuing its annual Toxic Release Inventory—or TRI—Report in 1988. The reports show intense amounts of pollution released in Africatown coming from the two paper mills. At the time, Mobile County, which includes Africatown, ranked in the top five counties nationally for the amount of pollution released into the air annually. There are several chemical factories located a dozen or more miles up the Mobile River from Africatown, and another group a dozen miles to the south on Mobile Bay. These are responsible for a portion of the annual emissions that led to Mobile's top five ranking. But an analysis of emissions coming only from the Africatown zip code in 1988 is stunning.

One hundred percent of the nearly 1 million pounds of chloroform released in Mobile County in 1988 was released in Africatown. Chloroform is classified as a probable carcinogen by the EPA. Chronic long-term exposure, such as one would experience living in the shadow of two paper mills, can cause liver disease and affect the central nervous system. One hundred percent of the chlorine dioxide in the county was released in Africatown. Nearly all of the 1.8 million pounds of hydrochloric acid released in the county in 1988 was released in Africatown. Nearly all of the acetone, methanol, xylene, chlorine, methyl ethyl ketone, and toluene released in the county were released in Africatown. The chemicals are linked to cancer, birth defects, fertility problems, kidney and liver damage, nose and throat irritation, asthma, and loss of hearing and color vision.

"As time went on, the Alabama pollution control laws got stricter and the paper companies decided they weren't going to spend the money to install the new pollution control equipment and they moved out," Womack said. "But they were in the area for about seventy years, polluting the air, polluting the area, polluting everything, including the people in the community."

Pastor Christopher Williams, Sr., leads the Yorktown Missionary Baptist Church, one of Africatown's three main houses of worship. He became pastor in 2006, after he retired as an

Alabama state trooper. Williams said he conducted fifty funerals in his first two years as pastor, out of a congregation of about one hundred people. The pastor at nearby First Hopewell Baptist, also in Africatown, conducted a similar number. Williams estimates that 75 percent of the people he buried died of unusual types of cancer, not often seen except in cases of industrial exposure. He reached out to county and state officials and asked them to investigate the area for a possible cancer cluster. Without investigating, officials denied the area had a cluster, and they wouldn't even come to town for a meeting with residents.

"If you're doing funerals every weekend, that's a cluster. If people are dying of cancers that are caused by chemicals, that's a cluster. There's no question," Williams said. "The biggest problem as to why it's not considered a cluster is that the people are black in that community and they are not rich."

Eventually, Pastor Williams found his way to Dr. Raoul Richardson and Dr. Mohammed Baheth, with Baheth Laboratories, an environmental testing laboratory affiliated with the University of South Alabama. Williams asked them to help identify what was killing his congregation. The duo started attending community meetings in Africatown.

"The more people we met, the more people we saw die. We were actually having multiple people we had just talked to die of cancer in between meetings," Richardson said. "We'd talk to someone and two weeks later, they'd be dead. We knew they couldn't afford to pay us. But we couldn't just sit around and watch them die, so Doc and I told them we'd do it."

The scientists agreed to start collecting samples in 2014. Baheth has played baroque trumpet and piano with symphonies around the world, and holds twenty-one patents for everything from a new treatment for prostate cancer (which he used to cure himself as the first test patient) to a share of credit as part of the team that created the original formula for unleaded gasoline. In collecting samples around the fences surrounding the paper mills, he wore a white lab coat. His activities did not go unnoticed.

"I'll be honest with you. I just got pissed off," Baheth said, explaining the decision to identify himself so prominently as a scientist. This being Alabama, Baheth said the companies responded by having an official from the state environmental agency visit his lab. The regulator inquired about Baheth's work in Africatown, and according to Baheth threatened to revoke various certifications required to operate the lab. Dr. Baheth, who is also a former sheriff's deputy, didn't take it well.

"I told him to go home, have a Coke and a smile, and then shut the fuck up. I'm not going to take that kind of treatment, threatening me when they are letting people die." Soon after, Baheth said a lawyer offered him $1 million to abandon the Africatown study. A month after he declined, Baheth was in a traffic accident that left him badly injured. He said officials determined his brake lines had been cut.

Baheth and Richardson collected six years' worth of sampling from Africatown, and their research was at the heart of a billion-dollar lawsuit filed by residents of Africatown charging International Paper and Kimberly-Clark with contaminating the water and soil with chemicals that may have killed hundreds, possibly thousands, and could continue to do so until they are cleaned up. Baheth's samples revealed high concentrations of dioxins and furans, the same compounds that hurt so many Vietnam War soldiers exposed to Agent Orange.

"The soil samples show it is everywhere in the community. How could it not be after a seventy-year exposure of that magnitude?" Baheth asked.

Baheth and Richardson were both stunned when they discovered that lawyers representing the one thousand plaintiffs in the class had circulated a letter stating, "The soil testing that we performed showed that the dioxin and furan pollution was merely at background levels." Richardson said his sampling data showed contaminant levels in soil ten times above expected background levels. But it was too late. Ninety-five percent of the plaintiffs agreed to settle based on the letter from the lawyers. In the face of a $1.8 billion claim, some Africatown residents received awards as high as $8,000, with some receiving as little as $200 from the suit. And for that, they had to give up the right to ever bring a case again.

"I don't know what the lawyers are talking about when they say we only found background levels. Our data are way above the World Health Organization background. They quit returning my calls right around the time they sent the settlement letter out, but we never heard a word about it until it was too late," Richardson said.

The pollution remains in Africatown, Richardson said, and will never go away unless it is cleaned up.

"It is fine for the lawyers. They are not the ones eating out of those gardens in Africatown. They are not the ones eating fish out of those creeks in Africatown," Richardson said. "The people in Africatown who continue to be exposed to dioxins and furans at these levels, they are going to continue to die of cancer, whether the case is settled or not."

The mills are not the end of the pollution story in Africatown.

The area immediately around the community was historically home to numerous chemical plants, paint factories, and heavy polluters such as electroplating shops, most long since closed. All of those industries leave contaminants behind, though none of the individual factory sites may approach the intensity of what lies in the old Hickory Street Landfill, which sits a few hundred yards from Africatown's Lewis Quarters neighborhood.

I stumbled onto the landfill, which has been closed since 1970, by accident. Paddling around in a kayak one day in 2007, I found myself at a bend way up Three Mile Creek, just down the hill from the cemetery and Cudjo's old homestead. The creek is where Cudjo's son Pollee told his parents he was going fishing the last time he was ever seen. As I paddled under the Telegraph Road bridge, a group of older African-American women were fishing with cane poles and worms next to the sawmill and lumberyard that surround Lewis Quarters. I pushed a little farther into a tributary, One Mile Creek, and found myself surrounded by a stunning amount of trash. Styrofoam cups, plastic bottles, basketballs, shopping carts. I got out of the boat to take a picture of all the garbage along the bank and stepped into a weirdly iridescent liquid oozing out of a rusty barrel at the water's edge. Then I noticed heaps of really old tires coming out of the mud, and more barrels. I climbed up a hill about thirty feet high that began at the water's edge and found a broken test well with the state environmental agency's logo on it. These are commonly placed around Superfund sites to monitor whether contaminated groundwater is flowing away into the environment. Unwittingly, I had happened onto the old landfill, which sits right on the edge of Africatown, well away from the elite society in downtown Mobile. Though I'd never heard mention of it, the site had been considered a candidate for Superfund cleanup since the Superfund laws were passed in 1980, but it never happened. Just walking around the property, I could tell they'd put a protective cap of red clay over the landfill at some point and it was failing. I started working on a story for the newspaper right away.

It turns out the cap was put on in the 1980s. The state environmental agency noticed it was washing away and compromised during an inspection in 2005, but never did anything about it. Clay caps have a habit of failing in south Alabama due to heavy rainfall. (Mobile is America's rainiest city, with an average of seventy inches annually, compared to about fifty-five in Seattle.) A 2006 report prepared by the Alabama Department of Public Health and the federal Agency for Toxic Substances and Disease Registry (ATSDR) offers insight into what was in the landfill. "Prior to 1970, the landfill accepted any kinds of wastes without restriction. Some of the products were electroplating sludges, solvents, organic and inorganic chemicals, heavy metals, cyanide and reactive sulfide wastes," the report reads. The phrase "reactive sulfide wastes" screams paper mill to environmental toxicologists, and refers to sulfur compounds that generate toxic gases and acids when exposed to water. Under modern environmental law, all of the compounds listed in the report must be disposed of in a specially designed hazardous waste landfill. Such landfills include an impervious liner to contain the contaminants. (Unsurprisingly, the largest hazardous waste landfill in the United States is in a small Alabama village called Emelle. The population is 90 percent African-American. The landfill was sited there by a group of white county supervisors over the objections of the people of Emelle.) The report says: "Former employees of the dumpsite stated that it was not uncommon to see numerous drums with a poison symbol on them. . . . It has been reported that heavy equipment operators would crush the 55 gallon drums containing ignitable liquids, and they would explode. A fatality was reported when an equipment operator crushed a drum and it exploded, burning the bulldozer and the operator." The report goes on to note that "there has never been a documented removal action or cleanup of the materials placed in the landfill."

At one point in the early 2000s, the city of Mobile tried to turn the fifty-seven-acre dump into a public park, but had to abandon the idea when testing revealed extremely high levels of heavy metals and other pollutants in both the groundwater and the protective cap at the site. That is a worrying finding. It means the pollutants are moving into the creek both from the soil as they escape through the cap and from the numerous springs weeping out of the creek bank.

The way the Superfund list works, a site is put through an EPA process called the Hazard Ranking System. In 2002, I completed the online training course that teaches regulators to use the Hazard Ranking System and its associated computer program called PreScore. Using data from various environmental tests that had been performed up to that time, I calculated that the Hickory Street site would earn a score of about 42. Anything above a 28 qualifies a site for the first stage of a Superfund cleanup. The primary thing the system is designed to do is determine if there is a pathway for human exposure to pollution. I'd paddled right by an obvious human pathway on my way up the creek, the old women fishing with cane poles. I used to see them there all the time as I drove over the Telegraph Road bridge.

If anyone was going to be exposed to the mercury, chlordane, hexavalent chromium 6, and all the other chemicals known to be in the dump, it was them, or the kids I sometimes saw swimming by the bridge. I warned the women that I didn't think they should fish there anymore. They laughed and said they'd fished there all their lives and weren't going to quit now. I wrote several articles, but nothing ever happened. The state promised to test fish from the creek but never did. The city made noise about starting a new monitoring program, but never did. I see people fishing at the bridge to this day.

I recently told Mobile municipal judge Karlos Finley and his double first cousin Eric Finley about stumbling onto Hickory Street Landfill. They told me a most unusual story that illuminates the kind of contamination Africatown's residents have been exposed to for seventy years. The cousins opened the first tour business that carries people around Africatown and other sites of note in Mobile's African-American history. Their family has a long history of promoting and protecting Africatown. The city of Mobile's African-American Heritage Trail is named in honor of their aunt Dora Finley, and their grandfather was the doctor who taught Africatown's midwives how to deliver babies. When they were growing up, their grandparents lived next to the Hickory Street Landfill when it was going full swing. Their memories provide a bizarre peak into the 1950s and '60s on the edge of Africatown.

"When the dump was active, you could go and just drop off anything. There were no rules or fancy environmental terms like 'landfill' or anything like that. Kids played there," Eric Finley remembered. "My cousins, other kids from Africatown. They probably still do today. There's not a fence or anything along the creek to keep them out. Who knows what they were exposed to playing in there."

But far from addressing this sort of pollution legacy, the state is instead authorizing new polluting industries to be placed on top of the old industrial sites. Joe Womack has become the point man for a movement to protect Africatown from exactly this. He is warm and genial, but when riled, the former Marine major comes out. The group had a recent victory, when they blocked the creation of a new oil storage tank farm on part of the old International Paper campus. The tanks were to store oil-rich tar sands, which were to arrive by train car straight from Canada.

Womack started his fight long before there was any hope of finding the *Clotilda* and attracting positive attention to his hometown. One of the galvanizing events for him was the day in 2013 when a pipeline company showed up at the Mobile County Technical School, tore down the fence around the baseball field where Cleon Jones and the other major leaguers learned to play, and began laying a pipeline designed to shuttle the Canadian tar sands from a railyard at the state docks on the edge of Africatown to a refinery in Pascagoula, Mississippi. Womack went to the Mobile County school superintendent to ask how the school system could allow a pipeline to be run right through the historic campus and beneath the ball field and playground. The school property, originally purchased from Timothy Meaher, had been donated by the families of Africatown's founders in order to coax Mobile into providing teachers for their children. Womack was told there was no way to stop it as the pipeline company was allowed to use an old easement on the school property that dated to the 1950s. The company has the right to renew the easement indefinitely for about $9 a year.

Riding around Africatown with Womack, he takes notes when he sees a rezoning sign in a yard. Every time he passes a vacant lot, he says, "we need to put a house there." When he sees an unoccupied house that needs a little work, and the lawn mowed, he says, "we could move a young family in there." Africatown, he says, is ready to be restored to its former glory. All it will take, he says, is for the city of Mobile to quit thinking of Africatown as a dumping ground for industry.

"The city has conspired with business to site things in Africatown. There is no doubt. If you look at the map, there is no place in Mobile to put heavy industry and dirty industry. So they try to move it here," Womack said. "That's what this lawsuit is about. Making right what they've done to Africatown all these years."

Chapter 10

FINDING *CLOTILDA*

fter concealing the slaves on the various plantations
and successfully conspiring with Judge Jones to avoid
prosecution for his crime, Timothy Meaher spent the
next thirty years enjoying the fame his association with the *Clotilda* had brought. He was frequently interviewed by newspapers and magazines from around the country, which treated the
Clotilda story as a swashbuckling adventure. He had become
enough of a celebrity in his lifetime that the *New York Times*
published an obituary upon his death, declaring him "the importer of the last cargo of slaves brought to the United States."
But even after the Civil War, Meaher worried that federal officials, or the former slaves, would try to press charges against
him for illegal slaving or kidnapping, respectively, if they were to
locate the wreck. The fact that federal officials had been unable
to find the ship when Meaher was arrested days after the *Clo-*

tilda arrived had been critical to his escape from prosecution. He was especially worried after his incarceration and prosecution for blockade running made him well known to federal officials in the postwar years.

I believe Meaher intentionally used his numerous media interviews to throw people off the trail of the wreck. In 1890, during one of his last interviews, Meaher revealed that he retired as a steamboat captain when he was legally compelled to allow African-Americans to rent cabins on board, rather than force them to ride below with livestock and other cargo. He also gave an account of the *Clotilda*'s last voyage in the interview, and said the ship was sunk in a place called Bayou Connor. Other sources quoting Meaher—including numerous historical documents and the half dozen books about the *Clotilda* and Africatown written between the late 1800s and today—variously place the wreck in Bayou Connor, Bayou Corne, Bayou Canot, the Mobile River, and the Spanish River. These places all exist, but they are not where I found the ship. By suggesting the wreck was in Bayou Connor or these other locations, Meaher sent searchers miles north of where the ship had actually been burned and scuttled.

The ruse worked. For 160 years, the fate of the *Clotilda* remained a mystery. The first efforts to find it began almost as soon as the ship was destroyed. Officers of the U.S. District Court in Mobile spent five months searching unsuccessfully for the ship and the Africans in 1860. During the next sixty years, people came to routinely—and incorrectly—identify several wrecks in local waters as *Clotilda*, often pointing to various design features supposedly shared with the ship. Some of the mistaken identifications happened simply because several old shipwrecks around Mobile Bay were quite prominent into the early part of the twentieth century, with parts of the ships visible above the water's surface even from a great distance. Compounding matters was Mobile's four-hundred-year history as a seaport. More than 280 shipwrecks have been located in Mobile Bay and the swamp immediately to the north. Most remain unidentified. Some of them are ships that sank as early as the 1600s. Others are ships or barges that were intentionally sunk after they'd become too worn-out to sail. Wooden ships like the *Clotilda* had a fairly short working life of about twenty-five years. Built before the revolution in construction techniques brought on by the mass production of screws, nuts, and bolts in the 1870s and '80s, the wooden sailing vessels of the *Clotilda* era were held together with nothing but giant nails. Decades at sea, with the constant stress of rising and falling waves, gradually loosened them, making the ships leakier and leakier, until eventually they were no longer seaworthy. As a result, several bayous around Mobile Bay are well-known "ship graveyards" where old vessels were beached or sunk to get them out of the way of the shipping channels and rivers. Based on precise descriptions of the *Clotilda*'s design filed in the federal archives in Atlanta after the ship was built and registered, we know none of the wrecks "positively" identified by the experts of the day in ship graveyards and other places could have been *Clotilda*. That did not stop sightseers from paying a few dollars to hire boats to take them to the supposed scene of the crime to see one of the imposter ships. Even the city of Mobile got into the act in the 1950s, removing pieces from one of these incorrectly identified ships and putting them on display as relics from the *Clotilda*.

There were numerous efforts to locate the *Clotilda* in the

1980s and '90s, some by amateur sleuths and some by people and companies specializing in finding sunken ships. Often, companies hired to map obstructions in the main river channels under federal or state contracts would keep an eye out for nineteenth-century sailing vessels, in the hope of stumbling upon the infamous ship. After novelist Clive Cussler made international news with his successful 1995 effort to locate the wreck of the Civil War–era *Hunley*—the first submarine to sink an enemy ship in combat—he said that his next search would be for the *Clotilda*. Coincidentally, both the *Hunley* and the *Clotilda* were built in Mobile. Oddly, the Alabama Historical Commission refused to allow Cussler permission to search for the ship, despite the fact that his team had located dozens of historic wrecks. Cussler's rejection was due to another *Clotilda* search then underway. That effort was led by Jack Friend, a noted historian and eccentric from Mobile who authored the definitive history of the Battle of Mobile Bay, where Admiral Farragut is said to have yelled, "Damn the torpedoes! Full speed ahead." Friend had allies on the state historical commission who rejected Cussler's permit application in order to give native son Friend a chance to find the ship. Despite countless hours of research and thousands of dollars spent hiring a maritime survey company in the early 2000s to explore a portion of the vast Mobile-Tensaw Delta, Friend came up empty. Given the hundreds of unidentified shipwrecks around Mobile, and the fact that the delta encompasses hundreds of thousands of acres, this was not surprising.

The delta is a gigantic swamp, about thirteen miles wide and fifty miles long. It is one of the largest continuous wetland complexes in the United States. Dozens of rivers and creeks twist and snake through its ghostly stands of Spanish moss–draped cypress and broad meadows of cattails and marsh grasses. There are a lot of places to hide something as big as a ship in the delta, precisely why Meaher and his conspirators chose the seclusion of the swamp for the end of their journey. I have made a career out of studying and exploring the delta, with more than twenty years spent traveling the nooks and crannies of the vast wilderness. I produced a documentary and a book, *Saving America's Amazon*, about the system, along with hundreds of newspaper articles. I also earn part of my living running nature tours in the delta, taking people deep into its remote interior aboard my boat. Over the years, I've encountered a number of shipwrecks, usually nothing more than the ribs and keel still visible, but I'd never considered looking for the *Clotida*. In part, that is because I wasn't familiar with Africatown's origin story as the place where the last slaves brought to America settled after slavery, and didn't understand that the ship that brought them here was missing.

That changed when my friend Jeff Dute, a manager at the Bass Pro Shops sporting goods store near my house, called and suggested I look for the ship in 2017. Jeff gave me an abbreviated version of the story, and said he'd just heard John Sledge, a city of Mobile historian, on the radio saying the fate of the ship was one of the nation's great unsolved mysteries. Hunting for the wreck of a schooner sunk before the Civil War sounded so outlandish, like looking for pirate treasure, and I told Jeff so. But, after we hung up, I typed "Clotilda" into Google and started to imagine the places in the delta one might hide something as large as a schooner. If the ship was truly hidden somewhere in the swamp, I figured I had a better chance than most people of finding it.

My initial research, digging into Sylviane Diouf's book and then a trove of historical documents at the Mobile library, showed that the lives of the captives who arrived aboard the *Clotilda* had been well-documented. Yet the mystery of the ship's fate lingered. During the thirty years he lived after the *Clotilda*'s arrival, Meaher had left his trail of misleading bread crumbs for would-be ship hunters. But as I read over them, many of his claims fell apart just based on my knowledge of the swamp. The *Clotilda* was twenty-six feet wide, and needed four feet of water to float. Both measurements meant the ship was simply too big to traverse much of the giant swamp's interior, including some of the places Meaher mentioned specifically by name. But to visiting journalists, the bayou names Meaher spouted off were as exotic as the wilds of Dahomey. Only a small handful of people in Meaher's day, or indeed even today despite the presence of Google Earth and GPS, would know where some of these locations are. Additionally, then as now, the delta's many sloughs and channels have multiple names, depending on which of the several towns around its edges you come from.

One of the most persistent *Clotilda* hunters was the Mobile-based historian Jack Friend. He spent his time and money chasing down the story Meaher told in one of his last major interviews, in 1890, which had been treated as the definitive account of the *Clotilda*'s fate by nearly everyone who wrote about the ship. Upon Friend's death in 2010, his papers were donated to the history museum in Mobile. I spent an afternoon in late 2017 going over Friend's *Clotilda* research with John Sledge, a city historian and writer who wrote *The Mobile River*, an authoritative history of the city's seaport. He shared Friend's interest in the *Clotilda*, and the two had been close friends. Buried in one of the boxes of Friend's papers was a formal report compiled by the survey company he hired for his *Clotilda* search.

The survey started at the mouth of Bayou Canot and headed north, encompassing the places once known as Bayou Corne and Bayou Connor. The crew used side-scan sonar, a magnetometer, and a sub-bottom profiler. Together, the three techniques paint a picture of the riverbed and any objects sitting on it, detect any metal items, such as anchors or ship fittings like nails, and probe a dozen feet below the muddy bottom looking for things that might be buried under river sediment. Friend's search turned up nothing in any of the locations suggested in the books and documents.

My own research had already suggested a different location, farther south, next to Twelve Mile Island in the Mobile River, a few miles north of both Timothy Meaher's plantation and shipyard. Going over the primary historical sources, a significant discrepancy caught my eye. In his interviews, Meaher had claimed the slaves were off-loaded from the *Clotilda* to his steamboat in the Spanish River, and then the *Clotilda* was towed to Bayou Connor or another spot and scuttled. This sequence of events had been repeated in numerous articles, and in several books about the *Clotilda* in the last hundred years. It had been repeated so often, it had come to be accepted as fact by generations of historians.

But as someone who frequents these locations regularly, I knew that the Spanish River and Bayou Connor are miles apart, with lots of lonesome and secluded swamp in between. Why would you unload the slaves in one spot, then spend another hour towing the slave ship north before burning it? It just didn't make sense. Multiple witnesses—including Captain Foster, the

Meaher brothers, and their trusted slave James Dennison—
all agreed that the *Clotilda* had been towed into the swamp
through the Spanish River in order to bypass the port of Mobile,
which sits on the Mobile River. But the Spanish River is particularly narrow, with bars so shallow they can ground even a
rowboat, never mind a steamboat or oceangoing sailing vessel.
An old riverboat captain like Meaher could have accomplished
the treacherous trip towing the *Clotilda* through the Spanish in
the dark, but I can't imagine that there would have been room
enough anywhere in the river for the *Clotilda* and a steamboat
large enough to carry 110 slaves to pull up alongside each other
for the transfer of the captives. The river is only two miles long,
and the channel as it runs today is not big enough for such a
transfer between boats that would have been more than sixty
feet wide if lashed together side by side. Plus, the Spanish River
runs into the Mobile River within sight of the downtown port,
which our band of criminals was trying to avoid at all costs. It
seemed the last place one would pick to make a discreet transfer
of more than one hundred chained captives. Better to keep heading north, toward the plantation where the slaves were to be
stashed, and make the transfer in a more secluded spot.

   After we examined Friend's papers, I told Sledge my theory
that the ship was along the back side of Twelve Mile Island.
What's more, I told him I thought Friend and the authors and
researchers who had repeated Meaher's description of where the
ship was burned had been duped.

   My theory was based partly on something I had noted in
a journal account by Captain William Foster, who actually
sailed the *Clotilda* to Africa. The account had been available
to Friend and the historians who wrote about the ship, but for

some reason, all of them seemed to discount its description of where the *Clotilda* was destroyed in favor of Meaher's seemingly more detailed version in the 1890 interview. I learned of the existence of the captain's journal from a member of the Meaher family, who has chosen to keep his identity secret. He told me that he first saw the journal when a local dance teacher who was a descendant of Foster's offered to sell him the captain's possessions from the ship, including the desk, chair, and clock from his cabin. Meaher declined to buy the items, then was offered two journals handwritten by Captain Foster. One, Meaher said, was so faded as to be almost illegible. I believe this was the ship's log Foster kept on board during the actual voyage. The other was the handwritten and slightly embellished version of the ship's log that Foster wrote years later.

The member of the Meaher family who told me about the journal got the dance teacher to agree to donate the later version of the journal to the Mobile Library, though not the furniture and clock. (I have since confirmed that Foster's descendants still have other *Clotilda*-related items, including the original journal Foster kept during the voyage. I have appealed to them to donate any artifacts they have for the new Africatown museum, or to the Smithsonian, but the relatives have cut off all contact since I made the suggestion. Perhaps they will read these words and be inspired.) Foster wrote his account in 1890, thirty years after he sailed *Clotilda* to Africa, and it is clear it was an attempt to claim some of the fame Meaher had been enjoying. It is titled "The Last Slaver" and mentions Timothy Meaher only once, with Foster describing the captives Meaher paid for as "my slaves." It clearly burned Foster to see Meaher celebrated as having brought the last cargo of slaves to the country when the steamboat captain had actually remained safely behind in Mobile, while Foster faced four mutinies among his crew, a hurricane, and several narrow escapes from the anti-slaving fleet during the voyage.

The twelve-page journal contains a tantalizing tidbit regarding the destruction of the ship. Foster recorded the scene this way: "At Twelve Mile Island I transferred my slaves to a river steamboat and sent them up into the canebrake to hide them until further disposal. I then burned my schooner to the water's edge and sunk her."

Now, this made sense! Twelve Mile Island would be a perfect place to both burn a ship and swap illegally imported slaves from one vessel to another. Much more remote and discreet than the Spanish River. The northern tip of Twelve Mile Island is twelve miles from the port of Mobile (hence the name), meaning it is about seven miles farther from downtown Mobile than the Spanish. Plus, the water around Twelve Mile Island is plenty wide for two ships to tie up side by side. While the west side of Twelve Mile Island was and still is the main river channel, the east side of the island is desolate and never visited by commercial traffic. What's more, Cudjo told Zora Neale Hurston the ship was burned at Twelve Mile Island. Now, when the actual burning happened, Cudjo would have had no idea where he was, and would never have heard of Twelve Mile Island. But when he was enslaved, he spent the next five years working on Meaher's steamboats. At 87, during his interviews with Hurston, he was able to call out the names of 21 river landings along the Mobile River—where Twelve Mile Island is located—in perfect order. It seems certain he would have learned the location where the ship was set on fire during that time along with the name of the island. Especially because fellow captives like James Dennison participated in the towing and destruction of the *Clotilda*. Furthermore, a newspaper article from 1917 relied on a "Kogo Lewis" as its primary source. It is almost certainly Cudjo who tells the reporter that the *Clotilda* "was afterwards towed up to Twelve Mile Island and burned to the waterline." As I dug in on my research, I discovered that the Meahers had owned the land around the east side of the island since the 1850s. What better place to transfer a cargo of illegal slaves and burn and sink a ship than alongside a chunk of remote swampland you own?

I had a location. All that remained was to find a ship. For that, I planned to make use of the lowest tides of the year, which typically occur in January. On the second day of 2018, I headed up the river toward Twelve Mile Island. I actually launched my boat at Meaher State Park, which is named for one of the brothers, who drove one of the steamboats as they moved the Africans and the ship into the Delta. Thanks to the "bomb cyclone of 2018" then ravaging the northeast, a stout north wind had blown much of the water out of Mobile Bay. Tides in the delta were about three feet lower than normal. After a twenty-minute run in thirty-degree weather, I was at Twelve Mile. Almost immediately, I found the bones of a ship. At normal water level, the vessel would have been completely underwater, but on this day, it was largely uncovered. I took aerial photos with my drone, and closeups of the construction techniques and types of wood. I later took Winthrop Turner, a shipwright expert in nineteenth-century ship construction, to the site. He identified the vessel as a schooner built between 1840 and 1875. That fit, as *Clotilda* was christened in 1856. His descriptions and my photos were enough to intrigue a pair of marine archaeologists in nearby

Pensacola. The University of West Florida's John Bratten and Greg Cook were part of a team that discovered and explored a dozen Spanish galleons from the 1500s sunk in Pensacola Bay. They knew their stuff.

Within a few days, they were on my boat headed to the ship. Their team made careful measurements, took lots of photos, and concluded that we had a ship that was definitely built in the 1850s or 1860s, and appeared to be precisely the same width as *Clotilda*. We were unable get a reliable length for the wreck, as it disappeared into the mud, but the team estimated it was somewhere in the neighborhood of one hundred feet. That was pretty close to the *Clotilda*'s known length of ninety feet. I spent three weeks studying the wreck further, and assembling everything known about the ship. On January 23, 2018, I published a story with the headline "Wreck Found by Reporter May Be Last American Slave Ship, Archaeologists Say." The story went viral on an international scale. I was hailed as the man who finally found the *Clotilda*, the last slave ship.

Two months later, it was announced that an international team was coming to Mobile to investigate the wreck. The team included the Slave Wrecks Project, the Smithsonian Institution, the National Park Service, Divers with a Purpose, the Alabama Historical Commission, and a marine archaeology company called Search Inc. The leader of the investigation was Search's Jim Delgado, a celebrated marine archaeologist who had led one of the last expeditions to the *Titanic*.

I spent a lot of time that first day talking with Dr. Delgado, who was most interested in hearing how I had homed in on this particular stretch of the Mobile River. We talked of the discrepancies in the historical record, the realities of geography regarding the locations mentioned, about Jack Friend's survey, and Foster's journal account. After about three hours, he pointed toward a pair of divers trying to find the end of the ship. Using long metal poles, they were able to probe through the mud and find the outline.

"You see the divers are measuring it, with John at this end of the tape," Delgado said, pointing to a man holding a large measuring tape on a reel a few feet from us. "Right now, they are at 157 feet, 4 inches."

"That's a big boat," I said. "It's too big."

"Well, it is too big. So . . ." Jim stared at me for a minute, his mouth puckered in, like someone holding bad news they don't want to tell you. It was the first inkling that I had likely made a massive journalistic error. "I don't want you to take this too hard. This is how you look for ships. It's not easy. I mean, you came out here and found a ship of the right design, from the right era, in the right place. That's pretty impressive. And look at the attention you've brought to this story, and the area. It's international. I don't want you to feel badly. Or be embarrassed. You've done something incredible, even if this is not it. I think you have figured out where it is. I think *Clotilda* will be found right around here."

I remain grateful to Jim for trying to let me down easy. He spent about forty-five minutes at the stern of my boat, both of us in dry suits, him trying to keep my spirits afloat as I faced what was certain to be a public humiliation. I think he knew I was going to take it hard. And I did. It was a long night when I got home. I'll say that. And much whiskey was drunk. I knew exactly how far the story had spread, how many people on both sides of the Atlantic were excited. In the two months since the first story, I'd even taken the ambassador of Benin to see it. As a reporter, I prided myself on seldom ever having a correction, despite doing complex, in-depth investigative reporting. Now, on the biggest story I'd ever broken, a story that had spread worldwide, my central premise was wrong. My father, Howell Raines, a career journalist and Pulitzer Prize winner, tried to soften the blow. "You published a piece full of caveats. You quoted archaeologists, you took experts to the site. You used the word 'may' in the first sentence and everywhere else. You're totally covered from a journalism perspective." Perhaps I was. Sort of. From a journalism perspective. But in the court of public opinion, in our sound-bite world, my sound-bite was that I'd found the last slave ship.

The next morning, a little bleary from the night before, I showed up in Africatown for the press conference where they planned to reveal to the public that it was not the right ship. The list of all the reasons this could not be the *Clotilda* was excruciating to hear in detail, for it highlighted how badly my ship had missed the mark. Several descendants refused to believe the archaeologists, insisting the scientists were wrong, that the ship had to be *Clotilda* and the state was trying to hide the truth on behalf of the Meaher family. I could see the disappointment all around me. Two months before, I had been invited to speak to several hundred Africatown residents crammed into this same room, the morning after my first story. At that meeting, residents talked excitedly about putting the wreck on display in a new museum in Africatown and what the discovery would mean for the moribund town and its forgotten history. During the next two months, as I interviewed dozens of people in Africatown, I came to understand what made the story resonate with the descendants and the entire world. The enslavement of millions of people spread over four hundred years was largely an anonymous crime in that we know nothing about the victims or the perpetrators beyond rough tallies of how many people were sold in various ports. No record of who they were or where they came from. But the *Clotilda* is different. Thanks to family lore and the books and articles written over the last 150 years, we know many things about its African passengers, including who captured and sold them, how their lives turned out, and where their descendants are today. The *Clotilda* story resonates because it is the origin story of the African diaspora globally. We know of the lifelong sense of loss the survivors felt, of the rich cultures they came from, the horrific fates that befell their African families left behind. The possibility of the ship's discovery had animated the community, setting off a flurry of meetings and celebrations.

The news from Delgado had the opposite effect, delivering a crushing blow to morale. People were crying as the presentation concluded. One of the descendants, Thelma Maiben-Owens, who runs the community garden in Africatown, had followed my work closely, and I'd noticed her watching me during the meeting. I'm sure my emotions and personal disappointment were easy to read on my face. After the presentation ended, she wrapped me in a hug and quietly sang the words of a gospel song in my ear, "There's a bright side somewhere, don't give up and don't give in." As she let me go, she looked me in the eye and said, "Don't you stop until you find it, Ben."

Later, as I left the meeting, two guys who worked for a company called Fathom Undersea Research and Engineering introduced themselves to me. I recognized the company they worked for, as it had recently located a Belgian ship from the 1700s off the Alabama coast. They told me that a decade prior, they had tried to look for the *Clotilda*, while they were being paid to search the Mobile River for two Civil War ironclad warships. They said their survey carried them up the river close to the bottom of Twelve Mile Island. They told me they figured, as I had, that Meaher had always lied about where the ship was. Even before my conversation with them was over, I knew exactly what I was going to do. These guys had done a high-tech survey of the river below Twelve Mile. Jack Friend had searched the river beginning right above Twelve Mile. But no one had ever searched Twelve Mile Island itself, which is precisely where the captain of the ship said he burned it. I would immediately conduct the first ever modern survey of the Twelve Mile Island section of the Mobile River. I just needed to come up with about $10,000 to pay for a survey boat.

Ten grand was a daunting amount of money for a newspaper reporter, but Thelma's advice rang in my head. The next morning, I called Dr. Monty Graham, the head of Marine Sciences at the University of Southern Mississippi. Monty is an old friend, and he'd been following my reporting on the ship. I asked if he would bring a Southern Miss crew to Alabama to do a full-scale bathymetric survey of the Mobile River around the east side of Twelve Mile Island. He asked if I had a budget. Such surveys involve a boat equipped with hundreds of thousands of dollars' worth of survey machines connected to multiple laptop computers, which collect reams of data from the survey equipment in real time. Survey boats so equipped are commonly used in the oil industry. I told him I didn't have any money, but Monty didn't hesitate.

"I'd love to do something to help Africatown, and it'll be good for our grad students. How about next week?" The University of Southern Mississippi's hydrographic science team showed up. It was led by Max van Norden, Dr. Anad Hiroji, Marvin Story, Kandice Gunning, Ashley Boyce, Jennifer Rhodes, and Alex Hersperger. By the end of their search, Monty's crew had located eleven possible targets in the two-mile stretch of river. With so many big objects so close together, it seemed clear we were looking at a ship graveyard, which explained the presence of the first, wrong ship I'd found. This still fit with Foster and Cudjo's recollection of where the ship was burned. After all, what better place to dispose of a ship than the back of a secluded island where several ships had already been sunk.

It took a full week for the team to collate all the data and produce a three-dimensional picture of the river bottom. We began examining various underwater possibilities using coordinates from the 3-D picture. We immediately ruled out several of the targets before we even returned to the river, because they were simply too large to be *Clotilda*. But we settled on one in particular because it was about ninety feet long, precisely the length of the *Clotilda*. On the side scan sonar imagery the team produced, you could see a wooden deck, with missing planks and several open hatches. The bow and stern stood out perfectly. It looked promising. So promising I could hardly sleep. All I could think about was putting on my scuba gear. I lay in bed imagining myself dropping down on the wreck to explore it and coming up with the bell from the ship with the name *Clotilda* stamped on it. Ship's bells are considered one of the best ways to confirm the identity of nineteenth-century shipwrecks.

A week later, just two weeks after all the visiting archaeologists had left Mobile with no plans to return, Monty was on board my boat with the owner of the Underwater Works Dive Shop and my mechanic Joe Turner, who would captain the boat while we were in the water. It was early April, and the spring floods were on. The current was running hard and the river was so muddy it looked like chocolate milk. As soon as we began exploring the most promising wreck, the one I'd been lying awake imagining, we knew it couldn't be *Clotilda*. The deck was the only thing on the entire ship made of wood. The hull itself was made of iron, indicating a ship from the Edwardian era, right around 1900, not an antebellum-era wooden schooner like *Clotilda*. It looked like we were done. The best candidate from the Southern Miss survey was a bust. We agreed to head back to the dock.

As everyone packed up their dive gear for the run back, I called up the survey chart on my phone. I guess I was hoping to see something everyone had missed. A bathymetric survey looks sort of like a topographical map, except instead of lines getting closer together or farther apart to indicate changes in altitude, different colors are used to show changes in water depth. For our chart, most of the river was pictured in yellow, indicating a fairly uniform depth of about fifteen feet. But along the edges near the bank, the shallower depths were pictured in orange, and the shallowest areas in red. Scattered around on the river bottom out in the channel, there were a number of what surveyors call "anomalies." These were spots where water depth suddenly changed, due to an object lying on the bottom. The anomalies showed up on the survey chart in slightly different colors, either red or orange, depending how high an object rose up off the bottom. Many of the anomalies were clearly trees or natural debris on the bottom. Monty's team had spent a week homing in on the

anomalies they thought could possibly be *Clotilda* and marking
them on the survey. Peering over my shoulder, Chas Broughton
from the dive shop pointed at a slightly discolored area that had
not been highlighted. "What's that?" he said. I remarked that it
looked like a shoe.

"Not to me. That looks like a ship. Let's check it out." Monty
called the lab from the boat and described the spot to his tech.
She found it on the map and texted us the GPS coordinates. It
was about three hundred yards north of the first ship I'd found.
The tech said it appeared to be about ninety feet long. My heart
started beating faster. We anchored the boat over the spot and I
jumped overboard. Nobody else was willing to get back into the
cold water at the end of a long day, so I got in alone. I could feel
logs and other debris on the bottom. I started diving down and
picking the logs and branches up, moving them out of the way.
Monty and crew on the boat were laughing, saying I had discovered a pile of sticks. I kept pulling up logs. Then I felt something
bend beneath my foot as I put my weight on it. My first thought
was that it might be a piece of wrought iron, a sign that whatever was on the river bottom was made in the 1850s, like the
Clotilda. Keeping my foot firmly pressed against the bent piece
so I wouldn't lose it in the heavy current, I started sliding my
hands down my leg toward my foot. I had to do that because the
river was in flood stage, the water a turgid brown. It was impossible to see anything, even with a mask on, through the muddy
water. Diving blind, I used my leg as a guide, running hands
down thigh and calf, then over my dive boot until I grasped the
metal under my foot. I could feel that it was hammered through
a thick plank of wood with squared-off edges, clearly a piece of
hewn lumber, not a log. I tugged lightly on the plank, unsure if

it was just stuck in the mud or part of the larger structure I was exploring. After a moment, the old nails holding it fast gave way and it came free in my hand.

I popped back up on the surface and held the piece aloft. It was about five feet long, with several large, rusty nails poking out of it. They were square-cut, and clearly handmade by a blacksmith. I called to my friends on the boat, "Guys, we just found something from the 1850s." Monty and Chas got in, and within minutes we knew we had found a ship. A ship that appeared to be the same length as the *Clotilda*. Nearby on the bank, I spied a concrete survey marker that had been newly painted bright red, already an extremely odd sight on the riverbank in the remote swamp. In big block letters, the marker bore the name "Meaher," a reminder that the family still owned this stretch of shoreline, as it had since the 1850s.

A few days later, I called the Alabama Historical Commission to report that we had located the remains of another ship from the 1850s, and that it appeared to be about ninety feet long. After a stunned silence, I offered to provide them the coordinates to the ship as well as our full bathymetric survey. They got Delgado on the phone and everyone began asking me questions about the find. I told them it was the only object we'd encountered that could possibly be the *Clotilda*. It would take an international team of archaeologists a year to confirm the find, but that moment when I pulled up the piece of wood with the nails poking through it was the first time the *Clotilda* had seen the light of day in 160 years.

Chapter 11

FINDING A FUTURE IN THE PAST

The people of Africatown struggled to grapple with the attention and energy surrounding the announcement of the *Clotilda*'s discovery. The media came in full force, and from around the globe. There was excitement in the community, but also a fear of not having anything to show for all the buzz. Lorna Woods, whose great-grandparents were founders of the town, laid bare the challenge facing Africatown days after the ship's discovery was announced.

"Everybody's looking at us, but we don't even have a store where you can buy goods on your travels through Africatown. It's nothing to see and nothing to do," Woods said. "Many people have come to Mobile and said, 'But what about Africatown? You have it on the map, but what are we going to see? What are we gonna do once we get to Africatown?' Nothing is to show here in Africatown that would bring the history out. We don't

212

have it to show. I would love for it to be shown that this was the last place a slave ship arrived. We don't have a museum or a building or anything. Just a sign on the side of the highway."

In addition to all the reporters, four separate documentary crews were filming at the community's big celebration. Everywhere you looked, cameras and microphones were pointed at residents. I made myself useful by carrying news crews from around the world up the river to the desolate swamp where the ship had been found. I took reporters to the site two or three days a week for months after the discovery was made public. Every time I launched the boat, I made sure we left from Meaher State Park as a personal poke in the eye for old Captain Tim and his scoundrel brothers who'd helped the night the ship was burned. I also often bring along descendants or community leaders on these trips, so more of them can see the remote spot where their ancestors began their American lives. A lot of them find themselves crying as we drift over the wreck.

A Kenya-born soundman for CBS who made the trip said, "Man, when I heard we were going to Alabama to film a partially burned slave ship, I said, 'We should burn the rest of the thing until there's nothing left.' But now that I've been there, I don't feel that way anymore. It was powerful being there. I think seeing the actual ship, whatever's left, burnt and rotten in a museum, would be powerful too."

Long before the ship was found, a core group in Africatown worked to promote the *Clotilda* history, going back decades. For some, the goal was simply to honor their ancestors and the story of their struggle. Others wanted to use that history as a way to draw people in, to resurrect Africatown, to restore the prosperity and vitality they remembered from childhood. Cleon Jones, the baseball hero, became a one-man Habitat for Humanity with his Last Out Society, organizing volunteers to paint houses, mow lawns, and try to restore the community's curb appeal. Then there was the *Clotilda* Descendants Association, the Benin-Alabama Trade Forum, the C.H.E.S.S. Foundation, the Mobile County Training School Alumni Association, the Africatown Community Development Corporation, and several other groups pushing separate agendas, sometimes at cross-purposes, all those groups in a town of just two thousand people. They focused variously on successfully getting Africatown listed on the National Register of Historic Places, restoring the town's housing stock to attract new residents, creating business connections to Africa, fighting the expansion of heavy industry, working to clean up legacy pollution, restoring the town's access to the river, and trying to keep county officials from closing Africatown's aging school. Over the years, bitter feuds have sometimes developed between many of the leaders of the groups. In particular, there was conflict between people who still lived in Africatown and people who had long since moved away but remained active within the community groups. When the ship was found, friction between the rival groups threatened to thwart progress on any front. In the months that followed, on multiple occasions, the leaders of one or another of the different groups sent out mass emails demonizing leaders of other groups by name over disagreements about the best path forward.

An unfortunate truth quickly emerged in the glare of the media spotlight, especially after anthropologists from the Smithsonian Institution arrived to collect oral histories. What they found was that the story of the *Clotilda* lives on in official records and documents, and in the books about the ship, but not in most of the people living in Africatown today. Descendants are scattered across the country, and many are only recently learning the story of their *Clotilda* ancestors. Unlike the Gullah Geechee culture in coastal South Carolina, Georgia, and Florida, where descendants have kept ancestral stories, art, crafts, recipes, and an African-based Creole language alive, there is little hint of an African language spoken in Africatown, not in words used by residents, the names of streets, or anything else. The Gullah descendants—who were geographically isolated on barrier islands and remained socially isolated as those islands became playgrounds for wealthy beachgoers—have managed to turn their cultural provenance into a tourist draw, with museums, a heritage trail, and a healthy schedule of public events. Many of the people living in or tied to Africatown want to create something similar.

But much of the history has been lost. Or hidden. Or dynamited.

During the archaeological investigation, it was revealed that the chunk of the ship I first found was a few feet away from the main hull, which was partially buried in mud. It appeared the ship had been blasted with dynamite at some point in its underwater history, which knocked the upper sections off the main frame, leaving most of the hold, where the captives were kept, intact, because over the course of a century the river had filled the hull with mud, shielding it from the blast. Jim Delgado told me this detail months before the find was finally confirmed, but the moment he said dynamite, I knew it was the *Clotilda*. Joe Meaher, the oldest of Timothy Meaher's great-grandsons and a well-known racist, had been telling a story about dynamite around town for decades. Meaher, who died in March of 2020, told historian John Sledge, author of *The Mobile River*, that he and his father dynamited the *Clotilda* in the 1950s or '60s. The goal, according to Meaher, was to make sure nobody could ever find the *Clotilda* and help the descendants launch a lawsuit or kidnapping claim against the family's large Civil War–era fortune. This meant, of course, that Joe and his father knew where the *Clotilda* was all along, for the last century and a half. I think other people in their orbit knew where the ship was as well.

I say this because the day I published my story about the first ship—the one that was too big to be *Clotilda*—a man who grew up with the Meahers called and told me I'd found the wrong ship. When I asked him how he knew, he said, "I just know. That's not the *Clotilda*. You're getting people all stirred up over nothing with all this. You should just let sleeping dogs lie." Then, when I found the second ship, a year before it was even confirmed he confronted me in the grocery store and told me I was ruining Joe Meaher's retirement. When I asked if it was the *Clotilda*, he said, "You're getting them stirred up over nothing." Ultimately, Joe Meaher's dynamite boasts provided one of the forensic clues archaeologists relied on to positively identify *Clotilda*.

Another blow to the community's effort to reconstruct its story came in the form of Hurricane Katrina, which destroyed the closest thing Africatown had to a museum. It was a home-made affair, a welcome center set up in a mobile home across the street from the first church and the cemetery. It was destroyed by the hurricane in 2005 and never replaced. The site is now overgrown with weeds, supervised by two headless busts sitting atop a brick wall. One set of shoulders cemented to the wall belonged to a bust of Cudjo Lewis, the other to a former mayor of Prichard, John Smith, who championed the restoration of a connection between Africatown and Benin beginning in the 1980s. He set up a formal "Twinning Ceremony" making sister cities out of Africatown and Ouidah in Benin, the city where Foster bought the *Clotilda* captives. The ceremony was held in 1986 during the Africatown Folk Festival, which attracted a slew of prominent activists including Reverend Jesse Jackson, Congressman John Lewis, comedian Dick Gregory, and author Alex Haley. It also drew a delegation from Benin, including the archbishop of Cotonou, Isidore de Souza, a direct descendant of Francisco de Souza, the most infamous slave trader in world history. John Smith continued his activism as a private citizen in the early 2000s, establishing cultural festivals in Africatown and Ouidah featuring artists from both countries. He was interviewed backstage by a television news crew in Benin in 2004 at "Festival International Gospel and Racines." In grainy footage posted on YouTube, an interviewer asks, "What is Africatown? Is it a specific place?" Smith tells the *Clotilda* story, explaining, "It is a specific place where the people who came from Ouidah lived. Their families are there. Their families, their churches, their cemeteries." Dressed in traditional African garb, he describes how he believes African-Americans feel about Africa and themselves. "They have strange and weird feelings, and often negative feelings, stupid feelings about Africa. They have stupid and awful feelings about themselves, their mothers and fathers. It will require a process of education on the part of us who know better to get them past these awful thoughts about themselves and about their identity."

In 2006, Smith managed to get a bill on the ballot in Alabama designed to create a free trade zone for African goods on the edge of Africatown. A thousand-acre parcel along the river was donated toward the effort to house what Smith envisioned as "the Sub-Saharan Africa and Caribbean Trade Center," which would feature buildings designed to look like African-style huts, food vendors, and an open-air marketplace for duty-free African goods imported through the state docks. If the bill passed, Africatown would become the central entry point for African goods, from fruits and vegetables to clothing and raw materials for industry, delivered by container ship. Smith was ecstatic preparing for his vision, twenty-five years in the making, to become a reality. He died of a heart attack on election night when he learned the ballot measure had failed. His remains are interred in a museum in Ouidah. The Sub-Saharan Africa and Caribbean Trade Center dream died with him.

But part of his vision, a museum celebrating the *Clotilda* and her passengers, appears to be coming to fruition. Before the ship was even discovered, Africatown's activist groups applied for and won a $3.8 million grant from Alabama's share of the BP oil spill settlement money, to build a new welcome center on the hill above the cemetery, to replace the destroyed mobile home. Then, in the wake of the ship's discovery, another federal grant was given to create a "heritage center" in the community, which will be the initial facility designed to hold any relics found in the hold of the ship. But neither the welcome center nor the heritage center will be anything close to the scale and power of the new Legacy Museum and National Memorial for Peace and Justice in Montgomery, Alabama. To anyone who has seen the line of people snaking around the Smithsonian's National Museum of African American History and Culture years after it opened, or seen the packed parking lot at Montgomery's new museum dedicated to victims of lynching, the plans for Africatown seem far too small for the sort of exhibit the *Clotilda* story deserves.

Vicki Howell, a former journalist with the *Birmingham News* and president of MOVE (Making Opportunities Viable for Everyone), agrees. Howell was a key part of the team that created Birmingham's excellent Civil Rights Heritage Trail, and actually wrote the text on the dozens of signs scattered around the city's historic sites.

"When I looked at where they were talking about putting the welcome center, I said it wasn't big enough. But when I was told there was not going to be a museum, I said, 'Well, that's not going to do.' For me, we had to have a place that was big enough to be the kind of place where people not only spend money, but can spend time and learn the history," Howell said. Surveying Africatown's geography, she realized the long abandoned Josephine Allen housing project site, which encompasses forty-two acres of rolling hills, was a perfect spot for a nationally relevant museum.

Her team launched a national design competition inviting urban planners and architects to reimagine Africatown, filling its vacant lots with new homes and replacing the decaying and abandoned housing project with a cultural center on a grand scale.

Darron Patterson credits Vicki with thinking big and sticking to her guns when people in the community scoffed at what she imagined. He said the old guard, himself included, was thinking at first about what they could scrape together, not what the history deserved.

One design for the old housing project site would include a shopping district and a replica of the *Clotilda* floating on a lake, where passengers would be able to enter the hold of the ship where the captives were kept. The museum will be designed to house the actual wreck, if it is ever dug up out of the mud. However, the fate of the ship itself has now become a separate point of controversy, with descendants demanding the state of Alabama—which owns the wreck due to state and federal laws governing historic objects found in state waters—begin to excavate it.

Immediately after the find was confirmed, the Alabama Historical Commission suggested that instead of digging up the ship, perhaps it should be left in place miles from civilization, deep in the Mobile-Tensaw Delta, an alligator-infested swamp that is thirteen miles wide and fifty miles long. This suggestion for a "Pearl Harbor–inspired memorial" that could only be accessed by boat met bitter resistance in Africatown, with residents accusing the state of attempting to hide the most important piece of proof regarding what happened to their ancestors. The battle continues today, more than two years after I found the ship, with the state still refusing to commit to pulling the *Clotilda* from the mud, mostly due to an expected cost in the tens of millions of dollars. So far, Alabama has pledged one million dollars.

"Not digging up the ship, that's just stupid. The ship is the history. When I went to Memphis and I saw the Lorraine Motel where Martin Luther King was killed, I cried. That's the same history we've got here in Africatown. People are going to cry when they see the ship," said Lamar Howard, whose food truck feeds everyone at all the community celebrations. "The people here, we ain't fixing to get no reparations. There's no forty acres and a mule. There's not even a gas station. But if you've got an idea then you can come be a part of this. Help build the community. I'm going to open a store. I don't care if it is in a tent. I want to have something where people can come and go home with something to show they've been here. I don't care if it's T-shirts, or earrings, or books. I want them to be able to show they've been to Africatown. They say there is going to be a trail, from Atlanta to Montgomery, then when they do this museum here, that trail is going to come all the way here, to where it all started. But we don't have anything if we don't have the ship. You know that saying, the truth will set you free? Well, the ship is the truth. All the Black folks in America got here chained up on ships just like that."

The elation and international attention that greeted the discovery prove the ship has already become a cultural touchstone. The *Clotilda* is an internationally important artifact. It is the only ship ever found that brought enslaved Africans to America. There is a piece of a slave ship about the size of a brick on display in the Smithsonian Institution's National Museum of African American History and Culture, but it is from a South African ship that sank in port in Brazil, and has nothing to do with the American slave trade. Having the burnt, rotten hull of the last American slave ship on display would instantly make Africatown one of the most important sites in the burgeoning Civil Rights tourism industry. Museums in Benin have already asked to have small pieces of the ship to display in that country. To the community, having the wreck on display in a new museum is vital to both resurrecting Africatown's declining fortunes and reconnecting the people living there to their own history.

But even with the coming museum and facilities, the struggle to collect that history continues. There is a constant refrain among many Africatown residents, whether they are in their seventies or their forties, that they grew up not wanting people to think they were connected to the Africans.

That stigma is at the root of much of the suppression of Africatown's history, sometimes by the descendants themselves.

Darron Patterson, the Descendants Association president and great-great-grandson of founder Pollee Allen, finally learned he was a descendant by chance in 2010 during a visit to Africatown. His family moved to Texas when he was seventeen, and Patterson spent most of his working life in Detroit, removed from his Africatown roots and relatives. During his visit to his hometown, he encountered two women on the street who had been friends of his mother's. He was stunned when they told him he was a descendant and should join the Descendants Association. For the first time, at age sixty, he understood that his great-aunt "Mama Eva" was actually the child of one of the Africans. Had he known before her death in 1992, he could have asked her directly about her parents and the rest of the captives. But that opportunity had been stolen from him by his mother, because she was ashamed of the connection.

Eva Allen Jones—Mama Eva to generations of Africatown residents—was born in 1894, the year after Mary McNeil Scott visited Africatown with Noah Hart and saw the settlers in their small, remote cabins. Eva lived until 1992. She witnessed the rise of Africatown to the heights of the 1950s through the 1970s, and then the beginning of the decline. Her African father was fifty-one when she was born, married to a second wife—an American-born woman—after the death of his first, African-born wife. Cudjo and many of the *Clotilda* survivors gathered regularly at Eva's house when she was young, speaking in their native tongue. In her later years, she and Lorna Wood's grandmother were two of the last people left in Africatown who knew some of the original settlers and could tell stories about what they were like and what they said about their homeland. But neither woman ever learned to speak Yoruba, Fon, or any African languages, from their parents. Even during her childhood around the turn of the century, Eva said being connected to her African father and roots was cause for humiliation. "We didn't want kids laughing at us," she said, explaining why she never used the African name, Jo-Ko, that her father and his *Clotilda* survivor friends called her. Beyond the language issue, even Eva's recollections, captured in an interview taped in 1978, are fraught with memories that don't comport with established facts. For instance, Eva told her interviewer that her father and his people spoke Zulu and were from the Congo. The Zulu are the most prominent ethnic group in South Africa, more than twenty-five hundred miles south of Benin, while the Democratic Republic of Congo is fifteen hundred miles away from Benin and no one there speaks Zulu. Those words, Zulu and Congo, were popular in American culture to describe something African during Eva's lifetime, but they have nothing to do with the people who arrived on the *Clotilda*.

"It is not their fault, but so much has been lost," said Sylviane Diouf, author of *Dreams of Africa in Alabama*. "We have the story because we have the books by Emma Roche and Zora Hurston. Not because it was passed down." When researching her book in the early 2000s, Diouf said she tracked down some descendants living in the New York area. They knew of the *Clotilda* story and that it belonged to their ancestors. "But the things they were telling me, these were things I recognized from an article from the 1950s. They were claiming their particular ancestors hadn't actually been enslaved. They had escaped into the swamp and lived there until after slavery. This didn't happen."

Even coming from a family that was proud of the heritage wasn't enough to ensure the history was preserved. Garry Lumbers is Cudjo Lewis's great-great-grandson and grew up in Cudjo's house. He lived there with his grandmother, known as Sweeta, who was Cudjo's granddaughter and helped care for him in his old age. Cudjo taught Sweeta his African healing skills, relying on plants and other natural compounds, and into the 1960s, when Garry was a boy, people would still line up outside the house for his grandmother's traditional remedies. Garry's mother, Mary, was one of the young girls leaning against Cudjo's knee in one of the only surviving pictures of him. She was one of the children he grew his sugarcane for. Despite these close connections, Garry says most of what he knows about his family's story comes from the books written about them rather than from his relatives.

"I heard so many things about the ship. I heard that the ship was somewhere down there and caught on fire, and they jumped off the ship shackled, things like that. Or some of them didn't end up slaves. It was so many myths. To actually know the whole truth, the real truth we know now with the books, it's different," he says.

Cleon Jones, who made the game-winning catch in the World Series as a member of the 1969 New York Mets, says he too realized the myths he grew up with in Africatown needed to make way for the truth. "We found out as Black folks that history was a lie. We learned we can write, or rewrite, our own history."

Of late, Africatown has been holding a lot of gatherings

under the big bridge by the river to celebrate and honor the ancestors and the discovery of the ship. The bridge looms over the spot where the slaves camped rough in the first weeks after they were freed and left the plantations where they had been imprisoned. A plan is in the works to turn it into a park honoring the *Clotilda* story.

Chapter 12

RECONCILIATION

O uidah, Benin. The ancient dirt road is made of fiery red clay. It cuts a rusty slash through the incredible green of the sub-Saharan forest, where coconut palms and papaya trees fight for light beneath towering armies of mango and five-hundred-year-old iroko trees. Small motorcycles, often carrying two adults and three or four children, buzz by, passing Voodoo shrines dedicated to the millions of captives marched into slavery along this centuries-old thoroughfare.

The old slave route runs from the Dahomean royal palace in Abomey to the beach in the city of Ouidah, which was responsible for deporting between 20 and 30 percent of all the Africans who were sold and enslaved.

"They were led on foot from Abomey to Ouidah, which took about four days, and then were put on the ship you have discovered. This is the road that the people who were on the

Clotilda were led to and walked down," says Abomey's mayor, Blaise Ahanhanzo Glele. The mayor shares his last name with his ancestor, King Glele of Dahomey, who ruled the kingdom from 1858 to 1889. This makes the mayor both a prince and a descendant of the man who captured and then sold Cudjo Lewis and his *Clotilda* shipmates. The mayor invited me to lunch to ask me about my role in the discovery of the *Clotilda*, and to show me around the town where he was born, which was once the capital of one of the most brutal regimes in history.

Lunch was served outdoors in a shady glade, surrounded by hundreds of exquisite wooden sculptures, from giraffe-headed humans and enormous elephants to small faceless figures, whose heads look down or away to the side, meant to shame the living for the souls lost to slavery. It was a large gathering, with perhaps two dozen people. The mayor toasted us with pineapple whiskey homemade on his farm. Then the local La Béninoise beer was served with a first course of a whole tilapia, pan-fried and heavily spiced, almost like blackened redfish. A second course consisted of a small, long-legged bird, sliced in half and accompanied by mashed white yams, a spicy tomato garnish, and a fiercely hot green pepper sauce. When the bird arrived, the mayor remarked in English, "Our chickens ride bicycles." I understood this to be a reference to the diminutive size of the bird on the plate, with its long, skinny drumsticks. Only later did I come to understand that *"poulet bicyclette"* is something of a national dish in Benin, and signifies the diner is being treated to a wild caught chicken, rather than a farm-raised or imported bird, considered less desirable on the plate.

The conversation turned to Benin's slaving legacy and how to use it for good. The goal, the mayor said, is to reconnect people in America and elsewhere with their African roots, and bring them back—at least as tourists—to the countries their ancestors were stolen from. For many, Benin is that country. The 110 people deported aboard the *Clotilda* and all of the people involved in capturing and selling them lived inside the borders of modern-day Benin. This, the mayor said, was the story for most of the people deported through Ouidah, which historians agree was one of the top three slave ports in the world. "We have the whole story of slavery here, the captors and the captured, and we live with all sides of the legacy."

The entire kingdom of Dahomey was contained inside the modern-day boundaries of Benin.

The tens of thousands of slaves captured each year to sell to Europe and the Americas were all from smaller kingdoms either in Benin or in the border regions of the neighboring modern nations Togo and Nigeria. This means the scars of enslavement remain ever present in Benin, where most everyone's ancestors were either capturing or being captured as part of the slaving economy. This has led to an uneasy peace there between the descendants of the captors and the captured. Even today, there are villages all over Benin where the descendants of those who were captured, mostly Yoruba tribespeople like Cudjo, avoid interacting with their neighbors if they are Fon, the tribe of the old Dahomeans. The Fon remain Benin's largest ethnic group today, and many Fon are still followers of the native Vodun religion, which is the parent religion of the forms of Voodoo and Santeria in Brazil, the Caribbean, and the American South.

This internal divide shows up in modern politics. Benin's current president, Patrice Talon, is a Fon born in Ouidah. He was attacked during the last campaign for having slave dealers in his family tree. Often, understanding a person's tribal heritage in Benin can be as simple as looking at their face. Ritualistic facial scarification can reveal someone's tribe, religion, and cultural heritage. Members of the Fon tribe, which ruled the Kingdom of Dahomey during the slave era, are recognizable by distinct facial scarification patterns, which are typically carved into their flesh when they are children or infants. Cudjo and his shipmates bore a variety of facial marks, tooth filings, and tattoos, all linking them to specific tribes, areas, and religions. Scarification is still widely practiced today. During my lunch with Mayor Glele, I saw that both Sacca Lafia, the interior minister of Benin, and another man who is one of the nation's highest ranking military officers bore facial scars that link them to different tribes—one to those who did the capturing, the other to those who were captured.

Ancestor worship is a central tenet of Benin's native religion, and remains important even to those who have converted to Christianity and Islam. Most homes have a shrine dedicated to ancestors. The shrines are populated with carved wooden statues of various gods, parts of animals such as chickens or monkeys meant as sacrifice, palm oil, gin, and various leaves, herbs, and powders that are burned. The power of this part of the legacy of enslavement for Africans—seeking peace both with and for ancestors—was brought home to me when Hector Posset, then Benin's ambassador to the United States, came to Mobile to travel upriver with me to the area where I found the *Clotilda*. He said the *Clotilda* was considered a national priority by Benin's president due to the long-standing partnership between Benin and Africatown. I traveled up the river with the ambassador, who was dressed in a fine pinstripe suit and tie. He performed a Vodun ritual aboard my boat, on the back side of Twelve Mile Island, where the ship lies. The ritual involved gin spewed from his mouth into the Mobile River and various incantations spoken in Fon. As he delivered them, first in low, forceful tones, and then yelling, tears began to stream from behind his sunglasses. I asked him what he was saying.

"I am just begging them to forgive us, because we sold them. Our forefathers sold their brothers and sisters. I am not the person to talk to them. No! May their souls rest in peace, perfect peace. They should forgive us." After sobbing for a moment, the ambassador, wiping tears from his cheeks, asked to depart the area and said, "I feel so sad."

Later, over dinner in a seafood restaurant overlooking Mobile Bay, he revisited the moment and elaborated.

"I am a prince of Dahomey. It was my father's ancestors who did this," Posset said, explaining that he, like the mayor of Abomey, had royal lineage. "But my mother was Yoruba. Her ancestors came here to this country [America] forcibly, they didn't choose. And it was my father's family who sold my mother's family. This is why I wept. I was insulting those who sold them back home. No money, no articles, no stuff can buy a life, but we sold our people. Brothers sold their brothers and sisters. Fathers sold kids and wife. I will never blame those who came here. I will always beg them for forgiveness."

It was Posset who first told me of the superstition in Benin about sitting beside a door when visiting friends. Being captured in one of the giant annual slaving raids executed by the Dahomeans wasn't the only way people ended up enslaved. Oftentimes, he said, it was old-fashioned kidnapping, orchestrated by people who knew you in your village, sometimes as you were sitting inside your own home.

Several of the *Clotilda* captives were captured in similar fashion, snatched by roving bands of slave hunters and then sold or traded multiple times before they ended up in one of the Dahomean barracoons. Kanko, a *Clotilda* passenger remembered by her descendants for throwing a sheriff's deputy over the fence of her farm in Mobile, was captured as she walked alone to pick something up from the market for her mother. As she left for her errand, her mother warned her to be on guard because slave traders had been seen lurking in a certain area. Kanko, a young teenager, decided to detour through that area, hoping to catch a glimpse of the slave coffle. She never saw her mother again, and no one in her family would ever know what had become of their little girl.

"When people talk about slavery, they think they are talking about Africa," said Nathalie Blanc Chekete, with Benin's National Agency for the Promotion of Heritage and the Development of Tourism. "But slavery was something that happened once they reached America or Brazil. What happened in Africa was deportation, where Africans took other Africans away from their lands and families and sent them away forever."

This tragedy, which lasted more than two hundred years in Benin, left an indelible mark on the entire society, one that still reverberates. Chekete said it shows up in little ways, such as the superstition about sitting in a chair close to the front door, and in big ways, such as the existence of the floating village of Ganvie, which today is known as the Venice of West Africa.

Ganvie sits five miles from shore in the middle of Lake Nokoué, on the outskirts of Cotonou, Benin's largest city. Long, skinny wooden boats ferry tourists and goods out to Ganvie, which is home to forty thousand people living in a city built on stilts. There are bars, restaurants, hotels, and giant canoes filled with children on their way to the floating town's school. The residents are fishermen, plying their craft with nets and traps from small dugout pirogues powered by sails and oars. They fish—men, women, and children—mostly around elaborate artificial reefs created from reeds and trees to provide more habitat. Many of the reefs double as pens for aquaculture, where residents farm various species to harvest size. Most fascinating about Ganvie is the question of how so many people came to live in houses on stilts in the middle of a lake.

The answer is simple when set against the backdrop of Dahomey. The small Tofinu tribe lived along the edge of the lake in the early 1700s, and witnessed the destruction as several neighboring tribes were swallowed up and destroyed by the Dahomean war machine. Rather than face a similar fate, the tribe chose to move and make a life over open water in the middle of the lake. They built houses of reeds and sticks standing on stilts. The Tofinu regarded the move as the only way they could ensure they weren't captured and sold. The water served as a protective barrier because the Vodun religion practiced by the Dahomeans forbade traveling over the sacred lake before battle. And, on a practical note, few of the Dahomeans knew how to swim. The Tofinu tribe has remained in the middle of the lake for the last three hundred years.

There are more than a thousand underground villages in Benin, highlighting another widespread tactic used to foil the Dahomean raiding parties. Long since abandoned, the villages consist of networks of tunnels and rooms dug into the earth by hand. The residents would farm and conduct business above-ground during daylight hours, then retreat into the hidden entrances of their subterranean homes to sleep, thereby foiling the Dahomeans, who conducted their attacks almost exclusively at night to maximize the element of surprise.

New museums are being built in Benin, in consultation with the Smithsonian Institution. They are dedicated to unraveling Benin's role in this earliest human trafficking, and exploring the effect on the global African diaspora. They will house, among other things, twenty-six significant works of art, including royal thrones and friezes ripped from the walls of King Glele's palace in Abomey, and a cache of the exquisitely detailed seventeenth-, eighteenth-, and nineteenth-century metal sculptures known as the Benin Bronzes. They were stolen as spoils of war in 1892, when France overthrew the Dahomean Empire. French president Emmanuel Macron announced he would return the treasures in 2019, and provide a $24 million loan to build the facilities to house the artifacts. The challenge for the museums will be to capture the full scope of culture exported from Benin to the Western world. Even within just the small group of the *Clotilda*'s 110 passengers, we can see essential elements of Benin's culture—drumming, dancing, songs of lament, herbal healing remedies, cooking styles, and appeals to supernatural powers through offerings—delivered straight from Africa to Alabama. That culture was similarly carried inside the enslaved deported the world over, and is expressed all around us in churches, music, and art. When Lightnin' Hopkins sings, "I'm going to Louisiana and get me a mojo hand, I'm gonna fix my woman so she can't have no other man," he is drawing a direct line to Benin's Vodun worship, where offerings and charms are still used to manipulate the future and the fortunes of others.

It takes twenty-seven hours to get from Africatown, Alabama, to Cotonou, Benin's largest city. The last encounter with the Western world takes place in Charles de Gaulle Airport, as you stroll toward your gate through the glitzy international terminal, past storefronts for Chanel, Gucci, Prada, Dior, and Hermès. Seven hours later, they pop open the jet door and you step out into the warm African night and the twenty-four-hour-a-day bustle of Cotonou. French is the dominant language in urban Benin, but it will not help when you encounter one of the fifty-two native languages and dialects prominent away from the big city. Without someone who speaks at least Fon, the language of the old Dahomeans, or Yoruban, Cudjo's native tongue, you will quickly find yourself unable to communicate in the towns and places where the streets are not paved.

Hurtling along one of the two-lane highways that link Benin's far-flung cities is an almost psychedelic experience. The rush of colors and sights is overwhelming, with something demanding your attention everywhere your eyes fall. Mangos, papayas, bananas, pineapples, and oranges grow wild and in great abundance. Incredibly vibrant flowers fill the forests. Monkeys and four-foot lizards dash across the highway. Ten thousand minibikes share the road with you, in a traffic system that seems to grant right-of-way based solely on how fast your particular vehicle is capable of traveling.

The only slowdowns on the highways come from the speed bumps set up to mark medium-sized villages along the route. Dozens of buildings, ranging from mud huts with corrugated tin roofs to concrete and stucco edifices, crowd around the highways near the speed bumps. The large bumps are designed to bring all traffic to a standstill as the vehicles traverse them, giving villagers a chance to cross the wildly busy thoroughfares. They also provide merchants, hawking everything from palm nuts and peeled oranges to smoked fish, shoes, and children's toys, a chance at the truck drivers, cyclists, and other travelers passing by. White faces are seldom seen. I counted just twelve during my travels around the country outside of Cotonou.

Pull into the larger market towns, and the roadways are lined with stalls selling liquor, cell phones, flip-flops, baby dolls, handmade furniture, wildly colorful fabric, and lots of glossy, highly varnished caskets. Tailors are scattered all around, often using old-fashioned foot-operated sewing machines to turn out traditional African garments and Western-style dresses based on patterns and colors you might recognize from the latest Paris runway collection, or from a 1960s Sears catalog.

In Ouidah, the city where Captain Foster bought the *Clotilda*'s passengers, monuments to slavery and its victims are scattered all over town. Most were built in the early nineties, when various international groups helped fund their construction as part of "Ouidah 92," an event designed to help bridge the gap between descendants of the slavers and descendants of those they'd captured and sold. But there are some competing monuments as well, monuments to the slaving kings and to the most prolific slave trader ever, Francisco de Souza, a Brazilian long celebrated as "the father of Ouidah." De Souza was put in charge of Ouidah's slave markets by King Ghezo and is credited with organizing the markets to better facilitate the "trade noir," and working out an arrangement where the five main slave-trading nations built the barracoons required to house thousands of people at a time. Even today, de Souza's descendants are prominent and wealthy citizens of Ouidah, and still live in the old slaver's compound in the center of the city. They bitterly oppose government plans to wipe their family name from Ouidah's central plaza, which sits on the spot where foreigners paid for the people they bought. The family likewise opposes plans for the new museums to describe de Souza as the slave dealer who sold more people into slavery than anyone else in human history, as opposed to describing him as a simple "merchant" as the de Souza family museum in Ouidah does. When the current patriarch of the de Souza clan, Moise de Souza, was interviewed regarding his objections to the new museum, he said, "It's the reputation of our family. We don't want to be known for this dirty thing."

I heard an opposing message when I visited the palace of His Majesty Dada Daagbo Hounan Huely II—the spiritual leader of Vodun in Benin, and the leader of many Voodoo adherents globally—who said he was proud that his country was confronting its slaving legacy. Dada Daagbo, who, according to his business card, is also the "*Roi des Mers et Océans*," or the King of the Seas and Oceans, is, in essence, the Voodoo equivalent of the Catholic pope for the world's Vodun and Voodoo practioners. His chair in the palace throne room sits upon an elevated platform about two feet high. Visitors sit in chairs around a table below him. The wall behind the throne is covered in pictures of his ancestors, who have held his title going back to the slavery era. An enormous elephant skull serves as a table in front of the throne. Several small wooden figures, freshly carved, lie on the skull. A clay pot next to it holds handfuls of dark green herbs. A small bowl is full of what appears to be gunpowder. Charred herbs and charcoal spill off a tray. Bundles of sticks hang from a rafter, along with other ornaments. Small statues wearing tiny woven shoulder bags, perhaps to hold some sort of talisman, stand at attention here and there around the room. A table in the center is stacked with books and papers, while a satellite dish on the roof delivers the news of the world on a large television.

I already knew Dada Daagbo from a trip he made to Mobile to visit the wreck site with me. He is eloquent in conversation, quick with a parable, a joke, or a smile, and has a law degree and a history as a successful arbiter for labor negotiations. He dresses in long robes and tall hats with giant brims, heavily covered in beaded symbols that hold great significance for practitioners of Vodun. On my boat at the wreck site in Alabama, he pulled out a handful of cowrie shells plucked from the beach in Ouidah, rolled them back and forth between his palms for a minute or two, then spat onto them and cast them across the deck. Studying the strewn shells while speaking Fon in low tones, he carefully arranged them into two rows and then stood and began grasping handfuls of the long blades of wild rice emerging along the bank. Still speaking constantly, but just above a whisper, he tied the blades of rice grass into knots, but left them growing in the water. After a half dozen or so knots on different clumps of grass, he turned and addressed me in French.

"It's going to happen that people threaten you. Don't hold back. Don't have fear. No matter how fierce the threat, no matter what anyone tries," he said, warning that some people in Benin and America were going to be upset by the ship's discovery because of guilt over their ancestors' roles and that they might act out. This had happened in Benin when people were confronted with slavery artifacts, but the government pushed ahead, he said, especially in his hometown of Ouidah with its numerous slavery memorials, because "it is not hiding from this legacy."

He greeted me warmly when I arrived at his palace a little way out of Ouidah on the edge of the jungle six months later, but again offered a warning and suggested I keep a low profile during my travels in Benin.

"I tell you again to beware. There are evil people who will not like what you have done," Dada Daagbo said, "but you come to Ouidah and you are welcome here. You have come to the historical land that witnessed millions and millions of slaves. Ouidah is one of the first places that has tackled the truth. . . . We have the relics. We know what happened and Ouidah is telling the story."

All over Benin, the government still recognizes the old kingdoms, including Dahomey, as a matter of national heritage and treats the palaces as state treasures. I met numerous kings and princes in Benin, including Dada Kefa Sagbadjou Glele, the current king of Dahomey and the last living grandson of the King Glele who captured and imprisoned the *Clotilda* passengers. The modern King Glele still holds court on the grounds of the ancient palace in Abomey where so many thousands were sacrificed in the old days. Though he has no official governmental power today, he and the various kings are treated as religious figures. Glele required us to approach him on hands and knees as a pair of three- and four-year-old princes chased each other around the room. After the introduction, our small group was invited to take seats on the floor around the throne. Two women attending the king served us each a glass of water, then, after that was drunk, Johnnie Walker Black Label neat in the same short tumblers. Serving water before alcohol is a custom in King Glele's palace that dates to the slave days. Richard Burton, who first visited Dahomey in 1840, wrote that serving a glass of water in the Dahomean court "is a sign that treachery is not intended."

Natalie Chekete, with Benin's tourism department, said distrust stemming from the slavery era profoundly affects "the way our society works today, because we can witness a loss of trust, a lack of trust, in our society. We want to dig into that period of time to document where it comes from, but we have a feeling that when you have a neighbor who looks at your family and says, 'Ah, there's some people to sell. I'm going to get them,' you start losing trust in people, all across a society. And you pass that down through the generations."

Numerous papers have been published about the continuing distrust between the tribes on each side of the slavery divide in Benin, and government officials regularly brought up concerns about that distrust at a societal level in interviews with me. They pointed to the Rwandan genocide, which was spawned by tribal resentments, and said the goal is to prevent a similar tragedy in Benin.

"People in Benin I think tend to be very peaceful," said Pastor Romain Zannou over a breakfast in Cotonou of scrambled eggs, black-eyed peas, and a dozen kinds of fruit. "You know, in families, you will have a mother or father who is a Muslim married to a Christian. This is how it was in my family. My mother, she was a Muslim. When we go to the north, all of her family are Muslim and they still welcome us. There is a such a strong interaction that there is no room for fighting. Benin is small. We are all related."

Zannou is credited with helping launch the movement for a reconciliation between the tribes on each side of the slavery divide within Benin. But the need for such a reconciliation came to him while on a trip to the United States. Zannou's personal epiphany came during a visit to a religious conference in Virginia in the early 1990s, where he was dismayed by a standoffishness he perceived among African-Americans toward him as an African. Told that it stemmed from the belief that Africans were to blame for selling American Blacks into slavery, Zannou began apologizing to Americans for the actions of his forebears. He found that it opened a pathway to new friendships. He realized that the same sort of healing was needed within Benin, for descendants there on each side of the slavery divide.

"Still today, there are families who will tell their children, 'don't go marry in this tribe, or talk to them, because in slavery, they were those who chased our ancestors,'" Zannou said. He described the situation in many villages as being "like the Berlin Wall." Yoruba families would refuse to send their children to school with Fon children, or refuse to shop in stores owned by the rival tribe. "When I spoke to them, they said the only reason they weren't killing each other was because they would go to prison."

Zannou brought a group of African-American pastors to one of the divided villages.

"They said, we have come to forgive you whose ancestors sold our ancestors. We can't keep fighting amongst ourselves," Zannou recounted. He said the idea that the descendants of Americans who had been sold would forgive those who sold them opened the door for the two tribes to begin speaking to one another. Today, thirty years later, all of the children in the village attend school together, regardless of tribe, and the divide has disappeared.

"I realized this is what the whole country needs. The whole world needs."

Newly energized, Zannou followed an order God gave him in a dream, to begin ministering to the late Mathieu Kérékou, who had ruled Benin for close to two decades. Kérékou initially came to power in a coup in 1972 and ruled as a Marxist dictator until 1991, when he called for free elections and stepped down after he lost, establishing Benin as one of Africa's successful democracies. Five years later, Kérékou returned to politics and won an election as the democratically elected leader of the nation. Zannou showed up at Kérékou's home and had a brief conversation with the president, encouraging him to embrace Christianity. The ruler wasn't interested. Undeterred, Zannou returned again and again, asking to speak to the president each time. Told the president wouldn't see him, Zannou made a habit of sitting outside the presidential compound for hours a day, hoping for a meeting. Finally, after eighteen months, his patience won out, and Kérékou agreed to meet with him, inviting him into his office saying, "Pastor, you are a very persistent man." Slowly, over the course of many months, Kérékou was converted. He became a born-again Christian and embraced Zannou's message of reconciliation.

Kérékou became reconciliation's most famous advocate during a visit to America in 1999. He made international news when, at a church in Baltimore, he dropped to his knees and asked African-Americans to forgive his nation for its role in slavery, calling it shameful and abominable.

"Benin, my country, was the most important place for slave trade. . . . We are the ones—our ancestors were the ones who sold out your ancestors to the white people, and the white people bought your ancestors and got them into various countries that they sent them just to build their economies, in the plantation, in the factories, farms, just like in America here," Kérékou said in the Church of the Great Commission. Talking to Zannou today, you can see his influence in the former president's conversion to reconciliation activist.

"I believe this can also take place at a larger scale, and it must. People who think that slavery is all sins of the past, no need for reconciliation, I think there is evidence in America that this is not true, that the sin is happening yesterday and today, not centuries ago," Zannou said. "You see that when something happens to an African-American, shot by mistake by a white police officer, you see it come back, that sin and that pain it causes, full strength again. It is there on the faces. There are those who want to ignore it, because reconciliation is not an easy path. If it were, it would have happened a long time ago. But it must be our path."

I heard a similar message a few months ago, at a celebration for a new park in Africatown, where the *Clotilda* survivors first camped out after they were freed from slavery at the end of the Civil War. There, I spoke with Jason Lewis, a master chief in the navy who grew up in the now abandoned Happy Hills housing project in Africatown. Jason has also visited Benin, describing his time there as "incredible" and "life-changing."

He was disappointed at the turnout for the park celebration.

"This is so lackluster, and that's disappointing because these are the moments that count. This is a moment like Martin Luther King sitting in someone's house planning a bus boycott, a moment that nobody cares about. But then what they planned, it ends up electrifying America. That's the kind of moment we are in right now, except we are saying, 'let's promote this story of Africatown and how our people survived,'" Lewis said. "Like the Civil Rights Movement, this is a moment of reconciliation. Money doesn't matter. Reparations are nothing. What matters is reconciliation. Reconciliation. Making peace, moving forward. And so we hope we can make this discovery electrify the world the same way Civil Rights did in Selma."

For Lewis, the discovery of the *Clotilda* has global implications.

"Whoever did what back then with the slaves, here in Mobile, or in Africa, they have a chance to say, 'I apologize for what my great-great-grandfather did.' And then we as the diaspora, we have a chance to say, 'We forgive you.' But with *Clotilda*, we have a chance to say it on a world stage, where everybody knows this is the last ship to come in, and we have a chance to have the actual descendants of the people on that ship and the actual descendants of the people who perpetrated it. We have a chance to come together and tell the world, they forgave each other," Lewis said.

But the Meaher family appear uninterested in reconciliation. In fact, they can't even reconcile rifts within their own family, rifts tied directly to the Civil War–era fortune left behind by Timothy Meaher. Timothy's three oldest descendants—brothers Joe, Gus, and Robert—have been involved in various legal disputes over the money they inherited. More recently, in 2017, Gus and his children sued Joe in circuit court, accusing him of a pattern of theft stretching back more than a decade. The court filings state that Joe cooked the company books to hide the fact that he had stolen at least $850,000 from his brother and two nieces. The case was still unresolved when Joe died in March of 2020.

Meanwhile, the Meahers have steadfastly refused since news

of the ship's discovery to have anything to do with Africatown or the descendants of the people their ancestors enslaved. I have spoken with members of the family who refuse to be quoted. They maintain that the descendants are motivated by a desire to seek reparations from them, or to sue the family for kidnapping. Jason Lewis knows of their refusal, but is undaunted. He can forgive, he says, even if they don't apologize, because he has come to understand the true legacy of the *Clotilda* survivors. They overcame almost unimaginable adversity and banded together to create a community. They took turns building each other's houses. They built a church and a school. They reconciled with their past and the people who wronged them, and they moved on.

Chapter 13

CODA

Closure is elusive. Sometimes, it comes out of the blue.

In February of 2019, nearly a year after I'd located the first ship but before the public knew about the second ship, I received an email from a retiree living in Great Falls, Montana.

"My name is Michael Foster. In the past few weeks I found out about the *Clotilda*, the last slave ship to America. I am sorry you haven't found it yet. I hope it is found. This history made me sad that an ancestor of mine participated in this, selling Africans for money, putting them into slavery."

Working through the Ancestry genealogy website, Michael Foster figured out that his great-great-great-grandfather was Captain Foster's brother. Mike reached out to me, hoping that I could connect him with any of his relatives I had encountered during my search for *Clotilda*. I told him about Foster's niece who had tried to sell the desk, chair, and clock from the *Clotilda* to the Meahers for $18,000. The woman who offered the furniture for sale ran a local dance studio, but died in 2002, shortly after donating Captain Foster's journal to the Mobile Library. I had reached out to her daughters to see if they still had the furniture from the ship with no success. Perhaps they'd respond to Mike, an actual relative. He tracked down the brother of the woman who'd donated the journal and confirmed that the family still had *Clotilda* artifacts. But once Mike suggested in an email that they should consider donating the items to a museum, the family cut off all contact.

I told Mike, a Vietnam vet, that I had another mission for him. I asked if he'd be willing to come to Mobile to meet with the descendants of those enslaved by the Meahers and his ancestor, Captain William Foster. His immediate worry was how people would receive him.

"I just don't know what to expect. Are they going to hate me? Will some of them yell at me? It's a bad thing that was done to their ancestors. I don't know what I can do but say I'm sorry," he said.

"That's exactly what they want to hear," I told him. "I think you will find an incredibly warm reception. All they talk about is reconciliation. They want to forgive."

When I told Darron Patterson, Mama Eva's great-nephew, that I'd been in contact with a Foster descendant willing to come to Africatown, he immediately asked for the phone number. The pair got on the phone and started talking. Their common language turned out to be sports. Darron is a lifelong sports journalist, and Mike's email handle begins with an acronym short for "San Francisco Sports Fan." They struck up a quick friendship and began planning Mike's visit, set to coincide with one of Africatown's major annual celebrations.

A few months later, Mike arrived in Mobile. I picked him up at his hotel, and we sat in my truck just before he was to meet a group of descendants for the first time. I asked how he was feeling. He said he was nervous and excited, but told me he had removed his wedding ring and planned not to say anything about his own family so as not to put his wife or daughters at risk in case anyone wanted "some kind of revenge against me for what my ancestor did."

Given Mike's trepidation and fear of reprisal, I was impressed he came. This first meeting was set up with eight descendants in a bar named after Cudjo Lewis called Kazoola's. Mike walked into the courtyard where they were gathered, letting out a sigh as he passed through the doorway. Seeing the group, he said, "My name is Mike Foster." Lorna Woods broke the ice right away. She walked up to him and smiled and said, "And I'm Lorna Gail Woods. Mobile, Alabama, born and raised. Do I look like myself?" Everyone laughed as she did a stagey pose, then they took turns introducing themselves and who they were descended from. I could see Mike was starting to tear up a little.

With his voice quavering, he spoke a few sentences about their ancestors being ripped from their homeland and ended with this: "Well, I'm here to say I'm sorry."

Joycelyn Davis, Lorna's niece, stepped toward Mike and smiled. "The ancestors are happy. Who would have thought this moment would happen? It's courageous of you to come. To step up, to be the one, to come and represent. This is a powerful moment."

There was some hugging and a little crying. Darron called for hamburgers to great laughter. A reconciliation had begun. The next day, Mike went to the Africatown Ancestors Festival, held at Mobile County Training School, which is built on the spot where Cudjo asked Timothy Meaher to give the Africans some of his land. Foster quietly circulated through the crowd, being introduced to more and more descendants by those he'd met at Kazoola's. He shied away from being called up onstage to speak to the four hundred or so people in the school auditorium, which Darron really wanted him to do. Mike was the first descendant of any of the main actors in the *Clotilda* story to apologize publicly, and Darron wanted to thank him in front of the crowd. But Mike demurred. As the day wore on, I think I figured out why. The emotion of the moment was starting to overwhelm him. I noticed him tearing up every time he would say, "I just want to apologize for my family's role in this," to someone he'd just met. The descendants noticed too, wrapping him in hug after hug. Mike described it later as the most moving moment of his life, other than his wedding and the birth of his children.

There was another, more private moment the next day. It was a chilly Sunday morning, and I took Mike Foster, Darron Patterson, and Garry Lumbers up the river to the shipwreck just after dawn. We left early because Garry had to catch a flight back to Philadelphia before lunch. Darron is the great-great-grandson of *Clotilda* passengers Pollee and Lucy Allen, while Garry is the great-great-grandson of Cudjo and Cecilia Lewis. Out on the river, Darron and Garry told stories about growing up in Africatown, and cracked jokes with Mike about getting old. As we drifted along the shoreline where I'd found the ship, I was hit with a sudden realization.

"It's kind of a historic moment," I said. "The last time a Foster, an Allen, and a Lewis were here together was that night the ship was burned."

Nobody said anything for a minute. Garry looked particularly stunned. "Wow! That's kind of amazing. That kind of hits home. The last time was back then. Whoa. This just made my whole trip, man."

He threw an arm around Mike, and both of them grabbed Darron.

"We're going to have a little hug here. I think we're going to cry," Mike said. "I love you guys."

"We love you too, man," Darron said. I took a picture to commemorate the moment. It looks like a trio of old guys on a fishing trip, smiling and laughing after catching a big one.

Mike called me after he got back to Montana and said he kept breaking down as he tried to tell his family about his experience. I could hear him crying over the phone.

Later the same morning I spoke to Darron, who was still on a high from the previous day's events. I asked if he'd gotten closure from finally meeting someone involved with kidnapping his forebears and hearing an apology.

"It wasn't like closure. It was like opening a brand-new door to a room I didn't even know existed. I don't know if it would be different with one of the Meahers. Mike and I, we're like two long-lost brothers who just found each other again."

Darron said he and Mike were talking about traveling to

Benin together, to walk along the old slave route and visit the spot where their ancestors' lives first intersected.

"Maybe seeing a descendant of a slave from the *Clotilda* and the descendant of the slaver who bought the people in Ouidah, seeing us together laughing and hugging, maybe that can help them heal too."

Acknowledgments

Many people in America and Benin played a role in the discovery of *Clotilda* and the subsequent revelations about the lives of those touched by its legacy, both in the past and in the modern day.

I must start with my friend Jeff Dute, who first suggested I look for the ship. His call came out of the blue, sounded fantastical, and set me on course for one of the most profound experiences of my life. Thank you for imagining that it could be done.

A group of people helped unlock Africatown's history and participated in the researching of this book. Among the descendants, Lorna Woods, her niece Joycelyn Davis, Darron Patterson, Garry Lumbers, Thelma Maiben-Owens, and Vernetta Henson were generous with their time and memories. Joe Womack, Robert Battles, Charles Hope, Cleon Jones, Jason Lewis, Anderson Flen, Tori Adams, Carolyn Adams Lewis, LeBaron Barnes,

Lamar Howard, Greg Cyprian, Eric Finley, Karlos Finley, Reverend Christopher Williams, and Willie "Junebug" Jones helped bring Africatown's past and struggle for recognition to life.

One member of the Meaher family, who has chosen to remain unidentified, provided much insight into the family and its history. But, it is a fact that the *Clotilda* remained hidden for so long because the descendants of Timothy Meaher made it so, refusing to this day to share family records and artifacts that could shed much light on their family's dark legacy. I am told by intimate family friends that the Meahers have numerous *Clotilda* artifacts in their possession, including the steering wheel of the ship. It is to their personal shame that they have shunned every invitation from the people of Africatown and the global African diaspora seeking a reconciliation.

Like most historical mysteries, this one was at least partially solved in a library, and thanks to a team of librarians, archivists, and researchers. My first call to Deborah Gurt at the University of South Alabama was a fateful one. She connected me to Elizabeth Theris at the Mobile Public Library's Local History and Genealogy annex, and the expert staff there. The trove of *Clotilda* and Africatown documents, curated over many years, contained the primary clues that led me to the spot on the river where the ship was sunk. Historian John Sledge was a constant inspiration as I hunted *Clotilda*, and he provided vital clues that led to its discovery. Judge David Bagwell helped wade through the issues surrounding ownership of the wreck, and led me to records in the federal archives related to the ship, as well as the various court cases involving Meaher and his conspirators. Maureen Hill, an archivist at the National Archives in Atlanta, rounded up boxes' worth of documents related to the *Clotilda*, everything from the ship's design to lists of every item carried aboard in the years before the final voyage to Africa. Rodney Krajca, an archivist with the National Archives in Fort Worth, managed to find all of the records related to Timothy Meaher's arrest and trial for blockade running.

A lot of people spent time on the water with me doing the fieldwork it took to find the ship, and all deserve credit. At the top of the list is Dr. Monty Graham and the hydrographic science team from the University of Southern Mississippi, including Max van Norden, Dr. Anad Hiroji, Marvin Story, Kandice Gunning, Ashley Boyce, Jennifer Rhodes, and Alex Hersperger. Their riverbed map led us to the wreck. Jason Gillikin, Eric Lowe, Winthrop Turner, and Joe Turner all accompanied me and provided their expertise during days on the river. Dr. John Batten and Dr. Greg Cook, archaeologists from the University of West Florida, participated in the search and taught me a most important lesson about perseverance when hunting for something lost. Their mantra was "You don't know if you don't go," meaning the only way to find something is to actually go out and look for it, and keep looking for it when you fail.

Dr. Sharon Ingram, the chairperson of the Alabama-Benin Trade & Cooperative Forum, was my conduit to Benin, providing invaluable connections to people there, including my excellent guide Patrice Amoussou, a multilinguist called on to speak French, English, Yoruba, Fon, and several distinct African dialects all in the space of a few minutes at certain points during our travels. Prior to my arrival, Patrice traveled all over Benin on a motorcycle, arranging meetings for me with government officials, kings, princes, and religious leaders. He connected me to people I'd never heard of who turned out to be pivotal to the telling of this story.

In Benin, Pastor Romain Zannou helped me to understand the country's religious landscape, both in the past and the present, as well as the burgeoning reconciliation movement among the tribes touched by slavery. Dada Daagbo Hunan Houna II Guely and his wife, Diwata Desir Hounon Houna II, introduced me to Vodun and hosted me at the royal palace. Ambassador Hector Posset shared the still raw emotions connected to enslavement for the African descendants of both the captured and those whose ancestors did the capturing. Natalie Blanc Chekete, Wenceslas Adjognon-Monnon, Alain Godonou, Mawunu Feliho—all with Benin's central government—were invaluable in facilitating my travels around the country and my education in Benin's history. Blaise Ahanhanzo Glele and Bruno Adjovi, the mayors of Abomey and Ouidah respectively, welcomed me to their towns and spoke eloquently of the importance of remembering all of Benin's history, even the darkest parts. As somebody who makes part of my living on the water, the day spent on a boat with Isaie Akpodji, who led me through the floating village of Ganvie, his hometown, remains indelible in my mind. Gabin Djimasse guided me around Abomey, walking part of the slave route, circling the tree of remembrance, and correcting various historical inaccuracies that have come to be accepted as truth in much of the history written about Benin. I got a taste of Benin completely removed from the official meetings and government tours thanks to Abou Ismael, a taxi driver who befriended me on the street in Cotonou. Over the course of two weeks, Abou invited me into his home to meet his family, took me to his favorite restaurants, and to meet his friends at one of Cotonou's buzzing nightclubs, where patrons broke out in a spontaneous chant of "Obama! Obama!" when they learned I was a visitor from Donald Trump's America.

Special thanks to my agent, Paul Lucas at Janklow & Nesbit, for seeing a book in my search before I'd even thought about writing one. Priscilla Painton at Simon & Schuster decided to gamble on me and offered a contract just days after it was announced that the first ship I found was not the *Clotilda*. Despite that setback, she said she had a hunch I'd find it, and that the bumps along the way (like finding the wrong ship!) would just make the finished tale more satisfying. My editor, Hana Park, worked to make every page better as she helped reveal the powerful story inherent in *Clotilda*'s legacy. My sincere gratitude to my lifelong friend Will Thach, whose life was shaped by his experiences during the Rwandan genocide. Will traveled with me to Benin, helped capture the stories we heard there, and served as the first reader of this manuscript. Shannon and Jasper, my wife and son, supported me even when my hunt for the ship meant I lost my job at the newspaper I'd worked at for decades. Their encouragement made all the difference.

Notes

Chapter 1: The Bet

1 *edging toward war*: Romeyn, *Little Africa*.

2 *"large, well-ventilated cabins"*: Roche, *Historic Sketches of the South*, p. 96.

3 *"and all its citizens"*: Fuller, *Belle Brittan on a Tour*, p. 112.

4 *enslaved people in the South*: Letter from William H. Woodberry to Mr. Donaldson, Mobile Library Collection, October 20, 1890, http://digital.mobilepubliclibrary.org/items/show/1829.

4 *solidifying against the practice*: Romeyn, *Little Africa*.

5 *"under the officers' noses"*: Samuel Byers, "The Last Slave Ship," *Harper's Magazine*, 1906, p. 744.

6 *the most northern of the slave states*: Amos, *Cotton City*, p. 85.

6 *as they were in Virginia*: Letter from Alfred Witherspoon to Tariffa Witherspoon, Henry Cocke Papers, Spring Hill College, 1859.

6 *$1,800 each at auction*: *Mobile Daily Register*, November 8, 1859.

7 *16 billion pounds . . . today*: David Olusoga, "The History of British Slave Ownership Has Been Buried: Now Its Scale Can Be Revealed," *Guardian*, July 11, 2015, https://www.theguardian.com/world/2015/jul/12/british-history-slavery-buried-scale-revealed.

7 *nations engaged in slavery*: Dickey, *Our Man in Charleston*, p. 25.

7 *caught with loads of captives*: Jim Jordan, "Charles Augustus Lafayette Lamar and the Movement to Reopen the African Slave Trade," *Georgia Historical Quarterly* 93, no. 3 (Fall 2009): 263, https://www.jstor.org/stable/27809120?read-now=1&seq=18#metadata_info_tab_contents.

8 *"holier 'than what is written'"*: British and Foreign State Papers, Volume 45, 1854–55, https://babel.hathitrust.org/cgi/pt?id=mdp.35112204235248&view=1up&seq=1188.

8 *Cotton Fields: probable result*: Dickey, *Our Man in Charleston*, p. 83.

9 *the legal penalty was death*: Lalor, *Cyclopaedia of Political Science*.

12 *headed for Nicaragua*: Roche, *Historic Sketches of the South*, p. 70.

13 *by his father, Gazaway*: Jordan, "Charles Augustus Lafayette Lamar," pp. 247–290.

13 *"a cautious man, too"*: Borchers, *Thomas Lamar*, p. 132.

13 *his uncle in a fight*: Jordan, "*Charles Augustus Lafayette Lamar*," pp. 247–290.

14 *"as he pleases," Lamar wrote*: "A Slave-Trader's Letter-Book." *North American Review* 143, no. 360 (1886): 447–61. http://www.jstor.org/stable/25101128.

14 *the Middle Passage*: Jordan, "*Charles Augustus Lafayette Lamar*," p. 273.

14 *Africa from the port*: Lalor, *Cyclopaedia of Political Science*.

15 *"the Southern country"*: Dickey, *Our Man in Charleston*, page 100.

15 *"the federal government"*: The African Repository 35 (January 1859): 30, https://books.google.com/books?id=wrIVLxvh1F8C&pg=PA30&lpg=PA30&dq=africans+in+alabama+wanderer+new+york+times&source=bl&ots=YYR7jmn6ip&sig=ACfU3U0TA9bRcL_XZvxelzCr2oM3aHwtpA&hl=en&sa=X&ved=2ahUKEwiK_-Gq48TlAhVnk-AKHVnCAMsQ6AEwDXoECAgQAQ#v=onepage&q=africans%20in%20alabama%20wanderer%20new%20york%20times&f=false.

15 *the ship of slaving*: Jordan, "Charles Augustus Lafayette Lamar," p. 280.

16 *arrest and a fine of $250*: Ibid., p. 284.

16 *"Go Unpunished"*: "His Associates Go Unpunished," *New York Times*, May 29, 1860, p. 8.

16 *Washington in the eye*: "A Slave-Trader's Letter-Book."

17 *back in Maine*: "Death of Capt. Tim Meaher, Venerable Steamboat Man," *Mobile Daily Adverstiser and Register*, March 4, 1892.

17 *migrated south*: Diouf, *Dreams of Africa in Alabama*, p. 9.

17 *Alabama's largest city, by far*: Amos, *Cotton City*, p. xvi.

19 *"Kew might envy"*: Russell, *My Diary North and South*, p. 190.

22 *"American scientific racism"*: Dr. Scott Trafton, "Introduction to Types of Mankind," http://chnm.gmu.edu/egyptomania/sources.php?function=detail&articleid=39.

22 *"the horse and the ass"*: Darnell, ed., *Histories of Anthropologies Annual*, p. 142.

22 *"in a state of slavery"*: Ibid, "Statistics of Southern Slave Population with Especial Reference to Life Insurance," p. 141.

Chapter 2: The Voyage of the Clotilda

25 *like the* Clotilda: "Last Cargo of Slaves," *Globe-Democrat*, November 30, 1890, http://digital.mobilepubliclibrary.org/items/show/1793; Byers, "The Last Slave Ship."

26 *she could carry*: Vessel License for Schooner Clotilda, 1855, National Archives at Atlanta.

26 *and various plants*: *Clotilda Import Manifests*, 1860, Box 93, National Archives at Atlanta.

27 *"prove a fast sailer"*: *Mobile Daily Advertiser*, October 17, 1855.

29 *slavery was still legal*: "Chasing Freedom Information Sheet," http://www.royalnavalmuseum.org/visit_see_victory_cfexhibition_infosheet.htm.

29 *with 1,432 enslaved Africans on board*: *A Century of Lawmaking for a New Nation: U.S. Congressional Documents and Debates, 1774–1875, African Slave Trade*, p. 646, http://international.loc.gov/cgi-bin/ampage?collId=llss&fileName=1000/1095/llss1095.db&recNum=669.

30 *De Ronceray concluded*: *Enclosure with Consul De Ronceray's despatch* [*sic*]. *Key West, July 8, 1860*, Library of Congress, http://international.loc.gov/cgi-bin/ampage?collId=llss&fileName=1000/1095/llss1095.db&recNum=669.

30 *of the voyage itself*: William Foster, *The Last Slaver from U.S. to Africa, A.D. 1860*, 1892, Mobile Library, *Clotilda* Collection, http://digital.mobilepubliclibrary.org/items/show/1802.

31 *"rascality in general"*: Byers, "The Last Slave Ship."

33 *"the coast for export"*: Roche, *Historic Sketches of the South*, 73; *Mobile Daily Register*, November 9, 1858.

33 *to the true course*: Ibid., p. 84.

34 *"sprung main boom and other damages"*: Foster, *The Last Slaver*.

35 *"the most exciting race I ever saw"*: Ibid.

35 *"However, I made a bargain with my crew"*: Ibid.

36 *during the voyage*: Roche, *Historic Sketches of the South*, p. 85.

36 *"cargoes of Africans"*: *Enclosure with Consul De Ronceray's despatch* [*sic*], *Key West, July 8, 1860*, Library of Congress, http://international.loc.gov/cgi-bin/ampage?collId=llss&fileName=1000/1095/llss1095.db&recNum=669.

36 *load of red palm oil*: Hurston, *Barracoon*, p. 7.

36 *cover for the voyage*: Romeyn, *Little Africa*, p. 14.

37 *make all his runs*: *Clotilda Import Manifests*, 1860, Box 93, National Archives at Atlanta.

37 *"I thought she would intercept us"*: Foster, *The Last Slaver*.

37 *"The sea rolling at a fearful height"*: Ibid.

38 *up onto the deck*: Romeyn, *Little Africa*.

38 *"darted through waves like fish"*: Foster, *The Last Slaver*.

38 *the passengers on board*: Roche, *Historic Sketches of the South*, p. 85.

39 *"imminent risk of life"*: "Slave Dealer of 1690," *Cornhill Magazine* 14 (London: Smith, Elder and Co.): 254, https://books.google.com/books?id=B7gCAAAAIAAJ&pg=PA255&lpg=PA255&dq=Slave+Dealer+of+1690+Cornhill+Magazine&source=bl&ots=A_9NKXCaxd&sig=ACfU3U12HiGeHTAba0iIRi1yTMZYkBP9cg&hl=en&sa=X&ved=2ahUKEwiusYeL6N_lAhWBmOAKHeMnDy0Q6AEwAHoE

CAgQAQ#v=onepage&q=Slave%20Dealer%20of%201690%20Corn
hill%20Magazine&f=false.

Chapter 3: The King of the Amazons

41   *popularized in the next one hundred years*: Forbes, *Dahomey and the Da-homans*, p. 6.

42   *most unusual combat force*: Ibid, p. 23.

42   *would know her secret*: Natalie Checkette, Benin's National Agency for the Promotion of Heritage and the Development of Tourism, interview with the author, December 11, 2019.

43   *"in its merciless progress"*: Forbes, *Dahomey and the Dahomans*, p. 6.

44   *"cutting off heads"*: Ibid., p. 19.

44   *"leaving them exposed"*: Ibid., pp. 27–28.

45   *"and business seems brisk"*: Burton, *Mission to Gelele, King of Dahome*, p. 77.

45   *"the beauty of the prospect"*: "Slave Dealer of 1690."

45   *"wound around their necks"*: Foster, *The Last Slaver*.

46   *"a distinctly cucumber shaped shin"*: Burton, *Mission to Gelele*, p. 223.

46   *"manly and stalwart form"*: Ibid., p. 238.

46   *"Mohammed the apostle"*: Ibid., p. 241.

47   *"respect to the superior"*: Ibid., p. 253.

47   *"fill four ships"*: "Slave Dealer of 1690."

47   *"after detaining me eight days"*: Foster, *The Last Slaver*.

47   *"wisdom and exalted taste"*: Roche, *Sketches of the South*, p. 86.

48   *"My people sold me and your people bought me"*: Ibid., p. 86.

Chapter 4: Captured

49   *he adopted during slavery*: Roche, *Historic Sketches of the South*, p. 124.

51   *beer from banana mash*: Zora Neale Hurston, "Cudjo's Own Story of the Last African Slaver," *Journal of African American History* 12, no. 4 (October 1927): 651, https://www.journals.uchicago.edu/doi/abs/10.2307/2714041.

51   *to enter or leave*: Ibid., p. 651.

52   *the protective enclosure*: Hurston, *Barracoon*, p. 40.

52   *also had slaves*: Ibid., p. 23.

54   *"all day and not be tired"*: Ibid., p. 40.

54   *"let us fix a banquet for him"*: Ibid., p. 41.

55   *peacock feather*: Ibid., p. 42.

55   *the woman's parents*: Ibid., p. 22.

56   *Glele will attack*: Ibid., p. 44.

57   *war party set out*: Diouf, *Dreams of Africa in Alabama*, p. 46.

57   *"the yet living victim"*: Burton, *Mission to Gelele*, p. 257.

59   *on display in court*: Ibid., p. 256.

59   *"wid dem to Dahomey"*: Hurston, *Barracoon*, p. 46.

59　*"smokin' on de stick"*: Ibid., p. 49

60　*"made out of skull bones"*: Ibid., p. 52.

61　*Djimasse said*: Gabin Djimasse, interview with the author, Abomey, Benin, December 15, 2019.

61　*Cabinda, Angola*: Diouf, *Dreams of Africa in Alabama*, p. 51.

Chapter 5: Barracoon

64　*groups in large pens*: Foster, *The Last Slaver*.

65　*delays had left him nervous*: Ibid.

66　*"apart from one 'nother"*: Hurston, *Barracoon*, p. 54

66　*"Captain Foster spied me"*: Roche, *Historic Sketches of the South*. p. 113.

66　*"dey turn around and takee me"*: Hurston, *Barracoon*, p. 54.

67　*from another tribe*: Ibid., p. 164, note 6.

68　*"when they caught me"*: "Last Slave Ship Sunk Here Raised," *Mobile Register*, February 25, 1917, p. 12A, http://digital.mobilepubliclibrary.org/items/show/1792.

68　*"Man aloft with glass sang out"*: Foster, *The Last Slaver*.

69　*forced them to raise sail*: Romeyn, *Little Africa*.

69　*groups of six or eight*: S. L. Flock, "Survivor of Last Slave Cargo Lives on Plantation Near Selma," *Montgomery Advertiser*, January 31, 1932, p. 13, https://www.newspapers.com/clip/30441005/redoshi-renamed-sally-smith-last/.

69　*"bottom of de sea"*: Hurston, *Barracoon*, p. 55.

70　*"The negroes are packed below"*: Lieutenant T. Augustus Craven, *Executive Documents, Printed by order of the U.S. House of Representatives, During the second session of the Thirty Sixth Congress, 1860-'61*, p. 619.

71　*"It was frequently done"*: Percy Taylor, *Dothan Eagle*, December 4, 1935, p. 4, https://www.newspapers.com/image/538933651/?terms=Cudjo%2B lewis.

71　*up to fourteen knots per hour*: Foster, *The Last Slaver*.

72　*"we doan know"*: Hurston, *Barracoon*, p. 56.

74　*in wait for* Clotilda: Roche, *Historic Sketches of the South*, p. 92.

75　*twenty miles away*: Foster, *The Last Slaver*.

76　*the tugboat Billy Jones*: Romeyn, *Little Africa*, 1897.

77　*the ship at 9 p.m.*: Foster, *The Last Slaver*.

77　*a swarm of bees*: Roche, *Historic Sketches of the South*, p. 96.

79　*according to his wife*: Ibid., p. 97.

80　*"I transferred my slaves"*: Foster, *The Last Slaver*.

80　*much closer to Mobile*: Hurston, "Cudjo's Own Story."

81　*"wholly non-committal"*: "Last Cargo of Slaves," *St. Louis Globe-Democrat*, November 30, 1890, Mobile Public Library Digital Collections, http://digital.mobilepubliclibrary.org/items/show/1793.

Chapter 6: Into the Canebrake

84   *"four inches in diameter"*: Bartram, *Travels Through North and South Carolina*, p. 328.

84   *their foreign tongues*: Hurston, "Cudjo's Own Story."

85   *"rags an' pieces er corn sack"*: Scott, Mary McNeil, "Affika Town," *Wilcox Progress*, June 6, 1894, https://www.newspapers.com/image/308670655/?terms=affika%2Btown.

85   *"and vide us up"*: Hurston, *Barracoon*, p. 56.

86   *"by the same course"*: *Mobile Register*, July 14, 1860.

87   *captives from abroad*: "Annual Report of the Anti-Slavery Society," American Anti-Slavery Society, 1860, p. 29, https://hdl.handle.net/2027/nyp.334 33081995288?urlappend=%3Bseq=37).

88   *half in the canebrake*: Byers, "The Last Slave Ship"; Romeyn, "Little Africa."

89   *"chickens or geese"*: Roche, *Historic Sketches of the South*, p. 99

91   *Fon word for "elephant!"*: Ibid., p. 100.

91   *Cudjo told Roche*: Ibid., p. 57.

92   *were dismissed*: Final Record, U.S. District Court Southern District of Alabama, *United States vs. Burns Meaher, United States vs. John Dabney*, Federal Archives, Atlanta.

93   *ever paid the fine*: Admiralty Docket, U.S. District Court, Southern District of Alabama, January–April 1860, March–April 1866.

93   *"more cruel than death"*: "A Slave Captain to Be Hanged," *Telegram and Gazette*, December 7, 1861, pg. 1, https://web.archive.org/web/20041 115224136/http://www.letterscivilwar.com/12-7-61-slave_captain.html.

Chapter 7: Five Years a Slave

95   *most trusted servants*: Mary McNeil Scott, "Affika Town," *Wilcox Progress*, June 6, 1894, https://www.newspapers.com/image/308670655/?terms =affika%2Btown.

96   *"dem Affikins no more"*: Ibid.

96   *Cudjo told Hurston*: Hurston, *Barracoon*, p. 59.

97   *"bring 'em to de plantation"*: Scott, "Affika Town."

98   *"'I gittee you some mo' "*: Hurston, *Barracoon*, p. 60.

98   *as the sun set*: Roche, *Historic Sketches of the South*, p. 102.

98   *"We cry 'cause we slave"*: Hurston, *Barracoon*, p. 60.

98   *even one hundred years later*: Joycelyn Davis, interview with the author, May 2019.

98   *"say nothin' to us"*: Hurston, *Barracoon*, p. 62.

99   *"keep making yams"*: Hurston, "Cudjo's Own Story."

99   *"work, work, work"*: Roche, *Historic Sketches of the South*, p. 101.

101   *"he hitee you too"*: Hurston, *Barracoon*, p. 61.

101 *"tracings of tattoo marks"*: Russell, *My Diary North and South*, p. 188.

102 *"face of the Airth"*: Ibid., p. 189.

103 *"into their hungry maws"*: Ibid., p. 186.

103 *"I workee so hard"*: Hurston, *Barracoon*, p. 61.

104 *Liverpool in 1850*: Homans Smith, *Merchants' Magazine and Commercial Review* 45 (1861), p. 9. https://books.google.com/books?id=kAAd AAAAIAAJ&pg=PA9&lpg=PA9&dq=how+much+did+a+cotton+bale +weigh+in+1850&source=bl&ots=dUlKulr69c&sig=ACfU3U1Ue_Ym vUsWenHRMHJDDLUSP27yhA&hl=en&sa=X&ved=2ahUKEwjC3r PAlfTmAhWDGs0KHeP1C8gQ6AEwEnoECAgQAQ#v=onepage&q= how%20much%20did%20a%20cotton%20bale%20weigh%20in%20 1850&f=false.

105 *"on the berth deck"*: Frederick Law Olmsted, *The Cotton Kingdom*, p. 214.

105 *"must suffer exceedingly"*: Russel, *My Diary North and South*, p. 187.

105 *"squabble 'mongst deyselves"*: Scott, "Affika Town."

106 *Sylviane Diouf*: Interview with the author, August 2019.

106 homeland as *"A'tarco"*: Romeyn, *Little Africa*.

107 *"hit sho wuz"*: Scott, "Affika Town."

108 *in the historical record*: Hannah Dorman, "Finding Last Middle Passage Survivor Sally 'Redoshi' Smith on the Page and Screen," *Slavery & Abolition* 40, no. 4: pp. 631–658, https://www.tandfonline.com/doi/full/10.108 0/0144039X.2019.1596397?scroll=top&needAccess=true.

108 *"better talker than Cudjoe"*: Ibid.

109 *"a gracious Southern lady"*: S. L. Flock, "Survivor of Last Slave Cargo Lives on Plantation Near Selma," *Montgomery Advertiser*, January 31, 1932, p. 13.

109 *movement in that* city: Robinson, *Bridge Across Jordan*, 1991, p. 67.

111 *with freedom so close*: Dennison, *A Memoir of Lottie Dennison*, p. 38.

113 *three blockade runners were captured*: Cochran, *Blockade Runners of the Civil War*, p. 8.

114 *"for that purpose"*: Official Records of the Union and Confederate Navies in the War of Rebellion, *Report of Commodore Thatcher, U.S. Navy, forwarding the prize steamer Red Jacket, alias Grey Jacket, captured December 31, 1863*, Series 1, Volume 20, 1905, p. 753, https://books.google .com/books?id=pj1KAQAAMAAJ&pg=PA753&lpg=PA753&dq=us+na vy+grey+jacket+capture&source=bl&ots=JjWcUXXAIX&sig=ACfU3U 2vl_xYcXHD6I4EaCqJ-T2aUs6PCw&hl=en&sa=X&ved=2ahUKEwi4m Z6zmPfmAhVMKqwKHZMrCqUQ6AEwCnoECAkQAQ#v=onepage& q=us%20navy%20grey%20jacket%20capture&f=false.

115 *"and defeat his object"*: U.S. Supreme Court, *Steamer Grey Jacket vs. the United States*, December 1866, no. 84, p. 2, Fort Worth Archives.

116   *"had no redeeming feature"*: Cases Argued and Decided in the Su-
       preme Court of the United States, Volume 18, pp. 795–808, https://
       books.google.com/books?id=8-2QybslrLIC&pg=PA646&lpg=PA64
       6&dq=grey+jacket+timothy+meaher+us+supreme+court&source=b
       l&ots=l3se2M3fR0&sig=ACfU3U3qs_e2iVsuHbaY3MLxsZuTv3D
       -Bg&hl=en&sa=X&ved=2ahUKEwj54dGi4-DwAhXDVs0KHf27A sUQ
       6AEwEXoECBIQAw#v=onepage&q=grey%20jacket%20timothy%20
       meaher%20us%20supreme%20court&f=false.

118   *"surrender or retreat"*: Andrews, *History of the Campaign of Mobile*, pp.
       199–200.

119   *"not getting their share"*: Sledge, *The Mobile River*, p. 154, quoting Rix,
       Incidents of Life in a Southern City During the War (Mobile, AL: Iberville
       Historical Society Papers, 1865), pp. 19–22.

119   *"no mo' slave"*: Hurston, *Barracoon*, p. 63.

120   *"white livered brethren"*: Sledge, *The Mobile River*, p. 155.

120   *"We cain stay wid de folks"*: Hurston, *Barracoon*, p. 65.

Chapter 8: An African Town

123   *aboard the steamboat*: William Lochiel Cameron, "The Battles Opposite
       Mobile," *Confederate Veteran* 23: 306, https://archive.org/details/confed
       erateveter23conf/page/306.

123   *"his army affiliation"*: Dennison, *Biographical Memoirs of James Denni-
       son*, p. 42.

124   *"'for dem neither'"*: Hurston, *Barracoon*, p. 66.

125   *unclear from whom*: Roche, *Historic Sketches of the South*, p. 114.

125   *"Dey raise de garden"*: Hurston, *Barracoon*, p. 67.

125   *appeared in the press*: Scott, "Affika Town."

125   *African home villages*: Robertson, *The Slave Ship Clotilda*, p. 162

125   *their collective goal*: Hurston, *Barracoon*, p. 67.

126   *"government of the nation"*: Washington, *The Story of the Negro*, Vol. II,
       p. 28.

126   *"nothin' 'ginst us"*: Hurston, *Barracoon*, p. 66.

126   *"My people sold me and your people bought me"*: Roche, *Historic Sketches
       of the South*, p. 126.

128   *"how to behave ourselves"*: Hurston, *Barracoon*, p. 68.

128   *the decisions were just*: Ibid., p. 118.

129   *"by our current generation"*: Robertson, *The Slave Ship Clotilda*, p. 152.

129   *he said*: Ibid., p. 68.

130   *"buildee ourself a home"*: Hurston, *Barracoon*, p. 67.

130   *"give you property upon property"*: Roche, *Historic Sketches of the South*,
       p. 116.

131   *"Dey doan take off one five cent"*: Ibid., p. 68.

132   *"we got to stay"*: Hurston, *Barracoon*, p. 68.

132   *Timothy's death in 1892*: Mobile Probate Court, Land Registry map, 1920, St. Louis Tract, p. 18.

133   *plums, garlic, and okra*: Robertson, *The Slave Ship Clotilda*, p. 160.

133   *he'd learned in Africa*: Ibid., p. 159.

134   *"the social relations of life"*: Linden, *Voices from the Reconstruction Years*, p. 201.

134   *from voting Republican*: Roche, *Historic Sketches of the South*, p. 119.

135   *from the polling place*: Historic Chattahoochee Commission, 1979, Historical marker, intersection of U.S. Highway 82 and Barbour County Road 49 near Comer, Alabama.

135   *Meaher sneered*: Roche, *Historic Sketches of the South*, p. 119.

135   *and voted Republican*: Ibid., p. 120.

136   *he told Hurston*: Hurston, *Barracoon*, p. 73.

137   *"He was Cu Jo, dead and reborn"*: Daagbo Hounon Guely, interview by author, December 14, 2019.

137   *"might remember them"*: Roche, *Historic Sketches of the South*, p. 121.

137   *Uncle Charlie and Uncle Cudjo*: cudjolewisfamily.org.

138   *"never call me Eva"*: Chris McFadyen, "Legacy of a 'Peculiar Institution,'" *Azalea City News and Review*, September 15, 1983.

138   *"Yeah, I kin work for you"*: Hurston, *Barracoon*, pp. 71–72.

139   *"join de church"*: Ibid., p. 69.

139   *"mixee wid de other folks what laught at us"*: Ibid.

139   *next to Cudjo's house*: McFadyen, "Legacy of a 'Peculiar Institution.'"

140   *"much worn New Testament"*: Roche, *Historic Sketches of the South*, p. 125.

140   *"right back in church"*: McFadyen, "Legacy of a 'Peculiar Institution.'"

140   *"We Afficans try raise our chillun right"*: Hurston, *Barracoon*, p 74.

142   *"honesty and industry"*: *Mobile Daily Advertiser and Register*, March 4, 1892.

142   *"spoken of so often"*: Scott, "Affika Town."

143   *"woman's legitimate province"*: Eagle, *The Congress of Women*, pp. 131–134.

144   *" 'to her shipmates' "*: Roche, *Historic Sketches of the South*, p. 127.

144   *"cabins of the country"*: Romeyn, *Little Africa*.

145   *"where they reside"*: Ibid.

145   *" 'owrran k-nee ra ra k-nee ro ro' "*: Hurston, *Barracoon*, p. 74.

146   *screens became common*: Margaret Humphries, "How Four Once Common Diseases Were Eliminated from the American South," *Health Affairs* 28, no. 6, https://www.healthaffairs.org/doi/full/10.1377/hlthaff.28.6.1734.

146   *"but I cry too"*: Hurston, *Barracoon*, p. 74.

146   *entranceway of the house*: Diouf, *Dreams of Africa in Alabama*, p. 117.

147   *from African-Americans*: Wayne Flynt, "Alabama's Shame: The Historical

Origins of the 1901 Constitution," *Alabama Law Review* 53 (2001): 70, https://www.law.ua.edu/pubs/lrarticles/Volume%2053/Issue%201/Flynt.pdf.

147   *"If we would have white supremacy"*: State of Alabama Constitutional Convention 1901, Document 2, Address of Hon. John B. Knox, May 22, 1901, p. 7.

147   *those who lost out*: Ibid., p. 75.

148   *"de Affiky savages"*: Hurston, *Barracoon*, p. 74

149   *murdered man*: Diouf, *Dreams of Africa in Alabama*, p. 190.

149   *deep underground*: Journal of the House of Representatives, State of Alabama, 1896–1897, p. 652.

150   *died each year*: Blackmon, *Slavery by Another Name*.

150   *about $13 million today*: John Craig Stewart, "The Governors of Alabama," State of Alabama, 1975, p. 154, http://digital.archives.alabama.gov/cdm/singleitem/collection/voices/id/4485/rec/2.

150   *"in every respect"*: Letter from Edward M. Robinson to Governor Joseph F. Johnson, July 25, 1900, http://digital.archives.alabama.gov/cdm/singleitem/collection/voices/id/4485/rec/2.

150   *"fury and destruction"*: Letter of Messrs. JJ Parker and Samuel B. Browne to Governor Joseph F. Johnson, July 25, 1900, http://digital.archives.alabama.gov/cdm/singleitem/collection/voices/id/4485/rec/2.

151   *"His mama never leave him"*: Hurston, *Barracoon*, p. 76.

151   *"The community in general"*: Ibid., p. 165.

151   *had been murdered*: Ibid., p. 166.

153   *the mill any longer*: Ibid., p. 81.

154   *on the creekbank*: Robertson, *The Slave Ship Clotilda*, p. 159.

154   *"So many de folks dey hate my boy"*: Hurston, *Barracoon*, p. 88.

155   *"together in de graveyard"*: Ibid.

155   *"De house was full"*: Ibid., p. 89.

155   *"Den I jes lak I come from de Afficky soil"*: Ibid, p. 91.

156   *"dey know I lonely"*: Ibid., p. 92.

156   *"a much mended one"*: Roche, *Historic Sketches of the South*, pp. 123–124.

157   *"Cudjo finished"*: Hurston, *Barracoon*, p. 99.

157   *sweet to give them*: Ibid., p. 24.

157   *clothes and paper bags*: Eric Overbey, Doy Leale McCall Rare Book and Manuscript Library, University of South Alabama.

158   *"with brains and vision"*: M. Nathan Work, *Negro Year Book and Annual Encyclopedia of the Negro* (Tuskegee, Negro Yearbook Co., 1912), https://hdl.handle.net/2027/hvd.32044009670290?urlappend=%3Bseq=14.

158   *in the nation*: Ibid., p. 14.

159   *laborers doing the work*: Sledge, *The Mobile River*, p. 190.

159   *quarters for ten teachers*: Mobile County Training School Alumni website, http://www.mctswhippets.org/?page_id=325.

160 *"owed to society"*: Ascoli, *Julius Rosenwald*, p. 54.

160 *"between the two races"*: Booker T. Washington, "The Fruits of Industrial Training," *Atlantic*, October 1903, https://www.theatlantic.com/magazine/ archive/1903/10/the-fruits-of-industrial-training/531030/.

160 *teachers in Africatown*: "The Rosenwald School Program," Sears Archives, http://www.searsarchives.com/history/questions/rosenwald.htm.

161 *the state of Alabama*: Joseph Womack, "Africatown's High School—The Cradle of Mobile's Black Education," *Bridge the Gulf*, June 11, 2017, https://bridgethegulfproject.org/blog/2017/africatowns-high-school-cradle -mobiles-black-education.

162 *"where I want to be"*: Hurston, *Barracoon*, p. 89.

163 *"regarding the past"*: Percy Taylor, "The Last Slave," *Dothan Eagle*, December 4, 1935, p. 4, https://www.newspapers.com/image/538933651/?terms =Cudjo%2Blewis.

163 *he had memorized*: Emma Roche, "Last Survivor of Slave Ship Deeply Grateful to God, Man," *Mobile Press-Register*, August 18, 1935, http:// digital.mobilepubliclibrary.org/items/show/2195.

163 *"After he was too weak"*: Ibid.

163 *"Lord! God! I thank Thee"*: Ibid.

Chapter 9: Africatown—The Fall

167 *Black at night*: Lorna Woods, interview with the author, November 14, 2019.

168 *available for rent*: Tori Adams, interview with the author, January 22, 2020.

168 *"That's where the residents went to hunt"*: Joe Womack, interview with the author, June, 15, 2020.

170 *"There was little white stuff"*: Garry Lumbers, interview with author, February 9, 2020.

170 *"The stuff on the cars"*: Darron Patterson, interview with author, June 15, 2019.

171 *pave the streets*: Joe Womack, interview with the author, May 30, 2019.

173 *"running water and sewers"*: Roger Rapaport, "Grandson of Slave Ship Captain Rents Houses to Negro Families," *Southern Courier*, June 17, 1967, http://www.southerncourier.org/standard/Vol3_No25_1967_06_17 .pdf.

173 *"Wouldn't know how to use it"*: Jonathan Gordon, "Hard Times for Poor Folks," *Southern Courier*, March 16–17, 1968, http://www.southerncourier .org/standard/Vol4_No11_1968_03_16.pdf.

173 *as early as 1905*: Jay Reeves, "America's Last Slave Ship Could Offer a Case For Reparations," Associated Press, October 5, 2019.

174 *"People in houses next to giant plants"*: Joseph Womack, interview with author, May 30, 2019.

174 *"I ain't got no feelings about the Meahers"*: LeBaron Barnes, interview with author, March 9, 2018.

175 *"When the crack epidemic happened"*: Lamar Howard, interview with author, June 12, 2019.

177 *"There were lots of houses"*: Joseph Womack, interview with author, May 30, 2019.

178 *"The neighborhoods have become"*: Tori Adams, interview by author, January 22, 2020.

180 *"I can remember growing up"*: Joseph Womack, video interview, Africatown Storytelling and Pollution Concerns, April 2014, https://bridgethe gulfproject.org/blogs/joe-womack?page=2.

181 *"Was it a terrible odor?"*: Joseph Womack, interview with author, May 30, 2019.

182 *1988 is stunning*: Toxic Release Inventory, U.S. Environmental Protection Agency, https://enviro.epa.gov/triexplorer/release_chem?p_view=ZPCH&t rilib=TRIQ1&sort=_VIEW_&sort_fmt=1&state=&city=&spc=&zipcode =36610&zipsrch=yes&chemical=All+chemicals&industry=ALL&year=1 988&tab_rpt=1&fld=AIRLBY&fld=E1&fld=E2&fld=E3&fld=E52&fld= E53&fld=E54&fld=E51&fld=TSFDSP&fld=m10&fld=m41&fld=m62& fld=potwmetl&fld=m71&fld=m72&fld=m73&fld=m79&fld=m90&fld= m94&fld=m99&fld=on.

182 *"As time went on"*: Joseph Womack, interview with author, May 30, 2019.

183 *"If you're doing funerals every weekend"*: Christopher Williams, interview with author, June 20, 2019.

183 *"The more people we met"*: Raoul Richardson, interview with author, November 15, 2019.

184 *"I'll be honest with you"*: M. Allam Baheth, interview with author, November 15, 2019.

185 *"The soil samples show"*: Ibid.

185 *"until it was too late"*: Raoul Richardson, interview with author, November 15, 2019.

189 *"When the dump was active"*: Eric Finley, Interview with author, December 6, 2019.

190 *Pascagoula, Mississippi*: Glynn Wilson, "Mobile Alabama's Historic Africatown at Risk from Tar Sands Oil Storage Tanks, Pipelines," *New American Journal*, March 8, 2014, https://www.newamericanjournal.net/2014/03/mo bile-alabamas-africatown-at-risk-from-tar-sands-storage-tanks-pipelines/.

191 *"The city has conspired"*: Joseph Womack, interview with author, May 30, 2019.

Chapter 10: Finding Clotilda

192 *"the importer of the last cargo"*: "Last of the Slave Traders," *New York Times*, March 4, 1892, https://timesmachine.nytimes.com/timesmachine /1892/03/04/104119744.html?pageNumber=5.

194 *life of about twenty-five years*: James Delgado, James, interview with the author, March 3, 2018.

198 *caught my eye*: "Last Cargo of Slaves," *Globe-Democrat*, November 30, 1890, http://digital.mobilepubliclibrary.org/items/show/1793.

198 *from the* Clotilda: "Fort Gaines Museum Acquires 'Anchor Eye' of Last Slave Schooner," *Alabama on the Go*, June 1965, p. 29, http://digital.mobile publiclibrary.org/items/show/1795.

199 *on the Mobile River*: Foster, *The Last Slaver*.

202 *"burned to the waterline"*: "Last Slave Ship Sunk Here Raised," *Mobile Register*, February 25, 1917, p. 12A, http://digital.mobilepubliclibrary.org/items/show/1792.

Chapter 11: Finding a Future in the Past

212 *"Everybody's looking at us"*: Lorna Woods, interview with author, January 26, 2018.

215 *or anything else*: https://gullahgeecheecorridor.org/thegullahgeechee/.

217 *in world history*: Robertson, *The Slave Ship Clotilda and the Making of Africatown, USA*; p. 1.

217 *"about their identity"*: John Smith video from Benin broadcast, https://www.youtube.com/watch?v=INsCBKUvBIQ.

219 *"spend time and learn the history"*: Vicki Howell, interview with author, February 20, 2020.

221 *"ships just like that"*: Lamar Howard, interview with author, June 12, 2019.

223 *with established facts*: McFadyen, "Legacy of a 'Peculiar Institution.'"

223 *"it was passed down"*: Sylviane Diouf, interview with the author, August 21, 2019.

224 *"I heard so many things"*: Garry Lumbers, interview with author, February 9, 2020.

224 *"our own history"*: Cleon Jones, interview with author, May 30, 2019.

Chapter 12: Reconciliation

228 *if they are Fon*: Romain Zanou, interview with the author, December 19, 2019.

231 *"sent them away forever"*: Nathalie Chekete, interview with author, December 12, 2019.

236 *"for this dirty thing"*: Kevin Sieff, "An African Country Reckons with Its History of Selling Slaves," *Washington Post*, January 29, 2018.

239 *"is not intended"*: Burton, *Mission to Gelele*, p. 37.

239 *"down through the generations"*: Nathalie Chekete, interview with author, December 12, 2019.

242 *the Great Commission*: Sani, *Hatred for Black People*, p. 235.

Bibliography

Andrews, Christopher Columbus. *History of the Campaign of Mobile: Including the Coöperative Operations of Gen. Wilson's Cavalry In Alabama*. New York: Van Nostrand, 1889.

Amos, Harriet. *Cotton City: Urban Development in Antebellum Mobile*. Tuscaloosa: The University of Alabama Press, 1985.

Ascoli, Peter M. *Julius Rosenwald: The Man Who Built Sears, Roebuck and Advanced the Cause of Black Education in the American South*. Bloomington: University of Indiana Press, 2006.

Bartram, William. *Travels Through North and South Carolina, Georgia, East & West Florida, the Cherokee Country, the Extensive Territories of the Muscogulges, or Creek Confederacy, and the Country of the Chactaws*. Philadelphia: James & Johnson, 1791.

Blackmon, Douglas A. *Slavery by Another Name: The Re-Enslavement of Black Americans from the Civil War Until World War II*. New York: Doubleday, 2008.

Borchers, Donnis Mott. *Thomas Lamar, The Immigrant: 300 Years of Descendants*. Madison: The University of Wisconsin, 1977.

Burton, Richard F. *A Mission to Gelele, King of Dahome, with Notices of the So Called Amazon, the Grand Customs, the Yearly Customs, the Human Sacrifices, the Present State of the Slave Trade, and The Negro's Place in Nature*. London: Tinsley Brothers, 1864. https://burtoniana.org/books/1864-A%20Mission%20to%20Gelele%20King%20of%20Dahome/A_Mission_to_Gelele__King_of_Dahome%20vol%20I.pdf.

Cochran, Hamilton. *Blockade Runners of the Confederacy*. Indianapolis: Bobbs-Merrill Co., 1958.

Darnell, Regna, ed. *Histories of Anthropologies Annual*. University of Nebraska, 2007.

Dennison, Mable. *A Memoir of Lottie Dennison*. Boynton Beach, FL: Futura Printing, 1985.

271

Dickey, Christopher. *Our Man in Charleston: Britain's Secret Agent in the Civil War South*. New York: Broadway Books, 2015.

Diouf, Sylviane A. *Dreams of Africa in Alabama: The Slave Ship Clotilda and the Story of the Last Africans Brought to America*. New York: Oxford University Press, 2007.

Eagle, Mary Kavanaugh Oldham, ed. *The Congress of Women: Held in the Woman's Building, World's Columbian Exposition, Chicago, U. S. A., 1893*. Chicago: Monarch Book Company, 1894. http://digital.library.upenn.edu/women/eagle/congress/sheldon-may.html.

Forbes, Frederick. *Dahomey and the Dahomans, Being the Journals of Two Missions to the Kingdom of Dahomey, and Residence at His Capital, in the Years 1849 and 1850*. London: Longman, Brown, Green, and Longmans, 1851. https://dl.wdl.org/2527/service/2527_1.pdf).

Fuller, Hiram. *Belle Brittan on a Tour, at Newport, and Here and There*. New York. Derby & Jackson, 1858.

Hurston, Zora Neale. *Barracoon*. New York: HarperCollins, 2018.

Lalor, John J., ed. *Cyclopaedia of Political Science, Political Economy, and of the Political History of the United States by the best American and European Authors*. New York: Maynard, Merrill, & Co., 1899.

Linden, Glenn M. *Voices from the Reconstruction Years, 1865–1877*. San Diego: Harcourt Brace, 1998.

Olmsted, Frederick Law. *A Traveller's Observations on Cotton and Slavery in the American Slave States*. New York: Mason Brothers, 1861.

Pettaway, Addie E. *Africatown, U.S.A.: Some Aspects of Folklife and Material Culture of an Historic Landscape*. Madison: Wisconsin Department of Public Instruction, 1985.

Robertson, Natalie S. *The Slave Ship Clotilda and the Making of Africatown, USA: Spirit of Our Ancestors*. Westport, CT: Praeger Publishers, 2008.

Robinson, Amelia Platts Boynton. *Bridge Across Jordan*. Washington, D.C.: Schiller Institute, Inc., 1991.

Roche, Emma. *Historic Sketches of the South*. New York: The Knickerbocker Press, 1914.

Romeyn, Henry. *Little Africa: The Last Slave Cargo Landed in the United States*. Hampton, VA: Hampton Normal and Agricultural Institute, 1897. University of Virginia Electronic Text Center, http://xtf.lib.virginia.edu/xtf/view?docId=legacy/uvaBook/tei/RomLitt.xml.

Russell, William Howard. *My Diary North and South*. Boston: T.O.H.P. Burnham, 1863.

Sani, Shehu. *Hatred for Black People*. Bloomington: Xlibris, 2013.

Sledge, John. *The Mobile River*. Columbia: The University of South Carolina Press, 2015.

Washington, Booker T. *The Story of the Negro: The Rise of the Race from Slavery*. New York: Doubleday, Page & Co., 1909.

Illustration Credits

1. Joe Turner
2. Ben Raines
3. Ben Raines
4. Ben Raines
5. Ben Raines
6. Ben Raines
7. Frederick Forbes
8. Erik Overbey Collection, The Doy Leale McCall Rare Book and Manuscript Library, University of South Alabama
9. Courtesy of Doy Leale McCall Rare Book and Manuscript Library, University of South Alabama
10. Courtesy of Doy Leale McCall Rare Book and Manuscript Library, University of South Alabama
11. Ben Raines
12. Erik Overbey Collection, The Doy Leale McCall Rare Book and Manuscript Library, University of South Alabama
13. Ben Raines
14. Ben Raines
15. Ben Raines
16. Ben Raines
17. Ben Raines
18. Ben Raines
19. Ben Raines
20. Ben Raines
21. Courtesy of Daphne Search & Rescue

Index

275

About the Author

BEN RAINES is an award-winning journalist and filmmaker. His writing has appeared in the *New York Times*, *Los Angeles Times*, and other national publications, and he coauthored several scientific papers published in paleontology journals. His underwater film work has appeared in documentaries on public television, the Discovery Channel, and National Geographic. He wrote and produced the award-winning documentary *America's Amazon*, and its companion book, *Saving America's Amazon*, and directed *The Underwater Forest*, about the exploration of a seventy-thousand-year-old cypress forest found off the Alabama coast. Ben Raines lives in Fairhope, Alabama, with his wife, Shannon. He holds a degree in filmmaking from New York University and is a licensed charter captain who leads adventure tours in the Mobile-Tensaw Delta and to Alabama's barrier islands.